Karen grew up in a small country town in north-eastern Victoria, Australia. She spent her childhood riding horses through beautiful scenery of eucalypts, lakes, and snow-capped mountains and her love of landscape deeply affects her writing. She worked in a range of educational settings and holds a Ph.D. and M.Ed. (Hons) in the areas of fantasy. She is particularly interested in the power of the hero's inner journey which she explores through Deep Fantasy. Karen has travelled extensively overseas but enjoys nothing more than camping in the Australian Outback. She lives in Melbourne and now writes full-time. You can find out more about Karen and her books on her website.

Connect with K.S. Nikakis

Amazon:	https://www.amazon.com/author/ksnikakis
Twitter:	https://twitter.com/KSNikakis
Facebook:	www.facebook.com/ksnikakis
Goodreads:	www.goodreads.com
Website:	www.ksnikakis.com
Email:	author@ksnikakis.com

WORKS BY K S NIKAKIS

Non Fiction

Journey: Seeking the Sacred, Spirit and Soul in the
Australian Wilderness

Fantasy Novels Series

Angel Caste series:
Angel Blood
Angel Breath
Angel Bone
Angel Bound
Angel Blessed
Angel Caste – Complete 5 Book Series

The Kira Chronicles trilogy:*
The Whisper of Leaves
The Song of the Silvercades
The Cry of the Marwing
remnant hard copies only

The Kira Chronicles series:
The Whisper of Leaves
The Silence of Stone
The Secrets of Stars
The Thunder of Hoofs
The Crying of Birds
The Music of Home
The Kira Chronicles – Complete 6 Book Series

Fantasy Novels

The Emerald Serpent
Heart Hunter
The Third Moon
Messenger
I Heard the Wolf Call My Name
Finalist - Best YA Novel Aurealis Awards, 2019

Fantasy Short Stories

The Gift
The Tale of Prince Anura
Dragon Sprite
Glass-Heart
Finalist – Best YA Short Story Aurealis Awards, 2019

JOURNEY

SEEKING THE SACRED, SPIRIT AND SOUL IN
THE AUSTRALIAN WILDERNESS

K.S. NIKAKIS

First published by SOV Media Australia 2020
Amazon: www.amazon.com.au

Publisher: SOV Media
Melbourne, Australia.

Cover by AS Nikakis: http://asnikakis.com
Image: C Nikakis
Typography:
Dafont.com/Phil Campbell (Foxy Fonts). Donationware; Licence: Donation
Dafont.com/Roberta Stanic (Lumie). Licence: 100% Free

National Library of Australia
Cataloguing-in-Publication entry:
Nikakis, Karen Simpson
Journey: Seeking the Sacred, Spirit and Soul in the Australian Wilderness
ISBN 978-0-6482652-2-1

For my fellow travellers

Journey: Seeking the Sacred, Spirit and Soul in the Australian Wilderness

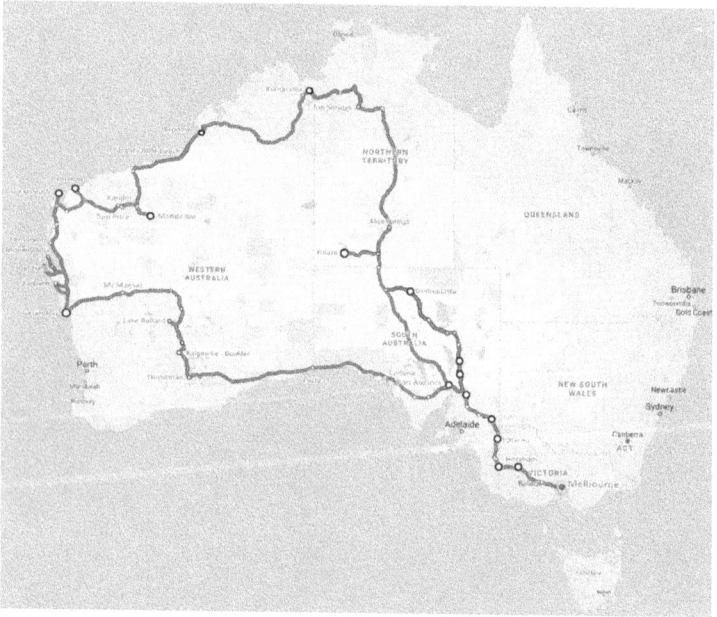

JOURNEY:
SEEKING THE SACRED, SPIRIT AND SOUL IN THE AUSTRALIAN WILDERNESS

We travel the highway,
the long graveyard of the wild and unwary
seeking change
but carrying our sameness with us.

DEATH DATE

Take a piece of paper and write down your birth date. Now, underneath, write down your death date. Cannot do it? Hmmmm. This is both excellent news and not so excellent news. It means you do not know how long you have to achieve all the things you plan to do and all the things you have no plans for at all, just vague, barely acknowledged yearnings.

This thing called life is a journey, right? Yes and no; it is really *two* journeys.

Describing life as a journey is hardly new, in fact, describing every threat, challenge and triumph in life as a journey is now a metaphor so over-used as to risk it becoming cringingly cliched. But this *cringingly cliched* metaphor for life's ups and sometimes devastating downs is restricted to the *outward* journey: growing up; career advancement and set-backs; happy marriages and not so happy ones; divorce; the delight of children or the fight to have them; life-threatening illnesses; grief for lost loved ones.

But there is a second, *inner* journey, that is far more important and yet in comparison, barely acknowledged at all.

This second journey, this *inward* quest, is vital to us all, for we are not just flesh and bone, but mind and spirit, and this *inner* journey belongs to this amorphous place that is so much harder to pin down.

It is so tempting to ignore it, especially when we are overwhelmed with events in the outer journey, but we do so at our peril. To ignore it is to risk journeying through life, *carrying our sameness with us* but, on the other hand, to acknowledge it *and* to actively seek it, is to live a richer, more fully-realised life.

My story, if you choose to read on, tells of my outward journey through the Australian wilderness of the Outback; a journey I use, with the help of poetry, prose and my Ph.D. in Joseph Campbell's hero journey, to tread the pathway of my *inner* journey. There are no chapter headings in my story, as there are no chapter headings in life. Rest when you must and journey on when you are able.

Welcome to the road.

WOOMERA

The way into the mind is a strip of black tarmac. It is May 23, 2019 and a clear autumn morning in Melbourne, Australia when we hitch our van on the back of our vehicle and head out. Australia's First Nation hunters used a *woomera* to speed their spears on their way but we use a Toyota LandCruiser 4x4 to speed *us* on our way *and* to return us, 75 days and 15,000 kilometres (over 9000 miles) later.

I share this *outer* journey with my husband (and sometimes two other couples) but the *inner* journey is mine alone. So, what do I learn from those 75 days on the road? What do more than 15,000 kms of Australia's desert inland and sapphire coasts reveal? What lessons, if any, are there in leaving behind the noise and clutter of my everyday life and journeying into the deep wild redness of Australia's heart?

Statistics tell me I can expect to live around 83 years but I do not want to live those same comfortable, unchallenging years over and over again and only truly live just a few years. At the risk of sounding cliched, I yearn for something more but what exactly, is harder to define. Australia is a prosperous peaceful country and I should be content but I am hungry for a richer, deeper life and this hunger keeps me restless.

What I *do* know, even before we set out, is that what I seek (*wisdom* seems too grand a word for it so I will call it *insights*) is not going to magically appear in my life simply by my failure to die. Age alone is not going to gift it to me. What I seek must be searched for and journeying into the wilderness is a time-honoured way of doing so.

The nomad, the pilgrim, the wandering hero of fantasy; all knew the importance of leaving the familiar behind and setting out into the unknown. The outer journey into the realm of the *strange* (over plains, mountains, rivers and seas) opens the door to the *inner* journey, where what they seek might be found.

But the insights the nomad, pilgrim and hero gained were not laying by the side of the road like carelessly discarded gems; they had to be *earned.* There is a price to pay for treading the path of the *inner* journey, that includes the shock and mental discomfort of the unfamiliar and the metaphorical death of the old self.

The famous mythologist Joseph Campbell identified the *twin* paths of the hero journey as the hero's *outer*, physical journey through the landscape, and the hero's *inner* journey through the psyche; a journey I call the *soul-journey*. I mean nothing religious by the term but for me it sums up the *importance* of the search for meaning (or insights) that so many of us are knowingly or *unknowingly* engaged in.

The privilege of journeying for pleasure was once confined to the wealthy and almost exclusively to men but I live in a time and place where journeying is accessible to many people and, if we *are* fortunate enough to set out *physically* like the pilgrims of old and *are* alert to the inner possibilities, then the soul-journey will unfold, not always in lockstep with our outer physical journey, but freed from the shackles of our old lives to begin.

MESSAGE STICK

Some time deep in Australia's past, a short length of wood was selected; painted or incised with the silent voice of symbols; and carried with the soft pad of unshod feet across Australia's vast red lands, on and on under the star-bursts of countless nights and through the gentle dawns of fierce suns until the message it carried was delivered.

Australia's First Nation peoples (the Aborigines) used message sticks to send their messages far and wide but *I* travel far and wide in *search* of messages. I am no barefoot traveller but one who journeys in a comfortable vehicle and sleeps in a comfortable van but being on foot, as First Nation people were, or with a pack, as a hiker might be, would not necessarily increase my chances of finding what I seek. I could travel all over the world in luxury or on a shoe-string budget and many people do and *see* nothing; *feel* nothing; *discover* nothing and so, to aid my quest, I set myself the task to write a poem a day.

I have always written poetry but it mostly gave way to novel-writing when my outer journey of work/study/managing a house/mothering meant I did not have time for both and I am keen to turn poet again.

Writing poetry might seem like an odd choice but poetry has the capacity to deliver an emotional punch to the guts; to stir and soothe and set us back on our heels; to strike with lightning force deep into the psyche and, like lightning, to illuminate what dwells there.

Poetic language not only creates *literal* meaning (meaning true of the *outer* world) but metaphoric meaning (meaning true of the *inner* world); crucial to understanding and expressing our soul-journeys.

Poetry works words extraordinarily hard to reduce broader, vaguer experiences to their essence, in the same way sugared-water boils down to a translucent gob of amber-coloured toffee in the bottom of a pot and requires a different way of seeing to that which guides us safely through the day. It requires us to pay *very* close attention to *what* we see and to *actively* consider what it *means*; it necessitates being alert to what *resonates*; to what *strikes a chord* within us and, as the journey unfolds and I hammer my rough words into more meaningful shapes, the poems become like stepping-stones into the inner world of the soul-journey and the insights I seek.

The Long Graveyard

We travel the highway
the long graveyard of the wild and unwary
seeking change
but carrying our sameness with us

To find the sacred
where spirit feeds soul
we must turn inwards

bear the darkness alone
and if blessed
arrive at a place of rest
and pause

at least for a little while
before we go on

The poems also have a second, unexpected effect: they bring into sharp relief the meaning of my stories and the stories become important to my soul-journey too. I should not have been surprised by this. The *impulse* that creates stories (and other art forms) comes from the unconscious; the realm of the soul-journey and the type of fantasy I write (Deep Fantasy) focuses on the heroes' inner journeys as much as on their outer ones.

If I were a painter, musician or photographer, the story of my soul-journey might be in the form of pictures, music or photographs and, were I none of these things, my story might remain in my un-conscious, unshared but no less profound. But I am a writer and what I discover in my search for insights takes story-form.

I hope my story aids your soul-journey too but if not, I hope it entertains, as all good stories should. Let us journey on together.

BIRRARUNG

If I were a First Nation Wurundjeri person, I might say, in a form of Woiwurrung (the language group to which I belong) that I am starting my journey from Birrarung but that would be before Europeans arrived in Australia.

And if I were one of those early Europeans, I might say that I am starting my journey from Batmania (named after John Batman who established the settlement) or Bearbrass as it was briefly known. But it is 2019, so I can safely say (presuming the city won't change its name again) that I am starting my journey from Melbourne (named after a former Prime Minister of Britain).

Birrarung; Batmania; Bearbrass; Melbourne: the names remind me I am not the first traveller in these lands and that others have trodden, ridden, or driven where we soon will. We are on the road by 9 am and I am glad to be away on time. We have people to meet (the two other couples we will travel with as it suits them and us) and schedules to keep.

Time is still important to me on this first day. We live in the north-west of Melbourne and it does not take long to retrieve our van from storage and join the strip of black tarmac known as the Ring Road. I consider my first poem as the traffic lights flick between red, gold and green and muse on how obedient we are to what are, in fact, symbols rather than literal, physical barriers.

Red, the colour of blood, is the colour of warning; green the reassuring colour of growing and life; gold or amber, the comforting colour of the sun. In this situation of stop – go, gold/amber gives us time to adjust between alarm and hope. Traffic lights are devices wrought of metal, glass and plastic, animated by electricity. Their colours are not driven by the fleshy pump of a heart or the sweet sap of a plant, yet our *recognition* of them (and obedience) in the outer world owes much to what they symbolise in the inner one.

The same blood-red travels with us as brake lights flash on all around. The traffic snarls and I suppress a mutter as we slow to a crawl. The couples we will journey with are a day ahead and I am keen to make up time. Drivers jockey for position around the van, as impatient as I am, and I do not breathe easily until we reach the open road.

Our tyres hum on the bitumen and I keep an eye on the mirror to check the van tows straight. The van is bigger than I am comfortable with and, thanks to work commitments, we have used only for brief hot, salty beach holidays. This is its first big trip, though not ours. We are old hands at camping; our equipment over the years a mirror of our *outer* life journey.

As a madly in love courting couple, we started off in a leaky two-man tent with leaky lilos (plastic blow-up mattresses); progressed to nonleaky tents and mattresses; then to a camper trailer (with two young children); then to a family tent (when our children outgrew the trailer); then to a touring tent (with adolescents); then a small caravan (on our own again); and now a big caravan (for extended travel) with a table that fits my PC for writing and my husband's PC for photography; a full-sized fridge; and a shower and toilet to make us self-contained.

BROKEN TRAILS

I mentally peel back the tarry layer of bitumen as we travel knowing that its smooth blackness overlays the prints of miner's boots
and ruts of wheelbarrows; the hoofs of pack-animals; the narrow,
metal-clad rims of cart- and wagon-wheels of the more prosperous;
the kinder feet of First Nation peoples; and before them, the massive
prints of Australia's mega-fauna.

Each traveller through time had a reason to set out across the lands:
the hope of gold and a better life; the seasonal need to seek game
and forage and fulfil ceremonial obligations; the instinctual need for
food, water and mates; or perhaps, like me, in search of something
harder to define.

This first morning of our journey remains cool and I breathe more
easily as we reach the Western Freeway and leave the traffic behind.
We head north-west towards Ballarat, one of many gold rush towns
in my home state of Victoria, and Kulin Nation country (a nation
made up of five First Nation language groups).

The freeway sweeps down over the flood plains at Bacchus Marsh
where First Nation people fished and hunted along the Werribee and
Lerderderg Rivers but the flood plains are now clad in neat orchards,
market gardens and the smooth green of turf farms.

We leave the flood plains behind for the long slow climb up the Pent-
land Hills. They give a sweeping view back to the city and I think of
the miners who trudged this way to Ballarat's goldfields in the hope
of a life free from poverty and oppression. The richer rode and the
poorer went on foot, pushing their possessions in wheelbarrows.

Ballarat is a regional city awash with gracious buildings, thanks to
the wealth generated by the gold rush of the mid 1800's. We visit it
often, given it is home to one of the couples we travel with but today
we bypass it and continue to Ararat and Stawell. The view from the
4x4 window is typical of this part of Victoria: broad green paddocks
divided with post and wire fences; gum trees (the common name for

the hundreds of species of eucalypts); darker stands of pines introduced by European settlers as windbreaks; sheep and cattle, heads
down grazing; crows feeding off roadkill; and the occasional hawk
like a child's kite against the sky.

Victoria has suffered less from the drought that grips Australia (and
in some parts, has gripped it for years) but Lake Burrumbeet (west
of Ballarat) is a broad brown pan of emptiness. The land grows drier
and stonier as we pass through Ararat and Stawell and head for the
wheat and sheep town of Horsham.

PURPLE PEAKS

Gariwerd's peaks purple the horizon and my heart lifts at the familiar sight. We have camped there many times, mainly in winter, when their cloud-cut crests shelter valleys a chime with bellbirds' pure calls. No one now knows whether *Gariwerd* is a First Nation Jardwadjali word or a Djab Wurrung one but the loss of knowledge has nothing to do with carelessness. Australia's First Nation people lay claim to being the oldest, *continuous* culture in the world and the loss of names and so much else came later with the European invasion.

For many years, the road signs identified the tilted sandstone ridges as the *Grampians* (named by European settlers after the Grampian Mountains in Scotland) but the signage now includes *Gariwerd*, their First Nation name. It seems ironic that, in a similar act of cultural erasure by invaders in other lands and times, the Grampian Mountains in Scotland were previously known by their Gaelic name of *Am Monadh*.

Some Australians are troubled by the bloody history of European settlement of First Nation lands and there is much on this journey that causes me to contemplate it and my place in history. If I were to walk backwards through time, in the many footsteps of my innumerable ancestors, I would find myself both the murdered and the murderer; the dispossessed and the dispossessor; the landless and likely, the landed; but I cannot. I am here in 2019, pondering the actions (and their effects) of people who lived in different times, with different values and different ways of doing.

Writers know the power of words as tools of destruction *and* of healing, and that words can act as the latter when they acknowledge the things that were taken *and* return them, and I am glad of the name *Gariwerd* as we drive on.

We reach the Wimmera Region and break at Horsham for a quick lunch and to stretch our legs. The word *wimmera* is a variation of *woomera*, the device that sends a spear faster and further, but we are still in familiar territory. We have been to Horsham many times because the second couple we travel with live here. It is warmer now; the air sweet with dry grass and the stand of dusty gums full of magpie-song.

Magpies are so common I barely notice them. I grew up in a small town three hours drive from Melbourne and their music forms the back-drop to my earliest memories. They are a bird with an astonishing vocal range with wonderful gurglings, burblings, rinsings and shout-outs but their glorious repertoire is balanced by their ferocious swooping during the nesting season. I used to beat them off as I peddled for my life to school and later too on horse-rides through gold-grassed paddocks, but nesting does not start till June and we are safe to enjoy our lunch under the gums.

Want to explore further?

This story is not a travelogue, loaded with descriptions of points of interest or popular tourist spots; nor is it a '*yarn* (story) *around the campfire*' narrative; nor a tale about *drinkin', shootin', fishin'*. The Internet is a pretty easy place to find out more about Australia but I provide some links at the end of some sections for those of you who want to learn more about my *particular* journey.

Gariwerd: https://visithorsham.com.au/activities/grampians-national-park/
Bellbird Song: https://soundcloud.com/wildambience/bellbird-forest
Magpie Song: http://www.magpieaholic.com/videos/
Magpie Swooping: https://www.youtube.com/watch?v=YGGTcY-frEZU

SHARDS

We would be forgiven for thinking that the soaring pillars that emerge in the distance belong to ancient Greek Temples but of course, they are nothing of the kind. First Nation peoples' imprinted Australia more subtly than mighty civilisations elsewhere and Europeans arrived here long after the demise of Ancient Greece.

Horsham marks the beginning of wheat country and the land flattens further as we head west, skirt Barringgi Gadyin (to the First Nation Wotjobaluk and the Little Desert National Park to the rest of us) and pass through the wheat towns of Dimboola, Nhill and Kaniva; small settlements marked by concrete wheat silos, that soar like stone shards (or Grecian pillars).

Further north in the *Mallee* Region (named after a small, many trunked eucalypt) these towering silos are adorned with giant murals, but here their undecorated grey concrete provides a muted backdrop to sulphur-crested cockatoos (known colloquially as *cockies*). The cockies wheel in brilliant white flocks and are so common, they become a companion bird on our journey. Their cries match their in-your-face attitude and have been compared to tearing bed-sheets. White flocks of corellas join them, a bird just as common and no more musical.

Warning signs appear as we near South Australia that prohibit the transport of fruit over the border to stop the spread of the pest-insect fruit-fly. I consider the nature of borders as we drive. Once only natural obstacles such as icefields, deserts, mountains, oceans and rivers hindered the movement of man and beast but now there are barriers even *within* the spaces we call countries some of which, like fences and roads, prove deadly to wildlife. As I note in my opening poem, Australian roads have indeed become the *long graveyard of the wild and unwary* and during this Outback journey, we are fated to see many times more dead animals than live ones.

But in the interval between travelling this road in May 2019 and now in mid 2020, as I hammer my raw thoughts, feelings and poetry into this story, the world has changed and barriers have taken on a very personal meaning. In May 2019, I had never heard of the virus that, by early 2020, has changed the world.

Australia closed its national borders, then its state and territory borders, then its regional borders. Then leaving home except for clearly defined and limited reasons became an offence and we each acquired our own personal borders: a circle of no less than 1.5 metres from the stranger. But I knew none of these things on that sunny day, early on my *outer* journey when the first stirrings of my *inner* journey were just starting to be felt.

We eat the last of our fruit as we drive in readiness for the border crossing and I ponder the role luck plays in which side of a border we end up on. I crossed Australia's coastal border in the 1950's, carried in the arms of my immigrant parents. Migrants were welcomed then but welcomes are scarcer now and even people deemed refugees under International Law, languish for years in Australia's off-shore detention centres and sometimes die there.

We pull up at the Quarantine Station which consists of more signage listing prohibited items; penalties for noncompliance; and several bright yellow, lidded-bins sturdily embedded in concrete. Flies form a hopeful cloud above the lids, attracted by the ripe smell of putrefying fruit and there are other things there too, propped against the plinth.

Caught Between

We arrive at the South Australian border
having eaten apples all day in preparation for this moment

NO FRUIT ALLOWED

We stop at the quarantine bin to discard our cores

Someone has left a net of onions and a bag of potatoes
propped against the side

These are legal, like refugees, but here they remain
neither carried over the border nor binned

Even the ants can go where they
cannot

No Fruit Allowed at other times and places has been/might still be
No Blacks Allowed; *No Jews Allowed*; *No Women Allowed*; prohibitions that existed/exist in our *outer* world; that we might encounter
on our *outer* journey but there are no prohibitions on our *inner* world
where our *inner*, *soul*-journey unfolds, *unless* we impose them.

These are the self-limiting thoughts and behaviours the poet William
Blake famously described as 'mind-forg'd manacles' and what I (less
famously) mean when I speak of 'seeking change but carrying our
sameness with us' in my opening poem *The Long Graveyard*. It is
the reason we travel; the reason *I* travel: to break free of these *manacles* and in the process, shed my sameness along the way.

Want to explore further?
Silo Art: https://www.visitmelbourne.com/things-to-do/tour-
ing-routes/silo-art-trail-touring-route
William Blake: https://www.poetryfoundation.org/poems/43673/lon-
don-56d222777e969

OLD ENEMIES

Maps are curious things because they show magical lands that do not really exist. The maps in the atlas we carry in the 4x4 and the Google maps that glow on our phones might just as well be of Allogrenia: the fictional forest world I created in my novels *The Kira Chronicles*. The maps we hold so dear, that guide us over the 15,000 kilometres of our journey, are simply scaled *representations* of what (most) of us agree to be the real world of roads, rivers, plains, mountains, towns and lakes.

Their blue coasts and red or black dashed-lines represent the ending of one territory, state or nation, and the beginning of the another. In the *real* world, on the *actual* ground, these borders were once far more fluid and organic; determined by traditional occupation; nomadic routes; ethnicity and culture; but in later times, the straightness of these borders more often reflects the wants of the last war's winner for resources, ports or prestige.

We drive on over the black-dashed line on the map into South Australia and are immediately transformed into Victorians, notable now because we are from *interstate* and later, because we are *Southerners*. How easily we are changed on our outer journey! The landscape changes too with great rows of dark emerald-green pines that march, shoulder to shoulder, across the paddocks.

These are windbreaks but old and broken with more silvered wood than resinous needles. Australia's First Nation people worked *with* this country, not against it, and had no need of such things. The windbreaks came later with the Europeans who, with visions of England's verdant pastures firmly in mind, cleared the land for crops and grazing and found themselves battered by icy winds or scorched by searing ones.

Windbreaks

They cleared the old soldiers away
the ones who stood against the wind
the ones who had strategies
for beating the ancient foe

The old trees sheltered the young
let the saplings thicken to find their strength
to protect the young in turn
before they fell too

And with the old soldiers gone
the wind roared its laughter
slapped its sides in mirth
flattened crop and pasture
took the soil and
in a final act of hilarity
sent it back in stinging showers

But not the rain
the rain it kept
for itself

And so, these settlers
these slaughterers of soldiers
brought in new troops
lines of pines
as proud as Redcoats
marching into
sniper fire

Those that survive are
supplicants to the wind
bribing it
with soft hymns in their needles
and the promise
of their own demise

We seem to make the same mistakes, even over two hundred years later, as if unwilling or unable to learn that this country is not Europe or England, or some other place. What I did not know then, as I considered the broken remnants of those windbreaks, was that the cumulative effects of European land management practices, long-term drought and the inexorable creep of climate change, were to soon result in the most far-reaching and devastating fires in Australia's recorded history.

FIRE GODS

When I was a child, the world turned to fire. Red replaced the blue sky; the air filled with a moistureless fog that thickened as the days went by; and carbonised bracken-fronds drifted down like over-sized snowflakes to land on skin and clothes with grey-ash kisses. But as a child, I had a child's trust that all would be well with the world again.

Australia's Black Summer begins less than a month after I eye those windbreaks on the first day of our journey. Dry lightning starts fires that engulf the nation from June 2019 to March 2020; burn out over 18.6 million hectares (46 million acres); destroy nearly 6000 buildings; directly kill 34 people (and hundreds more via smoke-filled air); incinerate over a billion animals, and likely cause the extinction of other, countless but less obvious organisms.

Fire, and the fear of being caught in it, rules the lives of thousands of country Australians like a vengeful god, but catastrophic fires are nothing new to Australia. The fire siren was tested every Wednesday evening in the small town of my childhood but if it sounded any other day or time, men ran and women worried.

One summer, the hill behind my house became a wall of flame and, as the fire threatened the town, every able-bodied man was out fire-fighting. Towns were defensible then; the fires nothing like the scale and ferocity of those now, with their lethal mix of flame-tornadoes and super-heated micro-climates. Now nothing is defensible and the advice to leave early increasingly becomes a forced evacuation, but I am old enough to remember other advice that now leads, like a blackened road, back in time.

The road looks something like this: shelter in your house or in a body of water, but not in a water tank (after people were boiled alive). If caught on the road, park with headlights on, stay low and cover yourself with a woollen blanket. This advice followed a tragedy where people abandoned their vehicles in a failed attempt to out run a grass fire. But then, in the 2009 Black Saturday fires, a friend of ours, his father and uncle, sheltered in their car and died.

In the same fires, one of the couples we travel with, loaded their car with their valuables: legal documents, wedding and baby photos, jewellery and, with their toddler, attempted to drive to safety. They were forced back by dense smoke; fought the fire from their house and saved it and themselves but lost the vehicle with its precious cargo.

Nothing in the outer world or inner world is static and as I contemplate the windbreaks and how Europeans changed Australia, I remind myself First Nation people changed this country too, most obviously through their selective and highly skilled use of fire. Perhaps their 60,000 years or so here gave them a greater understanding of their home; or perhaps their understanding of the world and their place in it was always different. I have no doubt my ancestors' view of *their* world and *their* place in it was different to mine too.

Even so, it is hard not to compare ourselves to others; to judge ourselves by others; to want to *be* like others we admire and *not* like those we do not. But these comparisons inhabit the outer world of our journey through life. The inner journey, the *soul-journey*, is ours alone to explore; free from the praise or prejudice of others; and free from *their* definitions *and* from our own *confining* ones.

We reach Bordertown as haze smudges the horizon. We had planned to spend the night here and wisdom dictates we stick to our plan. Kangaroos are active at dusk and hitting one won't end well for either of us but, aware of already being a day behind our friends, we head north on the Ngarkat Highway to the Mallee town of Pinaroo.

We have driven this road through the Ngarkat Conservation Park (named for the First Nation Ngargad people) several times before. (Note: English spellings of First Nation languages vary, especially the use of g, j, k, t and d) Ngarkat's 270,000 hectares (667,184 acres) sprawls on either side: a ripple of low sand dunes, heath and mallee, and home to kangaroos, emus and the rare mallee fowl.

We have never seen a mallee fowl and, in the 90 minutes it takes to reach Pinaroo, it is rare to see other vehicles too. This used to worry me, given phone coverage cuts out soon into the trip, but as we drive north, I am more concerned about kangaroos.

I lean forward in my seat and search the way ahead. We have *roo-shoos* fitted to the bull-bar (devices which emit sounds supposed to scare off kangaroos) but I do not want to test them. The kangaroos here are western greys which means they blend into the hazing air. They lurk, wraith-like, in the scrubby verges and then, as I annoy my husband by shouting warnings (he has better vision than me), the kangaroos turn back into bushes.

The shrieks of cockatoos fade as day gives way to night and it is fully dark before we reach Pinaroo. We have booked a site at the local caravan park but the small park is empty of any manager when we arrive. Other vans dot the space, lit by dim glows from their windows and, as we weave around them over the tussocky grass in a fruitless search for someone to pay, a camper tells us the manager will make his rounds later, as indeed he does.

By then we have discovered water gushes from under the van when we turn on the pump. We had metal sheeting fitted to protect the water tanks because this trip means unsealed roads but it seems something might have been punctured in the process and frustration adds to weariness. The manager is of no practical help but smiles sympathetically as he takes our cash. (No new-fangled EFTPOS machines here!)

The manager reminds me of men we have known in other country towns, who reach their sixties alone, either never having married or more often been divorced. They are simple men, bewildered when their wives find they are no longer enough, and leave them. The city is a dangerous place for men like these, where they are easily lost, but they are safe in small towns. They are the good blokes who help at the local footy club and who spend their evenings in convivial conversations at the pub. The town is their family and when they die, the local church is packed.

It seems to me that men like the park manager have no need to question where they belong although, I remind myself, I have no way of knowing that; I only really know my own feelings. I left my birthplace too young to have memories of it but knowing I was born elsewhere made me question my place as I grew up. I have since decided my questioning flows more from my soul-journey than my immigrant background; many native-born Australians share the same restless questing too.

Want to explore further?
Bordertown to Pinaroo: http://www.malleehighway.com.au/html/parks-sa-mallee.html

GOLD-WINGED ANGELS

My head is full of gold-winged angels as we head off the next day, in the clear, early morning light. I imagine their glow in the porcelain sky; the air-scythe of their wings; their sheer splendour as they hang above us and it takes me a while to trace the thought-thread back to the scatter of churches we pass.

They dot the paddocks, some seeming a long way from any town. Most are simple timber structures clad in peeling cream paint and a few have gravestones nearby. The churches in larger towns are far more substantial; often of bluestone or red brick, with soaring spires and stained glass. They perch on the town's highest points: Catholic, Presbyterian and Anglican, shoulder to shoulder, as if they jostle to be closest to God.

I like churches. I like their dark, meditative interiors; their shafting emerald and ruby-stained light; their gleaming wooden pews. Being married to a Greek-Australian means countless hours sitting (or more often standing) in Greek Orthodox churches for weddings, baptisms and funerals, and I am never bored, despite knowing little of the Greek language.

Unlike the Anglican churches I was raised in, Greek Orthodox churches are full of glorious iconography including gold-haloed saints and gold-winged angels (the ultimate source of my thought-thread). I always have plenty to contemplate in Greek Orthodox churches as the richly melodic chants and musky incense swirl around me.

Splendid iconography once adorned Anglican churches too but was scoured away during the Reformation of the 1500's. A church's iconography is powerful for the same reason that poetry is: its images are metaphors and symbols that represent and express the inner journey.

For instance, when we describe romantic love *literally*, we might say: *Love includes both joy and sorrow*, which is *literally* true. But when we use a *metaphor* to describe romantic love, we might say: *Love is a deep red rose on a thorn-clad stem.* This is *not* literally true (love is an emotion, not a plant) and yet it conveys a similar meaning.

But the metaphor's real power lies in doing *more* than conveying similar *meaning*. The metaphor also creates an *image* of a red rose: its red petals, green stem and curved thorns; it wakes recollections of *scent*; and it conjures *tactile* memories of *velvety softness* and *piercing jags*. It might also add a sense of timelessness because this metaphor for romantic love has a long history in Western culture.

Similarly, the gold-winged angels of Greek Orthodox churches conjure more than the literal meaning of a man with wings. Angels are powerful metaphors (my *Angel Caste* series features them) for the same reason dragons are powerful metaphors. While angels are sometimes described purely as messengers between God in the heavens and humans on earth, a *winged*-human, like a *winged*-snake (dragon), also symbolises the human craving for transcendence from a limited physical, earth-bound entity to something greater.

On a literal level, wings levitate humans and snakes from the ground, but metaphorically, this *higher* state is really a *descent* into a state of greater awareness (the unconscious); as meditation is; as a soul-journey is. I did not realise any of this *consciously* many years ago when I decided to investigate the purposes of dragons via a master's degree. All I knew was dragons fascinated me, as they fascinated countless others, and like me, those *others* I spoke to found it hard to explain why.

Dragons, in their various forms (snakes, serpents, worms) occur in countless cultures and while some may have arrived in a particular culture via story transference, most seem to have come into being independently. For instance, the Rainbow Serpent is central to Australia's First Nation creation stories (the Dreamtime); a culture, I have noted, that stretches back over 60,000 years.

Carl Jung, the famous psychoanalyst, called such wide spread symbols *archetypes* and as such, suggested they reside in the collective unconscious (shared memories) of all humanity (thus explaining their appearance in so many cultures). Being aware of and alert to symbols, especially archetypal ones is useful in making sense of our soul-journeys because, as I have noted, the unconscious where the soul-journey unfolds uses symbolic/metaphorical language, not the language we use in everyday life to, for example, buy a carton of milk.

I write Deep Fantasy novels, a genre that explicitly includes the hero's inner psychological journey, and so I deliberately employ such devices in books like *The Emerald Serpent* and the *Angel Caste* series. But such is the power of the unconscious that *unplanned* metaphors and symbols often emerge in my stories too.

My heroes' inner journeys are expressed through metaphors that readers are likely to recognise unconsciously, if not consciously, as a result of their frequency in myths, legends, books and films (and through the collective unconscious). Whatever the case, readers who enjoy the excitement of following a hero's outer journey are also exposed to the hero's inner journey and so are aided vicariously in their own soul-journeys.

Underground spaces like caves and tunnels are, like dragons, also archetypes. They represent the unconscious because, metaphorically, we *descend* from the outer world of consciousness to the inner world of unconsciousness. In the well-known story of *Aladdin and the Lamp*, Aladdin enters a cave (the unconscious) and is empowered by finding riches there, including a genie who grants his wishes; while Gandalf (in the books/movie *The Lord of the Rings*) enters the Mines of Moria to slay the Balrog and becomes his new, fully-realised *greater* self (Gandalf the White); and T'Challa (in the movie *Black Panther*) slays Killmonger, *in an underground tunnel*, to finally become King in every sense of the word.

Water serves as an archetype of the unconscious too. In *The Emerald Serpent*, the hero Etaine (an elf-like Eadar) suffers terrible trauma (including the murder of her baby son Ellair) at the hands of religious zealots (the Fada) and then lives a destructive life bent on bloody revenge.

To heal, she must enter the realm of the Emerald Serpent/Goddess which, like pre-Christian serpents and dragons in Western culture, is a symbol of constructive/healing energies. (It is hard to think of any dragon, worm, snake or serpent that does not reside in a tunnel, cave or water, that together, reinforce the power of mother earth/Mother Nature's healing/creative forces).

In *The Emerald Serpent*, Etaine firstly descends from the outer world of the Light Way (consciousness) through the Emerald Way to the underworld of the Serpent/Goddess in the Serpent Way (unconsciousness). In Excerpt 1, she focusses on the sound of the water to enter the Emerald Way. Her antagonism for Cormac (her former lover who inadvertently contributes to her suffering) is still strong.

The Emerald Serpent: Excerpt 1.

The Goddess's voice sang in the water's chime but Etaine's enjoyment was ruined by Cormac's prowl behind her, and she closed her eyes to shut him out. In an instant she was in the wondrous landscape of the Emerald Way where emerald drifts hinted the joy of Ellair's presence might still be possible.

In Excerpt 2, Etaine has healed sufficiently to help Cormac in the battle to defeat the Fada. They conceive a child (a symbol of new life and hope) to descend into the Serpent Way and then follow a spiralling tunnel that exits in a pool-filled cavern.

The Emerald Serpent: Excerpt 2

The pool was tranquil too but as Etaine stared into its depths, something moved. For a moment she thought a Fada body drifted back to the surface but then she realised it was a reflection. Light glinted off flecks of sinuous movement and, dry-mouthed with fear, Etaine slowly raised her eyes to the tunnel's walls. They were no longer made of stone but of muscle and skin; of overlapping scales that bunched and stretched as the Serpent tightened its coils about them.

Cormac's breathing was as harsh as her own and she knew that like her, he feared the Serpent would wreak revenge on them for the spring-fouling blood of the innocents; for the temples that crouched where the stars should have shone; for the Eadar's long neglect.

The coils drew ever closer and still neither of them moved. Etaine kept her grip on Cormac but the link between them now was so strong that he shared what she Remembered. The Serpent's mighty head uncoiled and swung towards them and Etaine forced herself to meet its eyes.

The Serpent's scales shone like burnished metal, but its golden eyes held depths that Etaine sensed were deeper than the times of Eadar and Fuaran and shifters; of the wild's creatures; perhaps even of the land itself. And then, imperceptibly, the Serpent lowered its head and Etaine felt the mote inside her blaze. Cormac jolted but Etaine's fear vanished as she understood the Serpent's satisfaction with what it found.

Etaine heals and becomes whole again by drawing on the strength of her unconscious and we embark on our own soul-journeys for the same reason: to become more complete human beings.

Similarly, in my five-book *Angel Caste* series, the hero Viv, who is half-human, half-angel (symbolising the human condition of physical-spiritual) is on a healing quest following an abusive childhood and adolescence. She sets out through the Rynth (a series of strange worlds) with her angel guide Thris but becomes separated and is captured by a cat-creature. The cat-creature represents her ties to her human-physical part, and her wings to her angel-ethereal part.

To escape its cliff-top lair, Viv must push through a pain barrier to liberate the wings she guesses are embedded in her back. Her wings represent her wish to transcend her human state (and the suffering of her abuse) as well as a literal means of escape.

Angel Caste: Excerpt 1.

Viv gasped as heat stirred in her back. Breathe, she exhorted, in, out, in, out. The burn escalated and Viv screwed her eyes shut as she fought to hold on to the vision of Thris's wings, but the pain was too great. Sobs rose in her throat and she was about to dash herself screaming against the stone when the pain suddenly extinguished.

Viv gasped in relief but was devastated to feel no difference. And then she glimpsed the edge of her shadow. Hardly daring to breathe, she turned so the new sun shone full on her back and there, stretched out on the cavern floor, was the shape of an angel.

Tears ran unchecked down her cheeks at its perfection, at her perfection. The wings were as shapely as Thris's but in proportion to her body and Viv reached behind her and tugged. There was a sharp sting, as if someone had plucked hairs from her head, but Viv barely noticed. The plume she held was the same dark bronze as her hair and so silken as to be almost slippery.

Viv brought it to her nose and inhaled the most beautiful fragrance.

Tranquility settled over her and she closed her eyes, at peace for the first time in her life, but then claws scraped on stone and her eyes flew wide. A second shadow had joined hers, immense and hulking, with small flattened ears. Adrenaline shot through her and in the split second she had left, Viv did the only thing possible.

She threw herself off the mountain.

Viv's struggle for healing and wholeness requires her to accept and unite the two parts of herself: her human traumatic past (that shames her) and the angelic heritage that makes her other than human.

In our own struggle to become whole, we too must confront and accept the parts of ourselves we dislike and that we have buried away deep in our unconscious, but more on this later.

SNAKES RESTING

The snake was coiled in our garage; head reared high, ready to strike. Australia has two of the deadliest snakes in the world: the eastern brown and the tiger, and this was a tiger, with a thick muscular body and (as we discover later), venom sacks filled to the brim. I have felt pure, unadulterated fear few times in my life but this was one such time. The fear was not for myself, but for one of our dogs who, due to my high-pitched calls to her, thought she was in trouble and slunk, not towards me and safety, but towards her kennel *and the snake*.

The floor vibrated behind me as my husband dashed past and into the garage, snatched *both* dogs by the collars (despite one dog being less than a metre [3 ft] from the snake) and threw them into the house. He slammed the door shut and by the time we had secured the dogs in the laundry, the snake had disappeared.

Disappeared does not mean gone and it took him and the snake-catcher another careful hour to locate it. The snake-catcher admired its size (and venom glands), safely bagged it up, and took it away to release somewhere more remote (snakes are a protected species).

I am contemplating the link between fear and anxiety as we detour to Berri, which is why I recall the terrifying incident with the snake, but I am more anxious than fearful about our water-leakage problem as Berri's orchards come into view. Tourist brochures tell the traveller Berri is in the Riverland, which means it is on the Murray, a river that rises in the Australian Alps, forms most of Victoria's northern border, and ends its life in the Southern Ocean near Goolwa, 2,520 kms (1,655 miles) away in South Australia.

Thanks to the Murray River's (irrigation) water, Berri is a major citrus producer and the last time we came this way, the air was drenched with the sweet scent of orange blossom. While the juicing company is long gone, the glossy orange groves remain, although there are more diesel fumes than orange scent in the air when we pull into the van repairers.

A brief discussion reveals they have enough of other caravaner's woes to keep them busy for several days and we head off again, west to Morgan (on the aptly named Morgan Road) and stop for a coffee and cake in the main street.

Morgan is another of South Australia's small towns of under 1000 people but was a busy river port in its heyday. At a time when the Outback's inhospitable wilderness made overland travel long and dangerous, the Murray's broad, brown waters were an important transportation route for paddle steamers, heavily loaded with goods.

The sun is hot on my shoulders as I trek to the café from our parking spot and I only notice the church, perched under shady gums, on my way back, laden with afternoon tea. The church is in the main street, which is uncommon and, despite being small, is of red brick not the usual timber. The ground is dry and dusty, and the smooth leaves of the gum that shelters it, dimmed with dust too.

Country Churches

These are no grand cathedrals
fought over by dynasties
there are no soaring buttresses here
or ethereal light from leaded windows
to hint at better times
beyond the veil

These are humbler buildings
of rough-hewn stone, or timber
and peeling paint
yet with roofs (of lesser pitch)
that still reach up to heaven
or at least away from hell

In these small settlements
power does not lie in the grand house on the hill
nor in the sprawling civic centre
but in these humbler places
that sit in parched paddocks or under gums
like snakes at rest
in summer heat

They hold the universe inside:
christenings, confessions, deaths,
secrets whispered along polished pews,
covetous glances at
a neighbour's wealth

The soul-stuff lingers here
long after the last pall bearer exits
or faith is lost
or the next generation
shifts away

It waits
like the close-packed bones
in the earth outside
for resurrection

I have visited mosques in Europe that were once churches, and
churches that were once mosques and, in the UK, there are cathedrals built on the foundations of simpler churches which in turn,
are built on the ruins of more rustic places of worship; sited near a
spring, or grotto, or cave where the wind's sweet music sang of the
sacred.

Such places were always special and remain so but European settlers
did not build their churches on sacred ground in Australia except
perhaps, by accident. They were (mostly) blind to the sacred in
Australia and to the extraordinarily rich and sophisticated culture of
its First Nation people.

You will notice that I use the word *sacred* often in this story but not with any religious intent. The dictionary definition of *sacred* includes *worthy of respect* but the term seems too small. My experience of the sacred involves profound feelings of peace, wonder, beauty and timelessness something the poet T.S. Eliot captures in his exquisite poem *Burnt Norton* that I cannot share for copyright reasons but which I encourage you to read.

WEAVINGS

I have often mused that dusk is a strange weaving of sunlight and darkness that creates a space between day and night that both struggle to claim and we leave Morgan behind as the afternoon slides towards the inevitable tussle. A delicate blue stretches unbroken from horizon to horizon and the sight reminds me how different Outback skies are, particularly at day's start and end, when the land's vastness dilutes the colour to the palest porcelain.

Burra is less than an hour away and a quick calculation tells me it is close to forty years since we first camped there as young marrieds. I find returning to places after long absences curiously unsettling. It is as if I have died, reincarnated, and abruptly remembered a past life. I am in the same place but am not the same person, either physically or mentally.

It reminds me that my journey between birth and death resembles weavings too; with different times in my life like the warp threads on a loom, and my experiences like the weft, passing over, under and ultimately through the warp, to create the fabric of my life.

Despite the existence of mediums, clairvoyants, palmists and card-readers (and their skill or lack there-of), I cannot see future patterns in my life-fabric only the patterns in my past, *if* I have the *in*-sight to identify them. At first glance, there seems to be random patches of this and that but the threads of my relationship with the man I marry began their pattern long before we met in person.

In 1957, the ships that carried his family back to Greece for a holiday and mine to Australia likely passed each other at sea; in 1971, I visited his city school's bush camp from my nearby country school when he was likely there; and from 1973-5 we certainly shared the same University Campus.

Other threads contribute to the pattern: my husband's friend from university and one of *my* university friends, with whom I lost contact after graduation, appear years later, as husband and wife. Her pattern forms part of mine as we battle infertility together and then ends when her life is taken by cancer.

Other threads in the pattern belong to a childhood friend and the only teacher I ever clashed with at Secondary School. I saw my childhood friend rarely, but it did not matter; we were always part of the pattern of each others lives. My friend died of cancer in her early fifties and the teacher I last saw as a 14-year-old, officiated at her funeral. Patterns can be obvious or subtle; regular or random, but whatever the case, there is much they can teach us. I finally met my husband when we both stepped outside the familiar to create different patterns. He is a born and bred city boy who, at university, said *yes* to a last-minute teaching practice opportunity in a country town and enjoyed it so much, applied for the school on graduation.

I am a country girl who grew up in Victoria's north-east and, wanting to explore the *unfamiliar* western part of the state, applied for schools there. Neither of us got our first choice of schools but our willingness to try something different meant we ended up in the same staffroom at the same time.

You might call our meeting, after so many near misses, a coincidence; the psychoanalyst Carl Jung might call it synchronicity (when meaningful but unrelated events occur together); and as a fantasy writer, I might call it magic. Its name is less important than the insight it offers, namely that, in taking a chance on the unknown rather than staying in the known, we create *new* patterns, rather than repeat the patterns of the past. It is about *truly* living each year not living one year over and over again. It is the reason we hitched the van on the 4x4 and drive west.

The patterns of my past also reinforce the uncomfortable truth that none of us have unlimited time to explore our soul-journeys. The young woman I reconnected with after university died in her early thirties without her longed-for children, and my best friend died of cancer at 52, a few months before her first two grandchildren were born. They were robbed of what I still have: the chance to create a fully-realised life.

I am a different person to the one who visited Burra many years ago but returning there unsettles me for a second reason. I often ponder how random the time and place of my birth (and everyone else's) seems to be and how different my life would be had I been born a hundred years earlier or in a different place.

Many of the miners who flocked to Burra's copper mines lived in primitive dugouts along Burra Creek. They were poor in their home countries (mostly in the UK) and they were poor in Burra and while they seized the chance for a better life, smallpox and typhoid claimed many.

Only time divides me from those miners with whom I share a genetic heritage. I came to Australia when sanitation and medicine were better, and human life held more value, and so once again, luck is on my side.

Want to explore further?
Paddle Steamers: https://www.environment.sa.gov.au/goodliving/posts/2019/02/paddle-steamers
Nikakis, K. S. 1995 *The purpose of dragons in selected children's literature in the twentieth century*. M.Ed. (Hons). Charles Sturt University, Australia.
Nikakis, K. S. 2010 *Dragon Tales – the role of the dragon in selected narratives* - Heidelberg Press, Australia. (Drawn from my master's degree)
The Emerald Serpent: https://www.amazon.com.au/Emerald-Serpent-Karen-Simpson-Nikakis-ebook/dp/B016GGTUXO
The Emerald Serpent Book Trailer: https://www.youtube.com/watch?v=bGpKxnpCEMg
Angel Caste – Complete 5 Book Series: https://www.amazon.com/Angel-Caste-Complete-5-Book-ebook/dp/B07RT15HW5
Morgan S.A*:* http://www.aussietowns.com.au/town/morgan-sa
T.S. Eliot: https://interestingliterature.com/2017/02/a-short-analysis-of-t-s-eliots-burnt-norton/
Burra S.A.: http://www.aussietowns.com.au/town/burra-sa\

STRANGERS

Ghosts assume so many forms I do not immediately realise I am
looking at one when the Barrier Highway takes us through Terowie,
a pretty historic settlement of well-preserved 19th century buildings.
Their painted wooden facades, broad corrugated verandas, and
turned veranda posts are typical of many country towns and of the
one I grew up in but, unlike my hometown, these deserted streets
bear the hallmarks of a *ghost* town.

The 2016 Census puts Terowie's population at under 200 and, as
I scan the carefully restored but mainly *empty* buildings, it strikes
me that Terowie mirrors the psychological state that precedes our
need to change. To the casual observer, it all looks to be in perfect
working order but there is no vibrant pulse of inner life beyond the
neat facades.

We reach Peterborough late afternoon and it is good to see the
familiar faces of our friends and be welcomed. We have known these
couples from the time we all ended up in that small, country school
staffroom where I met my husband We investigate our water leak
and the first (uncomfortable) task is to crawl underneath and gouge
out the silicon that caulks the metal casing. We peel it back to reveal
a badly connected pipe that, much to my relief, is soon fixed.

A leaking water tank can be more than an inconvenience in the Australian Outback; it can be lethal. We are not travelling in the hottest
part of the year when people can and do die when their vehicles
break down or become bogged but we still take the precaution of
carrying an extra 40 litres (10 gallons) of fresh water in the 4x4 (in
addition to the van's tanks).

Like many of the towns we visit, Peterborough relies on the tourist
trade for extra income, but there is nothing grudging about what it
offers. The town provides a centrally located parking area for big
rigs like ours, complete with water, clean toilets, and dump point (for
emptying caravan toilets). The locals are genuinely friendly too.

This is not always the case when we leave the cities behind and, as I consider the historical suspicion of strangers, I wonder whether the antagonism stems from inherited memories, when strangers could indeed herald danger, or whether it relates to a more modern phenomenon called politics.

Australia sells itself as a nation of bronzed beach and bush-folk but nations are always more complex than the face they present to the world. Australia is, in fact, one of the most highly urbanised nations in the world with around 90% of us living in cities or regional centres of over 100,000 people. And yet, rural Australians have long been extolled as *truer* examples of the down-to-earth, no nonsense, hard-working Aussie.

As well as the rural-urban divide, there are divides between states and territories that run north-south and east-west that reflect Australia's developmental timelines and the on-going geographical isolation of the far west and far north.

Setting out on any journey means encountering unfamiliar landscapes *and* unfamiliar people too. It is rare to meet anyone openly hostile to *Southerners* (as Victorians are sometimes called) but we do meet people with completely different world views, which is one of the reasons we travel. I have never known anyone to convince someone else to change their minds in arguments over climate-change or government policy but such arguments remind us of humanity's breadth *and* force us to think through our own beliefs, a process important to our soul-journeys.

Many divides are more ephemeral or at least more superficial than they appear, especially when we sit around a campfire and share food with tales of the road behind and the challenges of the way ahead. Our journey inwards might be unique to us, but countless others tread their own inward paths too and we often have more in common with them than outward appearances suggest.

Want to explore further?

Terowie: http://www.aussietowns.com.au/town/terowie-sa
Peterborough S.A.: https://www.aussietowns.com.au/town/peterborough-sa

PORTALS

When Viv steps into a rift (in *Angel Caste*) everything dissolves into a swirl of iridescent nothingness until she steps out again into the glittering and astonishingly different angel world of Ezam. Entering new worlds via ancient stone circles or black holes deep in space, is common in fantasy fiction but not quite so dramatic in the so-called *real* world and our portal into the Outback is far more mundane.

After some fun touristy activities exploring Peterborough's rail heritage, we head off along a sealed road into a moonscape of red sandy soil and spinifex (a spiky grass that grows in large tussocky cushions). The landscape confirms we have left the familiar safety of our previous lives behind and I am acutely aware that my welfare (even my life) depends on the continued movement of the mechanical device we drive and on any punctures we suffer not exceeding the number of spares we carry.

Our *mechanical device* is sophisticated but we soon pass the wreckage of other things that were once considered *sophisticated* and that proved no match for the Outback's inexorable heat and dryness.

Unforged

Shape-shifter metal
was once a vehicle, a water-tower, a bridge
but escaped the blacksmith's hammer
and the mighty machines' compression

and unforged

not by fire but by air and water
and the traitorous hand of
Time

To emphasise we are now truly in the Outback, we travel the *Outback Highway* north through Hawker, Parachilna and Leigh Creek to the historic, picturesque and well-known ruins of Farina. There is little roadkill along the way but plenty of other sobering reminders of lives once lived. Chimney stacks rise like limbless trees in the paddocks; fencing wire rusts in tangles; and the bizarre skeletons of derelict machines strew the ground.

In Victoria's wetter greenness there are ruins marked by great swathes of jonquils, where the bulbs continue to multiply long after the homestead's timbers rot away and even here, I see the occasional pink bloom of briar roses; a hardy rootstock that outlives its prettier, more fragile graft. The briars are scattered, probably spread by birds eating the rosehips but there are no other signs of gardens at the ruins we pass.

Later I explore in more detail how gardens are testaments to people's desire to bend Nature to their will but here, Nature will not be bent. The sun-seared earth devoured the gardens long ago along with the dreams of those settlers who fought to stay and failed.

STILLNESS

Prior to more sophisticated medical machinery, it was difficult to ascertain if someone was really dead, hence the stories of burying people with strings attached to above ground bells they could ring if they later woke in their coffins. Stillness was one way of judging death but Farina's ruins, despite being bereft of their original, life-giving citizens, are far from still. Instead, they are full of travellers like us *and* being restored by an army of volunteers.

Farina is more extensive and picturesque than the tumble of ruins we pass along the highway and the campground is popular too: a sprawling expanse of silty-dust sites marked by wooden tables and ash-blackened fire pits. We drop our nominal fee into the metal box fixed to the gate and find spots amongst the campers.

There are families; backpackers; and travellers like us; camping in everything from swags to $150,000 plus RV's and everything in between. The flies are waiting to greet us and we beat them off as we set up. They are greedy for the moisture of our eyes, noses and mouths and for the first time we don our fly-nets and head off to explore.

The westering sun douses the ruins in egg-yolk yellow so that the stone seems to glow and I snap phone photos as I walk, my thoughts on those who left here early and on those who tried to hang on. The sandy soil is overprinted with Nike and Adidas soles, and I think of the bare feet of the First Nation peoples; of the nail-studded soles of the early settlers; and of their children's tender soles.

Slyly

The stone was wrested from the ground
against its will
hewn into unnatural shapes
and forced to lie
straight edge
to straight edge

But the mortar was stone too
in another guise
and Time was on
its side

It loosed its grip slyly
over the years
and let the stone
go back
to the earth

Farina's pretty ruins adorn many a tourist brochure and yet life here
was anything but pretty. The settlement was eventually abandoned,
like the other ruins we passed, and I ponder at what point we walk
away from something dangerous, damaging or ultimately futile in
achieving what we really want.

We seem to be held captive by the warrior mentality of our warlike
history. We are either the victor or the vanquished, with little in between. One way or another, we are exhorted to *battle on*; *stick to our
guns*; *not to give up*. There might be an inherent nobility in standing
firm when all hope is gone in some situations, but thankfully, most of
us are not in these situations most of the time.

I am not suggesting all struggles are pointless or that defeat teaches
us nothing, because without struggle, we are unlikely to progress our
soul-journeys but knowing *when* to walk away is a victory in itself
although it is rarely seen as such. We might dress it up as a *strategic
withdrawal* or a *re-evaluation of a dynamic situation* if we feel the
need to defend our withdrawal or we might, with brutal honesty,
pause to evaluate what the struggle/situation is *really* costing us.

Time and money are obvious costs but there are less obvious and potentially far greater costs to any struggle such as the damage inflicted on our physical and mental health; the loss of joy in living; the
diminishing of our sense of self-worth; and the death of optimism for
the future.

We take back control over a situation *and* ourselves when we stand back and say: *You know what? This is simply not worth my time, attention, or energy.* It does not mean we should ignore something potentially dangerous; it means there are times when we need to distance ourselves from a struggle/situation to replenish the physical, emotional and spiritual reserves we need to move in more *fulfilling* and *rewarding* directions.

Missing

We see only what is lost

A roof gone
missing panes of window-glass
the silvered trunks
of limbless trees

Maybe we think of those
who lived here
missing too

The laughter of the young
the voices of the old

We do not see what is left

The sturdy walls, the chimney stack
and a briar rose
more stubborn than its graft
still dragging moisture from a ground
as hard as stone

By the time we return from our walk there are campfires dotting the darkness and murmured conversations drifting on the cooling air. The campground has pit toilets and coin-operated showers but we are self-contained and, keen to develop good habits, continue the miserly use of our own water. It is part of the paring away of things once thought necessary; a type of mundane decluttering in our outer journey that we must also perform on our inner one.

In my outer journey, I discover how easy it is to wash in half a bucket of water; soak our dirty clothes in the remainder; and finally dump the residue on the thirsty trees. We wear a smaller range of clothing too, alternating between a couple of tee-shirts and pairs of shorts in the heat; and a couple of windcheaters and tracksuit pants in the cooler evenings. Meals become simpler too as our focus narrows to what connects and centres us.

There is time in the long dusk to simply sit; to notice the prints of ants and birds in the dust; the birth of stars in the sky, and the rise of the moon in all its subtle shape-shifts. I track satellites overhead and thrill to the flash of meteorites. I smell the woodsmoke and listen to the crack of flames; I see how the colours bloom and die in the fire's heart and I think of how people have done this for thousands of years. Others chat but I mostly sit in silence and silence is mostly enough.

The pause at Farina gives me the chance to reflect on our time since leaving Melbourne and on our earlier trips into Australia's heart. We started our love affair with the Outback when we first camped in the Flinders Ranges in the 1970's and when our family grew to four, we used the two week school holiday breaks to dash the 1340 kms (832 miles) over three days to Alice Springs, camping at Port Augusta and Coober Pedy along the way. The sprint gave us six full days to explore the desert before we dashed back.

Those days were filled with snowstorms of corellas taking flight at our approach and the dangerous beauty of snakes sliding away from our tyres' rumble. Kangaroos and emus were common then too but most of *living* wildlife we see this time are crows and eagles at feast on kangaroo and emu corpses.

Eagles Feast

Eagles feast on roadkill
their disdain for cars
near-fatal

Crows eat too
more humbly
and more safely

Perhaps it is why
the tale fantastic
is crammed with the other-worldly
knowingness of crows

and not with
the arrogance
of eagles

On one of these earlier trips, we came across a herd of newly slain
camels that had strayed into the path of a road train. Road trains are
massive trucks that haul up to four trailers, rule the Outback roads
and, like rail-bound trains, cannot swerve or stop for animals (or
tourists).

Their bull bars smash through feathers and flesh alike and we have
seen decapitated cattle that have stuck their heads out. We do not
stick our heads out; we give road trains all the road they want. We
see no dead (or living) camels this time but the animal carnage that
litters the verges continues to shock me.

Deadway

The avenue of corpses runs for miles
this section of the highway
a cemetery
reserved for kangaroos

But there are places
where the emu gods intrude
to lay their own to rest

to let feathers stir
in homage to the passing draught
of cars

They rest less quietly
than kangaroos
whose desiccated hides
lie motionless

and yet nothing here
is truly at peace

Farina is only a few days from Melbourne but I am struck by how
death-steeped this journey already is. Apart from the roadkill, we
pass the ruins of single stations (ranches) and now pause at Farina's
more extensive ones: broken buildings that hold not just the death of
the settlement's communal life and the dreams of those who abandoned it, but the bones of those who were left behind in the earth.

We know *consciously* that death is part of life but few people welcome it unless as an escape from intolerable physical and/or mental
pain and I wonder if my outer journey is reinforcing the naturalness
of death to my inner, *unconscious* understanding.

Knowing life is finite adds a certain urgency to getting on with
things (however defined) but progressing our inner soul-journey
requires the *metaphorical* death of our previous self. We cannot be
both the happy child in the sandpit and the excited adolescent with
the keys to their first car; one life-stage must give way to the other, a
point I return to later.

There are many rituals that surround literal death and I happen to
live near a large cemetery which demonstrates some. At one end,
there is an avenue of marble mausoleums that are grander than many

houses. When I pass them on a walk, I wonder whether these mini mansions are about the *earthly* status and power of the deceased or of their still *living* relatives. But mausoleums might also be evidence of the desire to keep extended families together or be rooted in the need to protect the dead against scavengers and/or grave robbers.

Later in 2019, we visit London's historic Highgate Cemetery and learn it was established to allow deeper, more secure graves than those available in overcrowded churchyards. A few years earlier, we also visited the equally evocative Père Lachaise Cemetery in Paris and, as our Outback trek continues, I venture into smaller and more isolated cemeteries tucked away down dusty tracks.

Highgate and Père Lachaise Cemeteries are famous for their ce-lebrity graves but I have no interest in celebrities. Both cemeteries have exquisite funereal architecture with Père Lachaise's weeping, stone-shrouded figures achingly poignant and its Art Nouveau graves glorious, but beyond admiring their beauty, I have no real interest funereal statuary either.

What I *am* interested in, is harder to define. Cemeteries share some-thing special, even those with unkempt graves baking in the Outback sun or bounded by busy roads; they have a deep sense of quiet or a kind of stillness, where we sink deeper into our souls.

When we step through the mossy stone walls of Père Lachaise and Highgate Cemeteries, we step into an oasis of otherness where time escapes the measurement of the clocks outside. Graves in these cem-eteries can be old indeed (the earliest at Père Lachaise dates to 1142) but it is more than that. These cemeteries, like others, are sanctuaries for the living as well as the dead.

Mature trees form verdant canopies that give refuge to birds while lush growth fills the spaces between graves, making homes for other small creatures. The dappled shade and oxygenated air might con-tribute to the atmosphere of Highgate and Père Lachaise cemeteries too, but I feel the same in the exposed Outback cemeteries.

Cemeteries are places of death but not of endings, regardless of our religious beliefs or lack of them. Death is not an ending if we believe a soul (or similar) quits the body and goes somewhere heavenly, hellish or to another body. Death is not even an ending if we believe *everything* (however defined) ceases, because decomposition moves us inexorably back to a state ready for recycling.

Cemeteries add to my sense of the randomness of where I exist in place and time. Gravestones deliver potted histories of the dead and, in the Outback, I read of young men who drowned fording flooded rivers and of young women buried with the infants they died birthing. And again, I am reminded that time is finite and my soul-journey not something to be postponed.

Want to explore further?
Peterborough: https://www.peterborough.sa.gov.au/page.aspx?u=304
Spinifex: https://en.wikipedia.org/wiki/Triodia_(plant)
Farina: https://traveloutbackaustralia.com/farina.html/
Flinders Ranges: https://www.parks.sa.gov.au/find-a-park/Browse_by_region/flinders-ranges-outback/ikara-flinders-ranges-national-park
Australia's Wild Camels: http://www.bbc.com/travel/story/20180410-the-strange-story-of-australias-wild-camel
Road Train: https://www.volvotrucks.com.au/en-au/news/magazine-online/2016/jun/australian-outback-road-train.html
Père Lachaise Cemetery: https://www.google.com/search?q=pere%20fanchais%20cemetery%20Paris&rlz=1C1SQJL_enAU811AU811&oq=pere+fanchais+cemetery+Paris
Highgate Cemetery: https://highgatecemetery.org

EMU-TRACKS

The First Nation Arabana/Ngarabana tongue names the lemon-co-
loured blossoms of the mulga (a type of acacia/wattle) *utnadata* but I
see no characteristic wattle-clusters on the straggly mulga stands we
pass as we leave Farina behind, head north to Marla, and turn west
along the Oodnadatta (Utnadata) Track.

We have travelled the Oodnadatta Track before and, like other major
unsealed Outback roads, its condition depends on the weather and
when the last grader went through to smooth it. The track might be
closed after heavy rain but even when the usual aridity prevails, it
can be very rough indeed.

As the corrugations increase, we drop to third in our convoy; just beyond our friends' dust clouds. There is a complex theory behind the
formation of corrugations but the resulting ridges rattle the teeth and
literally shake vehicles and vans apart. There are stories of people
pulling up, only to discover once the dust clears, that they tow the
A-frame of their van with the rest of it having disintegrated along the
way.

These stories are likely exaggerations but they give a sense of the
state of the road. Our friends subscribe to a second theory that,
at higher speeds, vehicles skip along the top of corrugations, but
breaking something out here can mean waiting weeks for parts to be
shipped in and I am happy to go slower.

The land sweeps away flat to the horizon on every side and glittering piles of windscreen glass and rubber flung from tyres joins the
roadkill. Dust plumes mark other travellers in the distance and show
where the track cuts this way and that across sand and stone, and we
thud-thud on, making our own dust cloud until we finally arrive at
William Creek in the late afternoon, dust-clad but unscathed.

There is one caravan park at William Creek and we pay our fees
and circle the other campers in search of sites. They are hard to find
and we split up and finally pull into number 13. It proves as inauspi-

cious as the number suggests and we are set up before we discover the power pole is faulty. The manager solves the problem with a 25 metre extension cord plugged into another site.

The caravan park's only water is a lukewarm dribble in the showers and so fantasies about standing in gushing hot water remain fantasies. I have carried the association between water and caravan parks (as opposed to more rustic campgrounds and free camps) in my head from Victoria but William Creek breaks it. Water is scarce in the Outback and doled out accordingly, but the Outback's vast, wonderful sunsets are free and I take my share of the latest glorious offering as I stretch my legs.

Other travellers are in good cheer as they roll in, dust-covered (like us) from the track. Most are older couples or older men with their own rigs, travelling with friends. The media dubs them *Grey Nomads*: retirees with the time and money to finally explore their own lands but I wonder how many of our fellow travellers are simply interested in ticking off tourist *hotspots* and how many, like me, search for something else.

Oodnadatta Track

There are tyres along the edges
flung off in strips
or whole
and wheel rims
no match for

corrugations
corrugations
corrugations

Other travellers pass us or we pass them
headlights in the dust
or dust clouds in the distance
as fast as ghosts

We stop for the night and swap stories:
the bloke who blew two tyres
the man who only
discovers his back windshield is
gone as he pulls in
beside us

But there are deeper injuries
than vehicle damage:
a stroke
a time of darkness and despair
but back on the road again
travelling to who knows
where

*bloke – colloquial Australian for man

William Creek is not just a fuel and rest stop on the drive west; or caravan park, pub and general store; it is the base for flights over Kati Thanda-Lake Eyre. European explorers were right to guess that many Outback rivers empty into a vast inland sea, but evaporation means Kati Thanda-Lake Eyre is mostly a sparkling salt pan spread over 9,500 sq kms (3,667 sq miles) of red, sandy soil.

Yet every now and then, storms in the three states and the one territory its vast, sprawling drainage basin draws on, deliver enough rain for water to wend its way over hundreds of kilometres to fill the great, inland depression (15 m/49 ft below sea level), and then the birds come, and visitors like us, to fly over Kati Thanda – Lake Eyre as the birds do, if more briefly.

Many years ago, on a different trip with entirely different intentions, we met an older couple camped in the Flinders Ranges who suggested we join them on a visit to Lake Eyre South, as it was named then. (Kati Thanda, its First Nation Arabana/Ngarabana name, was returned in 2012.)

We agreed and it changed everything. The sky that day was a brilliant blue and the salt pan a vast expanse of glittering diamonds. We trekked far over it to find crystallised twigs and insects transformed by salt into exquisite, if ephemeral, jewels but it was not the lake's beauty that was life-altering; it was the couple's matter-of-fact comment that the Outback was just a three-day drive from Melbourne.

Until that meeting, the Outback had seemed as remote as another planet, but when we got back to Melbourne, we took out a map and compass, and drew circles around the city. One day's travel; two days travel; three days travel. How far could we get, in the usual two-week school holiday break, if we drove 11 or 12 hours a day? A long way, as it turned out, and so began our three-day dashes to Alice Springs.

And those six days of driving to and from the Outback were far from wasted time. Being confined all day in a vehicle and setting camp together each night, meant connecting more deeply as a family; something that lost none of its preciousness even as the lollies (candy) and toys of small children gave way to the books and PC's of adolescents. And even now, our (adult) children speak fondly of how special those times were.

That chance meeting in the Flinders Ranges all those years ago, reinforced why we journey in the first place. Staying *where* we are, both literally and metaphorically, risks staying *what* we are, and for all its comfortable predictability, that means a small life; not one enlarged by an inward journey that is, one way or another, accessible to us all.

The next day, we pay a lot of money for a small plane flight over Kati Thanda-Lake Eyre. Scenic flights are always expensive and we have helicoptered over the Grand Canyon and volcanoes on the Big Island of Hawaii; small-planed over the wonders of Kakadu National Park; and later in this trip, small-plane over the Bungle Bungle Range too.

We spend the money because we do not know what is coming: illness, incapacitation, death; or a virus with profound effects on the whole world and specific, nullifying effects on our travel plans. As I have pointed out, none of us know the date on our death certificates; only that we are here *now* and the flight might show us something soul-feedingly beautiful, or if not, certainly something different.

Deciding to take the flight also demonstrates the *dual* nature of making any decision, a duality that often goes unnoticed. In *deciding* to fly, we *decide* to experience something different. Had we decided *not* to take the flight, we would have decided *not* to experience something different, that is, to remain as we are.

This duality applies to every decision. If we decide to change jobs, we decide to experience something different (and open up new possibilities); if we decide *not* to change jobs, we decide *not* to experience something different (and *not* to open up new possibilities).

In any decision, we tend to focus on the consequences of *doing* something; not on the consequences of *not* doing something. In short, if we decide *not* to do something, we are in essence, deciding to stay *as we are*, which is fine, if we make the decision knowingly.

Silver Heart

Thermals bob us like corks on a hat
the plane a three-seater
the pretty Czech pilot
methodical
as she tells us our history
in a heavy accent

Well not *our* history exactly
but some strange blend
of what is accepted
as true
at least by some

Kati Thanda:
at least we have given
the name back
which is a start

The rain fell far away
and came here
like us

over the red dust
to settle
low and salty
in the country's
silver heart

We look down
as the pelicans do
see swirls of empty waterways
saltbush
the emu-tracks of wind

But there is another seeing
etched into the landscape
the scarification
of initiation
that tells of a knowing
we can never share

Birds gather whenever Kati Thanda-Lake Eyre fills but people still debate how they know to fly inland to Australia's (usually) arid interior. Regardless, it is a relief to see so many *live* birds after so much death.

We are too high to make out the smaller birds like banded stilts that gather on the shore, but the pelicans are obvious. They glide beneath us and congregate on the water's edge, drawing Kati Thanda-Lake Eyre's visitors as much as the flooded saltpan, but my interest soon shifts to the surrounding country. I was lucky to grow up in a rural area where I spent many happy hours horse-riding along bushy trails and I continued my love of landscape by studying geography in my first degree.

Like so much of Australia's centre, the land below is a nameless red colour: a cross between rust and blood; and ancient, with great throws of nubbed ridges, dry creek beds, and smudges of green that hint at subterranean moisture. I am enthralled by the grand sweeping vista of a land I have spent countless hours gazing at from the 4x4 window but I am also painfully aware of my cultural blindness.

As a geographer, I see fault lines, drainage basins, and the morphology of streambeds; and as a writer, I see the poetry of the land's vast sprawl, but I know I see through European eyes and not as First Nation people see it, and I feel my lack keenly.

Want to explore further?
Oodnadatta Track: https://www.hemamaps.com/explore/tracks/oodnadatta-track
Kati Thanda – Lake Eyre: https://auth-sa.southaustralia.com/travel-blog/kati-thanda-lake-eyre
Kati Thanda – Lake Eyre geology: https://earthobservatory.nasa.gov/images/145076/rare-filling-of-kati-thanda-lake-eyre

DUST STARS

We meet over breakfast, in the pristine early morning light, to consider the route ahead. We can cut west to Coober Pedy, to the quicker, *tarmacked* Stuart Highway, or continue north on the Oodnadatta Track. Despite the corrugations, we choose the latter, deciding the landscape is likely to be more interesting, and so it proves.

The land is flat, with the occasional low-swept hill, and pinkish soil strewn with stones known as gibbers. The stony downs or gibber plains have a fascinating geological history but I think of the effect of their jagged edges on our tyres and historically, on the hooves of the early explorers' pack animals.

We take a break at the Pink Roadhouse Oodnadatta, so-called because it is painted pink (!). Roadhouses are important landmarks in the Outback and serve as community hubs. Apart from providing fuel (and toilets) they can act as General Stores, Post Offices, and banks (via ATMs) and some have bars and food service too.

We refuel at most roadhouse we come to, regardless of need. Some fuel stops are over 200 kms (124 miles) apart and even when closer, a power outage or unpublicised closure might mean fuel is unavailable and, without fuel, no one goes anywhere. Outback roadhouses were once great sources of information about road conditions and other hazards but not anymore.

The traditional Australian proprietors (often a husband and wife team) who worked long hours in sweltering conditions in the middle of nowhere have largely been replaced by international backpackers who work for a few months to fund their travel and then move on. No amount of Googling (*when* we have coverage) replaces the knowledge the old-style proprietors accrued over the years.

In fantasy narratives, they are the Wise Old Man and Crone archetypes, but even without the old-style roadhouse proprietors, there are wise people on the road, *if* we pay attention. A joke around the campfire; a retelling of some yarn (story) at the shower block; a snippet of someone's trip shared at the fuel pump: wisdom comes in many forms.

The widow who travels with her dog; the widower who tags along with friends; the survivors of stroke and cancer: all are on the road again, seeking journeying's healing and what it might teach them.

I find the changing landscape endlessly fascinating: the sage green of saltbush and casuarinas; the pale gold of spinifex; the silver strews of windfall timber; the pink-rust-blood-red of stones and soil; and over all, the Outback's soaring skies. The radio is off and we speak little in the vehicle; simply sit and enjoy.

We pass more salt pans: smaller, drier and less famous than Kati Thanda-Lake Eyre but still beautiful. The track remains dusty and corrugated. It has not been graded lately and is popular, not just with southern tourists like us (who commonly set out around May/June after the ferocious Outback heat ebbs), but with road trains, the Outback's main form of transport of animals and supplies.

Dust (known as bulldust in the Outback) is our constant companion. Campers have tricks for keeping it out of their vehicles and vans but none are 100 percent effective. Dust, like the ever present flies, is simply part of the journey.

Dust

Dust covers our skin, our clothes
we breathe it in
and out
and curse its redness
and dryness

its endless ability
to seep and settle

But at night the stars take over
clean and bright
and it is easy to forget
that they are dust
and we are too

Spinifex and mulga punch holes in the gibber but bird life is limited to hawks and eagles, lolling about in the thermals, high in the
cloudless sky. There is less native animal roadkill now but more
cattle corpses. Cattle grids rumble as we pass over them to remind us
we drive through vast pastoral leases, mostly unfenced. Much of the
surrounding lands are, in fact, one huge paddock.

The track also dips over concrete floodways where rivers cross when
it rains. Flood markers tell us water can reach over two meters (6.5
feet) but it has not rained for months (or years) in some places out
here.

The drought means there is no risk of drowning or wet-bogging
although it is wise to remember that rainfall kilometres distant can
fill these riverbeds with fatal suddenness. The unwritten rule of the
Outback is not to camp in or near riverbeds, no matter how inviting
their soft sand looks.

The sun sinks and given we drive west it is a relief when it slides
below the horizon. Then Outback's magic truly begins. The land's
openness gives a 360-degree horizon, fire-rimmed where sky meets
earth and flowing up through hues of peach, yellow and pale aqua
to the deep velvet blue of the heavens' zenith. There is a hiatus as
stillness settles and then the silver of stars intrudes; scattered at first
and then crusted, layer upon jewelled layer, until their brilliance all
but obliterates the darkness between.

This glorious show is in full swing as we pull off the road onto a flat
area of gibber and form a circle with the vans. Our friends soon have
their *barbeque* going (a dismembered gas cylinder) and we feed it
with the wood collected along the way. Damper (a bread of flour and

water and whatever else we want to add) is cooked in the coals and foil-wrapped potatoes added.

Wood-smoke fills the air and orange fire sparks join the silver ones above. The fire creates a circle of people, and a circle has long been a symbol of inclusion, perfection and never-ending life. But I am not thinking about a circle's symbolism as my gaze flicks between the flames and the stars; I am simply letting myself *be*.

Want to explore further?
Gibber Plains: http://www.anbg.gov.au/photo/vegetation/stony-downs.html
Pink Roadhouse: https://www.google.com/search?q=pink+roadhouse

PLUNGE

The first wave is the worst. It is not the brief terror as the wall of water towers over me, although that is real enough; or the obliteration of sky by foam; it is the smash of chill water against warm flesh. The shock of the change always takes my breath away. We swim in Victoria's southern oceans every Christmas beach holiday, and even when the sand burns my feet, and lingering on its brilliant whiteness risks dehydration and sunburn, the shock is the same.

I am a creeper into cold water and even at the warm, indoor lap pool, I take the ladder. My husband is the opposite. He is a plunger. He jumps into the lap pool, sending a tsunami to slop the tiles and, at the beach, he runs past me and dives, while I loiter, knee-deep, dreading that first wave.

In 2010, however, I do take the plunge (of sorts) when I sign up for the 68th World Science Fiction Convention in Melbourne. I had never attended events of thousands of international writers and fans before and I find myself *on* panels and *running* them.

Writing is mostly a solitary occupation and my focus on the hero's inner journey means I spend more time looking inwards, writing-wise, than outwards but in 2010, I decide it would be good to mix with like-minded people and hear *different*-minded views on speculative fiction (science fiction, fantasy and horror).

Taking *the plunge* (both literal and metaphorical) is never easy. There were some heart-pounding moments at that first convention, but I find my feet and over the following years attend the same event in Finland and sign up for Dublin's later in 2019, which is why we have a firm return date to Melbourne.

I think about the effort (and often bravery) change requires as we head off the next morning, join the Stuart Highway at Marla, and turn north. In 2016, we shifted from a large house on 12.8 hectares (30 acres) into a small, suburban unit on less than half a house block.

Lack of space meant I gave away beautiful clothes and objects collected over years of overseas travel. I expected to really miss these things and was surprised to feel only relief in shedding them *and* pleasure in knowing that others might enjoy them.

Shifting house always necessitates change, in part because what suits the previous house rarely suits the new. This decluttering in the outward journey is mirrored in the inward journey where we cast off what we once thought was important; but the task in the inner world is harder than donating parts of ourselves to charity shops, even were it possible.

The mythologist Joseph Campbell noted that we must die to our old selves to be born as our new selves, that is, we cannot be *both* the happy child in the lolly (candy) shop and the young adult on the joyful threshold of independent life. One state *must* give way to the other *if* we are to progress. Growth, both physical and spiritual, is about change.

Change

Some disrobe first
leaving their former lives behind
like a pile of neatly folded clothes

Some jump in, fully dressed
some misstep and fall
while others must be pushed

The effects of change are the same:
a shock that takes the breath away
a floundering and then
a slow
making of sense

We must take the plunge
to find a new world
to make our own

until another world
beckons

It is a short 159 kms (98 miles) to the Northern Territory (NT) border
and there are prohibitions on carrying fruit and vegetables into the
NT too. Working out *exactly* what they are proves frustrating given
the signage is at odds with the Territory's website. The Quarantine
Check Point is unmanned, like South Australia's but unlike Western
Australia's, where Quarantine Officers search vehicles and vans.

Being an island has saved Australia from pests and diseases that
plague some other parts of the world but historical ignorance introduced birds such as the common myna, common starling, spotted
dove and rock pigeon; and pest animals such as rabbits and foxes;
and in more modern times, the cane toad.

Over the years, carelessness has added feral animals such as camels,
goats, deer, brumbies (horses), pigs, water buffalo, and the domestic
cat gone wild: a creature lethally efficient at hunting small native
animals With this troubled history firmly in mind, we conscien-
tiously eat the rest of the fruit as we drive and, as we cross another
dashed-line on the map, are confident the few vegetables we carry
are compliant.

The first thing I notice on the other side of that dashed-line is the
flash of metal through the mulga and then I recall seeing abandoned
cars on an earlier trip. Now as then, I puzzle over why these wrecks
have not been removed. Perhaps they were stolen and dumped and
then left there by owners unwilling or unable to pay for their retriev-
al, or perhaps they broke down and were abandoned as unimportant.
They might also be examples of *bush mechanics*, a method of repur-
posing vehicles practiced by some First Nation people.

Tin Cans

Cars rest on their roofs
red, white and blue
tin cans
shining in the sun

Robbed of movement
like flipped turtles
everything of value
stripped and yet
worth remains

a stillness
an anchor in the landscape
that the passing cars
lack

The wreckage seems like a terrible waste to me and I have to remind
myself that cultural practices vary. Western cultures use cars, houses,
jewellery and clothes to mark achievement, status and wealth but not
all cultures do. Nor is any culture static. Cultures change; sometimes
infinitesimally over many years and sometimes with dramatic speed.

In the outer world of our physical selves, cells rearrange themselves
without much personal intervention (apart from proper nutrition)
to change us from babies, to children, to adolescents, to adults, to
the aged, but in the inner world of our psychological selves, action
(either deliberate or accidental) is required to cast off the too-small
shell of our former selves.

This change happens at a broader, societal level too, when the old
give way to the young. It is the natural order of things and inevitable,
given we are mortal, but historically the old retained their importance as *fonts of knowledge*. Having lived longer, they had experienced more, and so knew more.

The mass transmission of information put an end to that and the accumulated experience of the old became less important. But information is not wisdom; wisdom is a very different beast indeed. While the young can be wise, the time and effort required to *develop* wisdom more often makes it the preserve of the old although, as I have already noted, wisdom does not result simply by the failure to die.

The inward journey (the soul-journey) of sifting, sorting and discarding what is no longer useful (the parts of our former selves) is about developing our own, individual wisdom (although it shares elements with the broader wisdom of others). This sorting process of experiences and beliefs to arrive at what is important and meaningful to *us*, is arduous and confronting. It means being brutally honest about the gap between what we believe ourselves to be and what, on closer inspection, we *actually* are.

My novels serve as one of my tools for this process and my *Angel Caste* series follows the soul-journeys not only of Viv, but of three angels: Thris, Ky and Ash. Thris thinks he knows exactly what attributes he needs to ascend to the next level in the angel hierarchy (and then *transcend*, the aim of all angels), and is confident he possesses them.

He pledges to protect Viv in their journey through the folds (other worlds), a task that will earn him merit to ascend, but when his angel body is weakened by Moth Fold's caustic fumes, he attacks Viv with devastating consequences for both.

Angel Caste: Excerpt 2

Ky's knowledge of the folds was limited, but the moment he plunged into the soft sand, he knew he was in Sand Fold and that he was safe. The creamy landscape of gentle hills rolled away on every side, undifferentiated except for a single dark shape on the next ridge. Ky sprinted down the sand hill and up the slope to Thris's prone form. He lay on his stomach and the stench of Moth Fold was so strong that it took all Ky's resolve to approach.

'Thris?'

*Thris made no response and Ky's shaking hands turned him.
Thris's eyes were so dark that for a ghastly moment Ky thought him
dead. Trembling from the smell, he stripped off Thris's pack and
clothes and used the sand to clean him. Thris's breathing eased as
Ky worked, and his eyes became less blank, but the bitterness remained and Ky wondered how much damage it had caused.*

'Thris?'

*Thris's eyes came to Ky, still horrifyingly dark. 'I am destroyed,'
he whispered.*

The old Thris is indeed destroyed but not, as he imagines, his chances of transcendence. The *limiting* beliefs of his old self can carry him
no further on his soul-journey and so must die/give way to new ones
if he is to continue. But it is far from an easy or pain free process.

Any journey is a disruption to our comfortable normality and the
unquestioned beliefs and assumptions that form our present selves.
(Of course, disruption can come in many forms apart from journeys,
such as divorce, job loss, accidents and life-threatening illnesses.)
Journeys expose us to different experiences that require different
responses which in turn, open the way for us to become the different
people we need to be to advance our soul-journeys.

The car wrecks we pass are too numerous to result from tragic accidents although we later pass white crosses that mark where people
have lost their lives. These are not uncommon along the sides of
both rural and urban roads and are sobering reminders of someone's
carelessness or suicidal impulse, and the on-going grief of those they
left behind. Cemeteries serve the same purpose, as do memorials,
large and small, like cenotaphs, steles, statues, installations, avenues
of honour (trees) and plaques.

The markers of the death of the old self during the soul-journey
are less obvious to others. We might commit to worrying less; to
excluding damaging people from our lives; to undertaking activities
we fantasised about doing but never thought we would. We might
declutter our physical surroundings; start volunteering; seek out reli-

gious or philosophical groups; or we might do none of these things, content in our awareness that we advance to a more meaningful destination.

We pull into a wayside stop for a coffee near Kulgera and discover the van's batteries no longer work. This means we have no water pump (so only jerry can water that must be poured from a spout) and no lights for free camping. We had intended to visit the Henbury Meteorite Craters but decide to head straight to Alice Springs to find a sparky (electrician). Our friends will keep to the original schedule and join us later.

The park proprietor in Alice Springs gives us the name of a sparky who we contact. He will come the next day, although no precise time will be given. There is nothing new in that. In Australia, the customer waits for tradesmen, not vice-versa.

Our friends come in that night, earlier than planned and the next morning, head off to explore Alice Springs with my husband. I volunteer to wait at the van, keen not to leave it unattended in case the sparky turns up and leaves again (as they sometimes do). The day drags on and I begin to suspect he is a no-show (as indeed he is).

Waiting

We wait in Alice Springs for the sparky to come

Our electricals have developed mystical tendencies
of the dark variety and we are
on the side of light

Midday passes and we ring again.

The sparky does his own scheduling;
we are tersely told to wait

His time is valuable like gold and silver
and precious stones, while ours
is dust

We wait on his pleasure and have no pleasure of our own

He does not come

Perhaps he had a blue with his missus,
a boozy day with his mates
perhaps he was the hero of some other emergency
saved someone else's day
forgot to ring

The electricals right themselves
or are righted by some force unseen
and we travel on

*Australianisms: blue – argument/fight; missus – wife/partner (mrs)

Our enforced delay in Alice Springs gives us time to reflect on the
possibility we might have drained our batteries by leaving things on
that should have been switched off while stationary and we use the
powered site to recharge them.

Even so, I am angry out of all proportion to the sparky's failure to
appear; an anger which, I decide, flows from my meticulous nature. I
honour my undertakings, no matter the personal cost, and I morose-
ly conclude that to progress my soul-journey, I must learn to rise
above this habitual (angry) reaction to the (perceived) unreliability
of others.

Want to explore further?

Bush Mechanics: https://en.wikipedia.org/wiki/Bush_Mechanics

Abandoned cars NT: https://www.abc.net.au/news/2016-12-03/burnt-out-cars-turned-into-art-in-central-australia/8089818

Feral cats: https://www.environment.gov.au/biodiversity/invasive-species/feral-animals-australia/feral-cats

Feral camels:http://www.bbc.com/travel/story/20180410-the-strange-story-of-australias-wild-camel

Angel Caste – Complete 5 Book Series: https://www.amazon.com/Angel-Caste-Complete-5-Book-ebook/dp/B07RT15HW5

Henbury Meteorite Craters: https://nt.gov.au/leisure/parks-reserves/find-a-park/find-a-park-to-visit/henbury-meteorites-conservation-reserve

DISPOSSESSED

The bang shocks me out of my reverie and for a moment I have no idea what has happened. I am one of those people who experience sudden noises the same as being physically struck and then I see it; a star-break in the windscreen.

We are heading out of Alice Springs but still within the town's bounds; on a tarmacked road; doing the speed-limit, as is the on-coming car; the provider of the stone. The break does not spread and we seal it with clear tape and decide against seeking a repairer. We are early in the trip and it seems silly to repair a star-break when we might lose the whole windscreen later.

We plan to stop for fuel and coffee at the Aileron Roadhouse, home to the *Big Man*, a statue I had never heard of. Australia has a lot of *big things* scattered around the countryside; constructed as tourist attractions in less sophisticated times. Over the years we have seen the big merino sheep, wool bale, earth worm, crayfish, trout, lobster, rocking-horse, pineapple and banana.

I do not have high hopes of the Big Man, especially after I learn it is of a First Nation man. In the 1960's (and even today) plaster figures of First Nation men complete with spears and white or red nappy/diaper-like loincloths could be seen in gardens alongside other garden ornaments like plaster swans and gnomes.

Equating First Nation peoples to swans and gnomes was/is largely born of ignorance but Australia has an appalling history of European dealings with First Nation people. The designation of Australia as *terra nullius* (empty land) by its European invaders, was used to justify its acquisition without treaty or payment and set the scene for massacres, land dispossession, enslavement, suppression of cultural practices and later, in the 1960's and 70's, the forced removal of First Nation children to be *assimilated* into European culture.

I explore the devastating effects of what came to be known as the *Stolen Generation* and the importance of *place* to *all* people in my

Deep Fantasy novel *The Third Moon*. The story is narrated by Warrain, a young man of Australian First Nation descent, who lives in
the far flung future on the planet Imago.

Warrain is haunted by inherited memories of his ancestors' brutal
experiences on Earth and the nightmare repeats when Warrain's
community of scientists is expelled from their Space Station by drug
affected Mechs (technicians) and he is forced to leave his mother
and unborn sibling behind. The scientists laboriously build another
Station but then, five years later, the Mechs pay them a visit.

The Third Moon: Excerpt 1

*My blood boiled like a fire-heated oil run at the prospect of being
robbed of my home a second time and I silently swore that I would
kill again and again, rather than let it happen.*

*'Micah would know the odds by now,' went on Rosco, as if he
spoke to himself. 'He will keep us alive to start again somewhere
else, but we will lose the women this time. The Mechs have seen
what we have got.'*

*My heart pounded so hard I had to steady myself against the
rancid wall. It was a fury fed not just by the theft of my immediate
family or of Station One's comforts, but by more ancient thefts committed thousands of years before on Earth.*

Warrain's search for a sense of place is integral to our soul-journeys
and I am still contemplating the dispossession of Australia's First
Nation people when the Big Man appears on the horizon. I feared the
sculpture would be a bigger version of the plaster garden-figures but
it is something else entirely and I am engulfed in the sort of thrilled
wonderment usually reserved for natural landscapes.

The Big Man is set on a hill some distance behind the roadhouse and
there are two more sculptures on the lower land next to the roadhouse, different to the Big Man, but just as powerful. As I stare from
the Big Man to the smaller figures of the woman and child, I do not
think of their creator or the manner of their construction; only of the
profound nexus between the three and the potential of art to aid our
soul-journeys.

Big Man

Big Man on the skyline
square shoulders
narrow hips
straight gaze

And *she*, the female
to his *he*
on the lowlands
her hand upon
their child's head
as she shows her *goanna*

He watches
protective
but sure enough
to leave her free

The sculptures convey a family connection that is both individual
and universal and reinforces my sense that our soul-journeys are
both individual and universal too.

Want to explore further?
Terra nullius: https://www.mabonativetitle.com/tn_01.shtml
Aileron/Big Man: https://www.ausemade.com.au/nt/destination/a/
aileron/aileron-information.htm
The Third Moon: https://www.amazon.com.au/Third-Moon-K-S-
Nikakis-ebook/dp/B071F77KMX

STORIES UNSPOKEN

The roadkill tells its own story; a story I do not know. Where a dead magpie hatched; first launched from its nursing-nest; sang and circled then flew too low or failed to hear the truck or van's rumbling roar; the lands where a dead kangaroo grazed and the dawns it counted before its muscular haunches carried it one bound too fast or one bound too slow across the highway.

I contemplate the ever-present roadkill as we journey but really, I am lost in my thoughts, aided by the uncharacteristic silence in the 4x4. In lots of ways, I am the opposite of my husband. He is extremely sociable while I am happy alone; he must have sound (what I disparagingly call *noise*), whereas I need quiet.

These differences can cause friction (which is why I have a separate room to write in) but he stops me from being a social recluse (which is a good thing) and I tone down his loud gregariousness (which, in my opinion, is also a good thing!)

The soul-journey is completed alone despite treading in the footsteps of countless others who have travelled the universal but individual hero path before us, yet the support of those (in the outer world) who care about us is crucial. My husband has never denigrated my writing (even in the long years before I signed my first publishing contract); has never criticised my need to be alone; has never hesitated to toss clothes in a bag and set off to support me at writing conferences.

But on this trip, for some reason, he seems as content as I am to contemplate the scenery in silence although he makes up for it when we stop: chatting to people at roadhouses, in country towns and at camp sites. Like many writers I watch and listen more than I speak, alert to what is *really* being said. The stories of strangers, spoken or unspoken, can help us decipher our own soul-journeys.

Stroke and cancer; the death of partners; job loss and redundancy: the people we meet are remarkably open about their suffering *and* their determination to keep going. I wonder if in *voicing* their fears, they can better face them and advance their own soul-journeys. Writing about this outer journey is certainly helping me better understand my inner one.

It might also be that, in having suffered, these people are reminded (and remind me) to savour every moment of the time remaining. In the hero stories of myth and legend (and more lately of fantasy), deprivation and suffering serve as powerful triggers for soul-journeys but many of us have little in common with such heroes.

I have lived a fortunate life in a fortunate country; am happily partnered; and have endured no major illnesses or premature loss of those dearest to me. Yet for those of us who have escaped tragedies (however defined), suffering might be more subtle and individualised. We all have different physical and emotional pain thresholds; what is physically or emotionally debilitating for one, is not necessarily for others, and yet in both cases, can prompt change.

From my early teens to my early forties, I experienced bouts of agonising pain every month (thanks to endometriosis which, during the 1970's and 80's, was barely recognised as a condition, let alone treated). I was made to understand, either explicitly or implicitly, that I made a fuss about the normal mild *discomforts* of menstrual cramps. Even when I was curled on the floor vomiting and begging God to make the pain stop, I half believed I was *putting it on*. After all, none of my friends suffered, so it must be all in my head (and so my fault).

As I grew older and sought more medical advice, the option of a hysterectomy was discussed but I wanted children and, at some point made a barely articulated *deal* with God (who I was unsure I believed in) that I would continue to suffer in return for Him one day granting me those longed for children. Unfortunately, endometriosis has dire consequences for fertility, something I did not discover until I was ready to start a family, and what followed were years of fury.

I was furious God had betrayed our *deal* and I was furious that friends and family became pregnant so easily (sometimes accidentally). I was not furious with *them*, of course, (I wished them only well), but their happy state was a constant twist of the knife in the wound of my failings, as those who suffer infertility understand only too well.

None of this was rational. The facts were I had a medical condition called endometriosis that causes severe pain every menstrual cycle and creates internal scarring that often prevents conception. But this was not well known at the time, at least by me.

High levels of distress (whether anger or anguish) can impede conception too and, in addition to starting treatment, I was advised to take up swimming. I was poor at first but as I ploughed up and down the pool, week after week, I got fitter and faster and calmer. Swimming was something I could control, when there was so much I could not control and, like many other forms of exercise, it was meditative.

Sliding through the water gave me the time and space to forgive myself for not believing the long years of pain were real, and permission to be angry and upset. It allowed me to acknowledge and accept my feelings; a process akin to ending a war with myself. That stage of my life was the hardest I have yet to endure but I emerged from it a changed person, although the change was not easy.

My suffering revealed unsettling things I had to acknowledge to progress my soul-journey. I started school early and struggled academically, which resulted in low self-confidence and a powerful fear of failure. I countered this by hard work which, I believed, would ensure the rewards I deserved.

I developed strong beliefs in fairness, hardly surprising given my strategy, but the strategy (of effort equalling success) does not work if *undeserving* people (however defined) are successful too, or if hard work does *not* deliver success or at least, avoids failure.

I could not overcome infertility by *working harder* (driving myself was actually counterproductive) and I raged at the unfairness of having suffered years of agony (through endometriosis) and not being rewarded with a child, while those who had suffered *nothing* at all, were *popping out* children (often unplanned).

I had to dispense with these simplistic and ultimately false beliefs or risk getting stuck in an endless cycle of bitterness. It was a struggle to shuck off this older version of myself and focus my energies on being well and happy and, when I finally had my children, I was gifted with an immense sense of gratitude and wonderment that remains, even now years later, when they are adult and off living their own lives.

My suffering was small compared to what many people endure but it is a trap to dismiss the very real emotional pain we feel because others appear to suffer more. Pain on all levels robs us of a joyful and meaningful life which, over the long term, can prove fatal. And even without the dire consequence of death, emotional pain can manifest as a gnawing dissatisfaction or sense of futility.

We might endure such feelings for years, distracting ourselves with shiny new possessions or holidays and end up embittered, or simply deeply regretful; or we might make abrupt life-changes that shock family and friends, such as tossing in prestigious and lucrative careers; leaving what appear to be good marriages; or setting off to exotic or obscure locations.

The trigger for change can be more obvious (redundancy, infidelity, surviving cancer) than the circumstances that *prime* us to make the change. In my case, the trigger to leave full time employment was a robbery (while we were overseas), but the circumstances (withdrawal of support for the degree I managed; long commutes; family cancers; the upkeep of a large house and land; a desperate want to write; watching my father die of dementia) had built for years.

However the change comes about, it is rarely easy, because the old, reassuringly known and comfortable life has to be left behind. As I have said:

The effects of change are the same:
a shock that takes the breath away
a floundering
then a slow making of sense

The soul-journey has no set duration and while it is not to be rushed, it should not be left to languish either. Changing ourselves is an active process; we must be alert and questioning and must undertake, what I have come to call, *the spade-work of the soul,* to bring it about.

It is not far to our next stop of Karlu Karlu better known by its European name of Devils Marbles. Karlu Karlu is an immense tumble of spherical granite boulders sacred to a number of First Nation peoples and we happen to arrive as the sun westers; the very best time to enjoy them.

The golden granite glows and shadows lengthen to fill crevices with darkness and throw silver-trunked gums into sharp relief. The small camping area is popular and our party of three takes up most of the remaining spots.

Karlu Karlu remains in use as a First Nation ceremonial site but there is disagreement over the boulders' mythical origins (the eggs of the Rainbow Serpent versus the hair [and sometimes spit] of an ancestral being). Like Uluru and Kata Tjuta, Karlu Karlu is sacred but I do not sense the sacred here as I do at those other sites. It might be due to Karlu Karlu's smaller scale or the noisy presence of others.

My first visits to Glastonbury, Tintagel, and Stone Henge in the UK (central to the King Arthur/Camelot myths/legends) were in winter and utterly different to later visits. I seemed to be the only person at Glastonbury. The ruined abbey was silent, even of birdcall; with a mist that streamered through its shattered arches and a hoar frost that rimmed its black, leafless trees with blossom.

I felt an intense sense of wonder, and peace, and of the sacred, that erased the boundaries of place and time. Tintagel was largely deserted too, with a grey, storm-tossed ocean and sacred too, in a wild, restless way.

There were other visitors at Stone Henge, but quiet and respectful as they wandered, like me, between the stones (which have since been fenced off). The great sweep of iron-grey sky pressed down as I lay my palms against the stones' warmer surfaces where, I knew, countless other palms had pressed through time.

It would be easy to dismiss my feelings on my first visits to these sites as being coloured by the romance of the Arthurian myths/legends and many fantasy tales *do* indeed use stone circles as portals to other times and places, but to discount my feelings would be to miss an important point, namely that, while myths are not true on an everyday, rational level (the realm of the outer journey), they persist because they *are* true on a psychological level (the realm of the inner journey).

Did Merlin really magic Uther Pendragon into Tintagel so Arthur could be conceived? Did the Ancient Greeks really expect to find Zeus lolling about in a golden palace atop Mt Olympus? Did Christians really (prior to the advent of flight) expect to find heaven floating above the clouds?

These myths (and legends) do not stand up to the hard gaze of science and so myths, in particular, have become synonymous with lies. But dismissing myths (and legends) closes the door on their potential to guide us on our soul-journeys. Myths endure, not because they are entertaining or quaint artefacts from less sophisticated times, but because, through their heroes, they tell us what we need to know.

We consciously crave heroes who, by definition, are not like us in the *outer* (so-called *real*) world but who *are* like us in our *inner* world, the place of the soul-journey. Mythical heroes are marked by things that set them apart: unusual births, incredible feats, and mysterious deaths. Arthur is the *once and future* king (which suggests the eternal nature of what he represents, as does the prophecy of Christ's second coming).

We gain comfort and strength from joining with others in our admiration of these heroes of books and films because their noble qualities exemplify the traits we aspire to, and their exploits mirror the trials we endure alone on our soul-journeys where *we* are heroes too.

BONES GLEAMING

The stars shroud Karlu Karlu in a timeless silver that makes the stones a fitting home for the Rainbow Serpent's slow slide of creation or the work of a different creator ancestor busy with his spit and hair in another sort of making. Both are gone with the sun's rising and we leave Karlu Karlu and continue north on the Stuart Highway, through Tennant Creek and past the Three Ways Roadhouse where the Barkly Highway joins the Stuart Highway from the east.

This is open desert country of red sand and sage-coloured spinifex and the travelling is easy until we turn west onto the Buchanan Highway and leave the bitumen behind. We thud-thud-thud over our old friends the corrugations and dusty scrub leans in or clumps away into the distance, interspersed with termite mounds. Bones gleam among the grasses, scoured by heat and the occasional pounding rains, and as daylight wanes, we pull off into the scrub and set camp for the night.

I am getting quicker at sorting our various systems as switching on the gas, pump, fridge and unlatching drawers and doors becomes habit. The night is still and star-doused but we are tired and do not linger around the fire. It does not matter.

We have a hatch above our bed and I watch the stars as I drift to sleep. Empty road trains barrel along the Buchanan Highway behind us so sleep does not last long. This is cattle country and their metal cattle crates clash and rattle as they roar past. I am glad to be off the road and hope that other creatures are safely off the road too.

Anorexic Models

Cattle corpses edge the roads
more elegant
than those of kangaroos

Cattle lie on their sides
legs crossed modestly
weathered hides draped
over bones
like haute couture on
anorexic models

Kangaroos lie with legs splayed
or are pressed into tarmac
like flowers in a book

to be carried on in the tread
of countless tyres

immortal
at least for
a little while

Want to explore further?
Karlu Karlu: https://theculturetrip.com/pacific/australia/articles/
the-devils-marbles-an-ancient-aboriginal-meeting-point/
Tennant Creek: https://www.aussietowns.com.au/town/tennant-creek
Buchanan Highway: https://www.ozroads.com.au/NT/routenumber-
ing/national/80/nr80.htm

UNHEARD

As I laze in bed the next morning, I muse whether silence is actually
a sound in its own right (despite its lack of sound waves). It is an
odd thought probably triggered by my wish for quiet amid the road
trains' roar last night. The 6th century mathematician/philosopher
Pythagoras postulated that the stars make music in his lovely poetic
(and mathematically-based) notion of the *harmony of the spheres*,
something I have contemplated as the Outback's star-show unfolds
each night.

If Nature does indeed *abhor a vacuum* then something must fill the
space that sound vacates. I later discover that our brains abhor a
vacuum too and tend to fill a sound-free space (a space hard to attain
on Earth) with all sorts of sounds.

I have plenty of vehicle noise to fill my brain as we head off to Top
Springs where we have a quick chat over coffee about the next part
of the journey. The Buchanan Highway continues north-west to our
destination of Timber Creek but the combination of blinding dust
and possibility of fast-moving road trains makes it a unanimous
decision to turn north along the sealed (albeit single-laned) Buntine
Highway, and head west again when we reach the Victoria Highway.

We pass herds of grey Brahman cattle that pass in single file like
ghosts among the trees. They move purposefully and I guess they
head towards a water source such as a bore-water trough. Brahman
were bred for Northern Australia's climate and their shoulder humps
and down-tilted ears make them very different to Victoria's black
Angus and red and white Hereford cattle.

Metal cattle yards appear next where cattle are corralled for transport
to market which explains the empty road trains last night. There are
termite mounds amongst the mulga too, adding to the hundreds we
have already seen on this trip but people have clothed them in shirts
and hats so they resemble an untidy assembly of scarecrows. I do not
find it funny, for the same reason I do not like animals being dressed
in human clothes or forced to parody human behaviour.

Whenever the Census rolls around, I write *Animism* in the box marked *Religion* instead of *None* because the latter suggests I have no spiritual beliefs. The *Oxford Dictionary* defines animism as the 'religious belief that objects, places and creatures all possess a distinct spiritual essence. Potentially, animism perceives all things – animals, plants, rocks, rivers, weather systems, human handiwork and perhaps even words – as animated and alive.'

While not a good fit my world view does broadly accord with my belief that the natural world (including humans) should be respected and, even if termite mounds did not house highly sophisticated communities in structures designed to control temperature, moisture and gas exchange, all which can be damaged, they should be left in peace, not interfered with for our amusement.

Peter Wohlleben's writings on the workings of Nature's hidden parts have revealed to me my ignorance of and disconnect from much of the natural world. It reminds me that, one way or another, our hunter-gatherer ancestors were intimately connected to the earth, not only because their physical wellbeing depended on it, but because their intellectual, emotional and spiritual welfare did too.

Some First Nation people manage to retain their spiritual connection to the land but their displacement (in Australia, by European invasion) too often severs their physical and intellectual connection. Even those who manage to retain access to their lands, have had their intellectual connection (their understanding of *how* the land functions) interrupted/erased by the invader's interference.

We were all First Nation peoples once; family groups/tribes who knew their territories intimately, but that is long past for most of us. Even had I stayed in my birth-country of England; I would not have been in my *particular* country. I was born in London but my ancestral names suggest Welsh and Scottish heritage, and my DNA reveals Scandinavian forebears. It is a reason I consider myself a member of *the lost white tribes.*

I am consciously aware of my loss of connection but I suspect many people feel their loss *unconsciously* as a yearning for something they cannot quite name. I explore this yearning for place in my Deep Fantasy novel *The Third Moon*, through the hero Warrain's struggles for a sense of belonging. And it is only when he understands *how* his new planet of Imago functions, that he is able to call it home.

The Third Moon: Excerpt 2

My moment of calmness lasted precisely that, a moment, because a plume of smoke abruptly streamed from the cleft above me. At first, I thought the peak was erupting, despite knowing Imago wasn't volcanic, and then I realised it wasn't smoke but butterflies.

Thousands of them poured into the sky, flashing gold as their wings caught the first rays of the early morning sun, and there, amongst the gold was a single blue, soaring higher than the rest.

As far as the eye could see, all along the coast, plumes rose from the peaks like the beacons the Ancients had used to warn of war, but instead of signalling destruction, Imago's beacons heralded renewal.

Tears streamed down my face as I at last understood what the maggots were, what she was. The planet's name made sense now too, but the human-maggot form wasn't the imago; wasn't the last manifestation of the planet's sentient life-form; this was; these wondrous brown-gold males and iridescent blue female that would ensure the next generation came.

I also suspect that those of us who do not *consciously* realise our disconnect from the land, sate our longing through the acquisition of *things*, as I did, but over time, *things* bring less satisfaction and owning them becomes more burdensome. *Things* must be stored and insured and, after we were robbed in 2016, I had no wish to replace the *things* that were stolen (except for jewellery gifted by loved ones, which was irreplaceable anyway).

I have noted the importance of decluttering for the soul-journey and, as I contemplate the termite mounds, I realise not only does decluttering leave space for more important things to enter but also the space for them to grow and mature. I recently read about the effects of *distracted* thinking on creativity and how, because of our busy-ness, our thoughts skip from topic to topic in a relentless cycle that prevents us from engaging in creative thought.

It suggested creative thought is achieved when we sit quietly and appear to do nothing. In reality, we are meditating, pondering, musing, daydreaming, and in doing so, giving ourselves the space and time our thoughts need to develop and expand; in other words, to blossom.

Decluttering allows us to reclaim that crucial time and space in the same way that journeying does when mundane physical and mental baggage is stripped away and, as I sit in the 4x4, I have the time and space to see the termite mounds, not just as lumps on the landscape, but in all their intricacies and strangeness, *and* as fellow travellers in this thing called life.

Termite Mounds

Termite mounds mark the soil changes
red, black, white and brown

blade-shouldered like stalagmites
or nubbed like
Snow White's dwarfs

Scattered through sage-coloured scrub
or close-packed
like gravestones or abandoned cities
Chernobyl, Fukushima

dead cities the green has
taken back

There is no green on the shoulders
of *these* cities and no death
despite their sombre hues

They might be quiet as graves
but within them
life seethes

We reach the Victoria Highway, head south-west through the Judbarra/Gregory National Park and cross the Victoria River, the first big water course we have seen since leaving home. It is a thin blue static line on the map but a broad brown moving one in reality and I discover that, at 560 kms (350 miles), it is *the longest singularly named permanent river in the Northern Territory*.

We sweep over its bridge, our tyres clacking like a train on the concrete joints and I spot ducks, pelicans, and storks on the brown water below. Big rivers were obstacles to European explorers (at least in the wet season) but thanks to modern engineering, we take just a few seconds to cross.

Water is crucial everywhere but particularly in arid regions and it plays an important role in the soul-journey too. Joseph Campbell and others have noted that the same symbolism occurs in myths and dreams, but that in dreams, the symbols are coloured/affected by the particular circumstances of the individual.

Most of our dreams disappear on waking and any remnants seem to be a jumbled rehash of the day's mundane events, but there are other dreams that stay with us, and these dreams can be useful to our soul-journeys *if* we can decipher them. Dreams spring from the unconscious and speak in symbols, not the language of our mother-tongue, and while some of these symbols are specific to the dreamer, others (archetypal symbols) are the same regardless of culture.

In a previous life, when I was exhausted juggling my various responsibilities, I started to dream I was driving my car when the brakes failed. I was going slowly, just dribbling along, but no matter how hard I pressed my foot to the brake pedal, the car continued to roll on. It did not take great insight to understand the car symbolised me, and the lack of brakes my lack of control over my life. My unconscious mind was telling my conscious mind I needed to change my circumstances (for my own good).

The car was the same model and colour that I owned at the time, so this symbol was particular to me, but another dream I continue to have uses the archetypal symbol of a house to represent me.

In this dream, I stumble upon a partially constructed house in a forest. I know I own it and it is complex and beautiful (wooden with gables and turrets and rooms coming off in all directions) but clearly unfinished and, in the dream, I constantly ask myself (or some hidden person) why I have not finished this house and why I do not live in it. There is also a troubling sense that I have somehow forgotten about it.

The psychoanalyst Carl Jung had a famous and well-documented dream of a house that represents a particular aspect of him (his psyche). In the dream he descends from the upper floors of consciousness via stairs and finally a trap door to the primitive part of his unconscious.

The house in my dream represents the things I want to achieve *creatively* but which get over-ridden by the more urgent demands of everyday life. The dream reminds me that a beautiful edifice of myself remains unfinished and, to emphasise the point, the house is in a forest, another common symbol of the unconscious.

The forest is where the orderliness of rational *conscious* thought (often symbolised by roads and paths) gives way to the wild emotions, instincts and other unruly things (like creativity) we banish to our unconscious. Consider Little Red Riding Hood's experiences once she leaves the path and enters the forest to be finally rescued by a *wood-cutter* (a restorer of order), and the horrors of Ratty and Mole's adventures in the Wild Woods (in Kenneth Grahame's *The Wind in the Willows*).

As previously noted, water serves a similar symbolic purpose (think of how many worms/dragons lurk at the bottom of wells) and I use the motif as water, snow, and ice in *Heart Hunter* to explore how the *state* of the outer physical world can mirror the *state* of the inner psychological world.

The hero (Chant) is set an impossible task by her people's shamanic leader: cross the impassable, ice-locked mountains and bring water (and fish) back to her land's frozen streams so that her people can eat. But the shaman's *real* (hidden) requirement is for Chant to progress her life stage from adolescence to adulthood.

Like the streams in her lands, Chant is *frozen*: stuck in her old ways of thinking and deaf to all advice. Her physical journey (which repeats the motif of water, snow and ice) provides tests that free Chant from her old self.

In Excerpt 1, Tel (who is completing his own soul-journey) retrieves Chant from the Vulturi who hold her prisoner. To escape with Tel, Chant must overcome her fear of water (which *threatens* her old self) to embrace her *new* self and partner with Tel.

Heart Hunter: Excerpt 1.

Shadows held the shore and as Tel turned towards Skeardin Head, there was movement in the dunes behind. It seemed Kablar's son, or his friends, weren't satisfied with the trade after all. Tel guessed the attack would come at the headland, where the rocks provided cover and which was far enough away for Kablar to retain his honour. Tel's body would be found later, in the water, like his father's.

But they had a start on their attackers. 'They follow,' he whispered, and shifted his grip to Chant's hand. 'Run!'

They fled along the hard sand at the water's edge stride for stride, and even with the old injury to her ankle, she was fast. Tel had to use every shred of his failing strength to keep up.

But as they neared the headland, she slowed. 'I can't cross,' she panted. 'I can't.'

'You must! They'll kill me if you don't!' She stared at him, wild-eyed. 'Go now! Go!' he ordered.

He pushed her forward and she clambered onto the rocks. The waves beat on the seaward stones and water surged and sucked about their ankles. Where he could he steered her into the shadows but he had no time to look behind him; any pause would cost him his life. Chant's ragged breaths were audible above the waves and he was no better; the remnants of marsh fever eating his strength. Then she stopped and he blundered into her.

The way ahead was a surge of water.

A spear clattered off the rocks and he grabbed her hand and leapt, taking her with him. A second spear passed so close the air whispered beside him. They clambered on, keeping to where the stones provided the best shelter. The desperate scramble seemed endless, Tel expecting a spear in the back at any moment. And then blessedly, open sand stretched before them and they broke into a run again, forcing themselves on until the shore provided no more hiding places.

Understanding the role of symbols in mythic and contemporary stories, *and* in dreams, is useful to understanding/progressing our own soul-journeys. There is extensive material on the Internet about dream symbolism (much of it *very* simplistic) but we are each the best judges of our own dreams *once* we understand more about our particular dream-language.

Want to explore further?

Hearing silence: https://www.wired.com/2015/05/big-question-can-silence-make-hear-things-arent/

Termite Mounds: http://www.withoutahitch.com.au/travel/under-standing-termite-mounds/

The Third Moon: https://www.amazon.com.au/Third-Moon-K-S-Nikakis-ebook/dp/B071F77KMX

Victoria River: http://www.aussietowns.com.au/town/victoria-river-nt

Carl Jung's Dream House: https://appliedjung.com/jungs-dream-house/

Heart Hunter: https://www.amazon.com.au/Heart-Hunter-K-S-Nika-kis-ebook/dp/B01M98H3HC

Useful reading

Joseph Campbell – *The hero with a thousand faces*

Carl Jung (editor) – *Man and his symbols*

Peter Wohlleben - *The secret network of nature* and *The hidden life of trees*

GREEN WEBS

Losing my mind? Acting mindlessly? I ponder the strange thing we call a *mind* as we continue along the Victoria Highway. We cannot dissect a brain, retrieve a bloodied piece of flesh, plonk it on the table and say: *Here it is; this is a mind* and yet our minds make us what we are. We need the mind's *conscious* aspect to navigate the outer physical world and we need its *unconscious* aspect to navigate the inner world of our soul-journey, but Western culture places far more emphasis (and value) on the outer world.

It leaves us, as *individuals,* to find a way to connect to our inner world and connect with it we must, if we are to become fully-functioning, fully-developed human beings. The Arts provide points of connection for us as engagers with its *products* (an ugly word for the beautiful things the Arts conjure) and/or as creative practitioners.

I have been profoundly moved by music, dance, pictures, movies, sculptures, gardens and all sorts of installations, while as a creative practitioner, I have painted, sketched, worked (very badly) with stained glass, built gardens, quilted and knitted, as well as wrangled words into poetry, short stories, novels and nonfiction.

The extended narratives (novels) I write, particularly in the subgenre of Deep Fantasy (with its acknowledgement of the hero's inner journey), have proved powerful tools of connection for me because, to explore the hero's inner path/soul-journey, I must explore my *own* beliefs and discover and address (as the hero must), my own assumptions.

Viv (in *Angel Caste*) and Etaine (in *The Emerald Serpent*) must turn from their destructive, self-sabotaging paths and take the far harder paths of healing and conciliation. As Etaine realises when she recognises the new path laid before her: *It required hope and trust, and the risk of being betrayed all over again, and Etaine doubted she had the strength to turn along it.*

In creating Viv and Etaine's stories, I soon realised that, even at the most mundane level (for instance, when another driver cuts me off in heavy traffic), it requires far more effort to think nice thoughts (the other driver is distracted; unwell; dealing with grief …) than nasty ones and that, in the grander scheme of world affairs, it is why the fight for peace is so much harder than the route to war.

We have an easy 324 kms (201 mile) drive to Timber Creek and the caravan park turns out to be a cool green oasis amid the red dust, with large trees and watered grassy sites. White ibis stroll about, aerating the soil with their long, curved beaks in their search for worms and grubs, and alert to discarded morsels from the park's human inhabitants. They loiter near the rubbish bins too, hopeful of overflow and living up to their colloquial name of *bin-chickens*.

The park's green is shocking after so much dryness, as are the crowds after the isolation of the Outback roads. There is a swimming pool and children in the playground; a laundry with washing machines and driers; a shop to buy ice creams and even enjoy a sit-down meal. The park is also a sanctuary where we rest for a while, safe in the familiarity of a world we have largely left behind.

I am reminded again of the unsettling effects of my return visit to Burra; of being in the same place but not the same person; and that we live a *series* of discrete lives rather than one seamless one, not just in our inner world of the soul-journey, but in our outer world too. During a *previous* life, I worked at a city school for four years, and travelled the same route to work every day and, for a long while afterwards, I would unthinkingly turn off the freeway as if I were going there.

Being in the Timber Creek Caravan Park, with its familiar comforts, invites me to slip back into my former, *easier* life, but we cannot return to earlier versions of ourselves, no matter how attractive they look in retrospect. We are not the same people, which is the reason we are no longer where we were. In *Angel Caste*, Thris recognises early that he is repeating the same *physical* journey (where he betrayed Viv and destroyed his chances of transcendence) but it takes him a lot longer to recognise he is not repeating the same *psychological*/soul-journey.

Angel Caste: Excerpt 3

Moth Fold was in its dark cycle and as the rift had delivered Thris into trees, he crawled into the first hollow he found and curled up. He had no idea whether it was the same forest he'd visited previously for he still had moments so blank he thought himself new. And yet, as he huddled amongst the roots, the extraordinary idea that Ezam's angelic hierarchy could be scaled more than once, floated into his head.

The notion was so bizarre that he wondered whether it sprang from the madness of his near dissolution. It suggested the Great Beyond might give angels a second chance to make wiser decisions and he wondered dully whether, given the opportunity, he would make wiser decisions. It had been here under the trees that he'd been all but overwhelmed by Viv's scent and resonance and yet had still believed he could control his want of her. It had been an act of arrogance that had cost him everything.

The moths stirred in their roosts in the branches above and Thris tensed. Something had disturbed them, something that now threaded its way through the trees towards him. He didn't have the strength to stand, let alone fight, and his heart pounded. Then he all but swooned in relief. It was Ky.

He came to a stop and dropped his pack. 'We need to travel together,' he said.

'Our roles preclude that,' said Thris, and faltered as he realised he'd used the phrase before. Hope flared as he wondered whether he was to be granted a second chance at ascension but then the scale of his violation slammed home and all hope evaporated.

The Timber Creek Caravan Park gives us our first close-up with a boab; a tree so strange I find it hard not to stare.

Bottle-bodied Wenches

Boabs are *she's*
their rounded bellies
full of water hoarded for
the hard times
every woman fears
will come

These are no shade-makers
these bottle-bodied wenches
yet they raise their knobby arms
spread their leaves
and hang onto them
for dear life

The sun laughs at their efforts
and burns holes through their green webs
but the boabs stand tall
and shawl the ground
with lace

No one knows how boabs came to be in Australia but as I contemplate the tree, I consider how we are drawn to difference, especially *rare* difference, and our consequent disdain for the commonplace. Albino animals capture headlines all over the world and might even be venerated, while unusually beautiful men and women have the potential to achieve material success unrelated to intelligence, skills, or hard work.

The heroes of book and film narratives are beautiful too, and for a reason: they represent the best of what we can be physically, emotionally, and spiritually. As the *chosen one(s)* of narratives, they stand out from the crowd of mundane, ordinary folk and yet these heroes of the outer world, are more than pretty icons. Their explicit feats in the outer world and less obvious ones in the inner world, inspire us to replicate what *we* must do as the heroes of our own outer and inner journeys.

Want to explore further?

Angel Caste – Complete 5 Book Series: https://www.amazon.com/Angel-Caste-Complete-5-Book-ebook/dp/B07RT15HW5

Timber Creek: https://northernterritory.com/katherine-and-surrounds/accommodation/timber-creek-hotel--caravan-park

Boab: https://www.australiangeographic.com.au/topics/science-environment/2019/07/how-did-the-iconic-boab-tree-get-to-australia/

ANCIENT RED

Many years ago, in a former life, I met a woman from the former USSR who was chaperoning a group of Russian students and was astonished to learn she needed an internal passport to move *within* her country. The idea was completely alien to me but the Western Australian border *does* have a sense of officialdom about it (thanks to its quarantine laws) that other Australian borders lack.

Having triple checked the relevant website, we know most of the foodstuffs we can take over but we were far less well informed on our first trip, when our newly purchased fresh fruit, vegetables, *and* honey were confiscated.

We join the queue of caravans, cars and trucks at the Quarantine Station and I unlock the van. We have consumed everything forbidden, or so I think, but have forgotten about a bunch of celery hiding in the back of the fridge and two, perfectly ripe and ready-to-eat avocadoes (sigh) all of which are unsentimentally confiscated.

At least I have remembered not to buy honey (my husband's favourite spread) but need not have bothered with my eye-watering effort of peeling an entire bag of onions because, I discover, onions are fine with their skins firmly in place.

We plan to spend a few days in Kununurra before our friends continue west along the Gibb River Road and we head south down the Great Northern Highway; skirt the southern edge of the Kimberley region; and continue to Purnululu National Park, home to the World Heritage listed Bungle Bungle Ranges. The other couples have been to the magic Purnululu before and are keen to try the Gibb River Road. We will meet again near Broome.

The caravan park sits opposite the Mirima Rock formations; a tumble of stone that blushes pink at sunrise and burns red at sunset. I have not worn a windcheater or long pants since staring in awe at the Big Man at Aileron and as the heat increases, I take a dip in the park pool. It is absolutely freezing (!).

We book a flight over the Bungle Bungle Ranges and the next morning finds us perched at the park gate in darkness, waiting for our 5.15 a.m. pick-up. The minibus driver turns out to be the pilot and her co-pilot drops us back later. They clean the plane too which seems to sum up the unpretentious, no nonsense work habits of many Australians.

The plane is more like a small private jet than the usual four-seaters we normally cram our selves into and is also less than half full, increasing our sense of privileged luxury. The Bungle Bungle Ranges, domed and striped sandstone formations, are extraordinary from the air, with sensuous curves that remind me of striped versions of Kata Tjuta. I am glad we make the effort to fly over them and am impatient to see them from the ground.

Metal Bird

We are rich for a moment
in a private jet
or at least a plane
with exclusive seating

No economy class here
with plenty of room to spread
but the land below
is all that matters

It rolls in waves of ancient red
with tree-lines that betray
moisture-sinks
and the shadow of a metal bird
that follows us home

That night we share a farewell drink with our friends and, as we watch Mirima fire in the sun's last rays, I muse that the aerial view of the Bungle Bungle Ranges is like our outer physical journey and that being among them will have the intimacy of our inner soul-journeys. But only time will tell whether my fanciful imaginings are true.

Our friends depart the next morning but we extend our booking a day to take an excursion to Wyndham, 122 km (75 miles) north and perched right on the Cambridge Gulf. We explore the historical port area, breathe the salty air, and watch the vast muddy waters of multiple rivers: the Ord, Pentecost, Durack, King and Forrest flow into the Joseph Bonaparte Gulf and from there, out into the Timor Sea. It is strange to have a horizon made of water after so much red earth and to have gulls replace sulphur-crested cockies and corellas.

On our return drive, we pull over at the Pioneer Cemetery; a lonely patch of windswept ground wedged on the road's narrow shoulder and little more than a stone-throw's from the sea. It is small and when I explore its stony slopes, I discover why.

Uneaten by the Sea

I walk amongst the graves
of those unclaimed
by old age

Children barely
from their cradles lie beside
others old enough to dream of futures
that never came

The plaque tells me this is
a Pioneer Cemetery
abandoned when coastal erosion threatened
but these pioneers were never quitters
and remain
uneaten by the sea

Want to explore further?
Kununurra: https://www.australia.com/en/places/broome-and-surrounds/guide-to-kununurra.html
Wyndham: https://en.wikipedia.org/wiki/Wyndham,_Western_Australia
Pioneer Cemeteries: http://lonelygraveswa.wags.org.au/index.php/resting-places/church-pioneer-cemeteries-burial-grounds/lonely-burial-sites-1-40

GROUNDED

He travels the fastest who travels alone, Rudyard Kipling famously wrote, and while I am unsure about speed, it is surprisingly liberating to travel on our own. As we head off the next day, we enjoy the self-ishness of following our own schedule but, in truth, no one is ever really alone in this part of the country when winter grips the southern states. Grey Nomads are out and about, their car plates revealing homes in Victoria and New South Wales, as are the locals: farmers, tradies (tradesmen), and the ever-present truckies (truck drivers).

It is another warm day with a gloriously blue sky and I smugly contemplate reports of Melbourne's miserable winter as we drive. It does not snow in Melbourne and the temperature rarely dips below 6 or 7 degrees Celsius (43 – 44 F) but the days can be grey and damp and the wind bitter-edged.

It is well known that the weather (particularly the quantity and quality of light) affects mood but I have read less about the effects of disruptions to other human cycles. Our sleeping and waking times are often dictated by commute, school and work times; as are meal times; exercise times; and even visiting the bathroom times.

Electric light erases the stars and urban horizons block the sun's rise and set; the moon's rise and set; and the moon's wax and wane. We walk on concrete, tarmac, crushed stone, compacted soil and plastic grass; birdsong is drowned by traffic noise, sirens and piped music; and any foray out is in the company of strangers, sometimes in bare-ly moving masses.

The decluttering important to the inner journey is more easily accomplished when we declutter our *outer* world by relocating to more natural environments (or at least *less* constrained ones). Free camping (away from the lights of parks) means going to bed with the sun's setting and getting up with its rising; eating when we are hungry; and going to the bathroom when we need to (not to fit in with schedules).

It means dust-covered feet; fumbling in the dark; seeing the moon change shape; marvelling at the stars. It means walking *where* we please, not choosing a route to avoid jostling others; not speaking or speaking as it pleases us, not merely to be polite.

Such things re-ground us, in the way we were grounded in our (more) primitive past. Then we ate when we were hungry; slept when we were tired; relieved ourselves when we had need. We watched the dark invade the land and blessed the sunrise that banished it; judged time by the moon's changing face and by what blossomed and fruited and died; knew the cries of our fellow creatures and their silence.

We are grounded when we reconnect with something vaster than us; when we acknowledge and reaffirm our oneness with something that has its own seasons, reasons and truths, in all their brutality and beauty.

We continue south to Purnululu but unusually, have no real idea where we will spend the night. What we do know is that we cannot take a double-axle van into Purnululu National Park. Our friends tell us of a depot where vans are stored while their owners head into the park with tenting gear. It is why the back of the 4x4 is stacked high with a tent; sleeping mats; gas stove and bottles; chairs and all the other paraphernalia we will need.

We follow the signs off the highway down a broad, unsealed road, and less than a kilometre in, discover the Bungle Bungle Caravan Park. It is a welcome surprise: neat, well-resourced and friendly. The manageress advises us to leave the van in their storage area (for a small fee) and visit Purnululu with the tent.

The 53 kms (33 miles) of road into the park is so rough it takes at least 3 hours each way and visitors commonly choose to stay there. We briefly consider the tedium of sorting out food and tenting equipment and repacking the whole lot afterwards and decide to head into the park early the next morning and return the same day.

Purnululu is the First Nation Kija/Gija word for sandstone *or* for fretted sand, and the differing meanings are not the only discrepancies in the information we glean. The range's name of *Bungle Bungle* is thought to come from *bundle bundle*; a grass that grows in the region though no one knows why the sandstone formations would be named after a grass.

Some information sources warn against calling the formations the *Bungle Bungles*, although *Bungles* is acceptable, while others, including state government websites, blithely refer to the ranges as the Bungle Bungles.

We unhitch the van and set up, but as I approach the showers later that night, an enormous brahman (cow or steer, I do not think to check), looms from the gloom. It is the last thing I expect to see next to a neat concrete path, next to a spotless ablution block. It shimmers like a ghost and regards me with luminous eyes as I search for escape routes.

The brahman is immense and motionless and for a ridiculous moment I wonder if it is a sculpture, or an apparition, but it is real, despite its stillness. I cautiously edge past it and it is mysteriously gone when I re-emerge after a wonderful hot shower.

We are on the road before seven the next morning and soon discover why it takes more than three hours to cover 53 kms (32 miles). The corrugations are so bad I fear our hefty 4x4 will shake apart and to add to the road's nastiness, gullies cut it crossways or cleave it in two lengthwise. There are jagged-edged rocks to threaten our tyres and loose gravel to invite roll-overs though none of these hazards slow the vehicles that speed past us, some towing camper-trailers.

We discover the road belongs to a cattle station when we finally reach signage that heralds the park and the road abruptly improves. We speed up and head for Cathedral Gorge, one of the park's main attractions and it is hot by the time we pull into the carpark, don our flynets, and set off through the beehive-shaped rocks.

The undulating, striated formations are spectacular from the air and even more so as we walk among them. The stone sweeps up on every side in vast, crestless waves; its golden sandstone dark-banded with cyanobacteria (a single-celled photosynthetic organism). The sandy track wends its way between the rounded peaks, over a stone-slabbed, dry creek bed and past sparse eucalypts, savannah and fan palms; and we sweat, drink from our water bottles, and swat at the flies.

Caramel-coloured skinks flash down crevices but we see no other creatures apart from the usual cockatoos, corellas and crows whose harsh cries echo off the stone. The track narrows and the stone soars skywards then closes-in to create a tunnel of deep, moisture-smelling shade that abruptly opens again into a vast, russet-hued amphitheatre. There is a mirror-still pool at its centre, edged by a sweeping beach of coarse gravel, and a scatter of people, quiet like us.

The pool is so bright it is impossible to tell where the rock ends and the reflections begin. I slow-pace around the amphitheatre's circular gravel floor, my gaze shifting between the walls and the water, as I breathe in the silence. Something I have no words for occupies this space and, as I draw it deep into my being, it simultaneously fixes me in place and sets me free.

Time ceases but at some point, a jumble of people pour into the gorge, chattering as they scramble onto rocks to take selfies by the pool. I do not know what those others feel as I nod to them as we leave; all I know is that, if I see nothing else of beauty during this entire journey, this moment alone has made it worth setting out.

Cathedral Gorge

There are places
with a special silence
where the stone gives way
and we sink

Here the air breathes
a different breath to spinifex
in the bright world outside

and words are too small
or too clumsy for what
is revealed

And yet in its naming
those first Europeans
sensed the sacred
here

and by entering their cathedral
the least we can offer
is silence
and a light tread

This is too much for some
who graffiti the air with chatter
and we leave
as they finally do
all of us washed
clean

Cathedral Gorge gifts me plenty to ponder because it contains two powerful symbols of the unconscious: stone (in the form of caves and tunnels) and water. I have described how I use water in *Heart Hunter* and was thrilled to see it used in a similar fashion in the film *Black Panther* (Marvel Studios, 2018).

After the death of his father the king, T'Challa must defeat challengers in a ritual fight to claim the kingship. The fight takes place in *knee-high* water that indicates T'Challa is only *partly* in the unconscious (where he needs to be *fully* immersed to make the *psychological* transition from prince to king).

He defeats the first challenger but, as a result of being *incompletely* in the unconscious, makes an *incomplete* transition to the kingship; being king in name only. Because he is not yet *fully* king, Killmonger defeats him in the second challenge. T'Challa must endure many trials to become fit to be king and finally defeat Killmonger (in an underground tunnel).

In *Black Panther*, the power of the pool motif is enhanced by the pool being circular in shape (symbolic of perfection and the cycle of life), a symbol I use in my Deep Fantasy series *Angel Caste*. It is in the perfectly circular, turquoise waters of the sacred lake of Astraal, that Viv finally chooses a *human* life of love and connection over an unattainable one of angelic etherealness *and* over her former life of hate and violence. It is here too that Thris achieves his longed for angelic transcendence and Ataghan turns from his violent life and commits to the healing Viv offers.

In Excerpt 4, a maelstrom is generated when the sacred lake is whipped to a life-threatening fury by an unstable rift. Viv dives into its depths to rescue Thris and when Ataghan follows to rescue her, he uses Viv's love for his daughter Fariye to convince her to relinquish Thris. In rescuing Viv, Ataghan also (symbolically) rescues himself.

Angel Caste: Excerpt 4

Ataghan's attention was on the Viv. She wove between the water-spouts, her wings flashing like metal as they caught the sun, but then she swooped low, oblivious to the clashing waves. There was someone in the water, and Ataghan yanked off his jacket, shirt, and boots.

'You're not going in after her, are you?' cried Baraghan in alarm.

Ataghan dashed the rain from his eyes. The squalls dulled Viv's wings, but he saw her struggle to lift someone, and then two waves soared skywards, clashed in an explosion of glass-grey water, and she was gone. Ataghan ran, and Baraghan cursed and ran too, towards the docks where there might be rope.

Ataghan plunged into the lake and ploughed through the icy water. Waves broke over him, blinded him, dragged him back, tried to drag him under. He focused on where the lake had taken her, reached the spot, and dived. She was a long way down, perilously close to a translucent maelstrom. His brain screamed at him to turn back to the world above, to flee the twisting column that threatened to devour him, but he kept going, caught her wrist, and dragged her back to the surface.

Her violet eyes were stark against her white skin, her gasps for air punctuated by sobs for the Angellus, and she struggled in his grip, as she tried to dive again. He only had one weapon and he used it.

'Ilris! Fariye needs you! Stay with me!' Waves buffeted them, and squalls slashed like whips. 'Ilris!' He shook her. 'Stay with me!'

Her eyes focused on him, filled with despair, but he knew he had her, and struck out for shore, keeping a grip on her hand. She swam too but it was exhausting, the waves battering them and the fume starving them of air. And then, when he could go no further, a rope slapped onto the water beside him, he gripped it, and Baraghan hauled them in.

As soon as he could stand, Ataghan swung her into his arms, staggered up the steps, and collapsed in the column's shelter. She'd curled into him, face buried in his chest, as if she could bear the world no longer, and he tightened his arms around her. 'Ilris,' he said, and kissed the top of her head, uncaring that Baraghan saw, then rested his head back against the pillar and closed his eyes.

Thris's closest angelic companions, Ash and Ky, are within the maelstrom. Ash, whose white wings indicate his nearness to transcendence, understands what they must do to mend the rift and save the worlds the rift threatens, and it is this act of selfless love, which delivers all three angels the transcendence they crave.

Angel Caste: Excerpt 5

Ky shrieked as the rift wall split and water gushed in, but the rent sealed again and Thris lay gasping on the floor. He blinked up at them in shock and they cried with joy as they hauled him into their arms.

The rift's violence lessened as they hugged him and, as the roar dimmed, a calmness settled over Ash. He knew what they must do now but he had no time to explain it, nor the words.

'Hold to me,' he whispered. They pressed against each other chest to chest, arms entwined, white-flecked bronze and black wings enfolded by Ash's white wings of transcendence.

'The trinity,' murmured Ky, calm suddenly.

'The love of three friends,' said Thris simply.

'The one,' said Ash, 'with the strength of three to mend the breach.'

Together they pushed their love outwards, a potent mix of angel essence, of spirit, of physical strength. They used their sweet angel breath to succour each other, but the strain was enormous and Ky the first to fail.

Ash and Thris knew the moment his heart stopped but neither faltered, and the rift began to mend. Ash knew when Thris's heart fell silent too, and he cradled him as he cradled Ky, his arm under his shoulders as he fell away, their wings like drifts of snow. And it was Ash alone who felt the last rainbow threads knit, and the rift become whole again.

Through their use of powerful mythic symbols, stories have the potential to aid readers' unconscious understanding of their own soul-journeys. Viewers of the film *Black Panther* or readers of certain books might be unable to explain why these stories resonate, but explicable or not, their power to advance the soul-journey is real.

The return journey from the Bungle Bungles proves no more enjoyable than the journey in and it is dark before we arrive back at the van. The brahman cow (or steer) fails to make another appearance, although the encounter seems stranger now that I have time to consider it.

The brahman's stature and stillness reminds me of cultures where such beasts are sacred and of the other shapes gods assume in myth and legend and, as I drift to sleep that night, I ponder our human need to give form to the sacred.

Want to explore further?

Bungle Bungle Caravan Park: https://bunglebunglecaravanpark.com.au/

Bungle Bungle geology: https://whc.unesco.org/en/list/1094/

Cathedral Gorge: https://www.bunglebungleguidedtours.com.au/news/cathedral-gorge-australia-kimberley-wet-season/

TRINITIES

I am still considering the sacred in all its manifestations as we head off the next morning and the thought-thread eventually leads me back to the *triskele* I use in *The Emerald Serpent*. The triskele is an ancient Celtic symbol of a three legged running cross with beautifully spiralled feet; a symbol I use to represent the triple form Goddess (nymph, matron and crone) and, by a curious turn of events, I am confronted by another trinity later that day.

Our destination is Fitzroy Crossing, 399 km (247 miles) west and, as lunchtime nears, we pull into a petrol (gas) station at Hall's Creek, fuel up and treat ourselves to pies for lunch. The midday sun beats down and we are parked in the shade of a broad, spreading gum behind the station enjoying our pies, when the threesome appears.

Fish on a Line

The child is having a hissy fit
stamping her feet, fists clenched in refusal
while mum walks on with the empty stroller
bare-footed across the petrol station tarmac
a glitter with broken glass

The older sister
fed-up with her younger sibling
picks up a stone and
hurls it back in her direction

I have seen goatherders in Greece use stones
to drive their charges forward
but this reverses
everything I know

The child follows like a fish on a line
using the slack to make her stand
not wanting to go on
but too frightened
to be alone

I consider the group as we continue our journey. Threesomes are common in myths and legends, and in their close relatives the fairy story and nursery rhyme. Think of Shakespeare's three witches in Macbeth; Greek mythology's three Weird Sister or Fates; Christianity's Trinity and Three Wise Men; the three billy goats gruff; the three little pigs; the three blind mice; Goldilocks and the three bears; the three (or six [2x3]) fairies in Sleeping Beauty; being granted three wishes; being whipped with the cat of nine-tails (3x3) and so on, and I wonder if it is why this latest threesome reminds me of one I saw close to twenty years ago.

I was in the usual traffic snarl exiting my workplace on a gloomy winter's evening in Melbourne when a wizard threaded his way across the road through the cars in front. *Just a student*, my *conscious* mind corrected, but tall and thin, with long red hair and beard, and dressed in a khaki army great coat (of the type bought from disposal stores by impoverished students).

I made it around the corner to the next traffic snarl where I saw the remainder of the threesome: the Madonna and Child. They also wove between stationary cars to cross the road and, like the student, were poor; dressed in grubby parkers (anoraks) over thin summer dresses.

I am not suggesting the three who crossed the petrol station carpark at Hall's Creek, or the young red-haired man and the woman and child in that chilly Melbourne evening are other than what they appear to be in the *outer* world, but they resonated, and I have learned to take note of things that do.

My (outer world) culture provides me with the words and concepts to label and define things meaningful to my *inner* world (though not to *express* them, which is why metaphor and symbolism are important) and the existence of these words and concepts (such as *Wizard* and *Madonna and Child*) tells me that what they define and label are neither new nor unique to me.

A wizard/magician/mage (and its equivalent in non Western cultures) is a common representation of the wise old man archetype whose power lies in his ability to harness both internal forces (wisdom, insights, awareness) and external forces (things/events in the outer world) to create an *extra*-worldly power.

One way or another, this power comes from within although developing the skills to wake, harness, control and exert such power is explicit in the outer world (Harry Potter must *learn* his *inherent* magic at Hogwarts in J.K. Rowling's *Harry Potter* books).

The wizard/magician/mage reminds us that we are more than just the flesh, blood and bone of the external world and that to be a *fully-realised* human being, we must acknowledge, nurture and draw upon our inner part. Likewise, the Madonna and Child reminds us that birth and mothering/fathering/parenting are not just about pain and mess; love and nurturing, but about the continuity of Life; of the cycle of the old giving way to the young; of the *natural* order of things (which includes our physical death).

And that brahman steer/cow I contemplated and that contemplated me at the Bungle Bungle Caravan Park? It reminds us that we are *all* creatures and, as such, are limited in our understanding by the particularities of our physical-creature selves, our consciousness *and* our unconsciousness.

I read of Mary Pool Free Camp in our camp book as we drive and we detour for a reconnoitre. Free camps allow 24 hour stop overs and range from flat areas adjacent to roads with no facilities, to large treed areas with phone coverage, dump points, water, toilets, fire places and rubbish bins. Some Grey Nomads spend their entire lives on the road on limited budgets, in fact, the cost of housing is one of the reasons some older Australians live out of their vehicles and vans, so *free* camps are popular.

This trip is the first time we have used free camps and we are totally converted by their sense of community and lack of strictures. Mary Pool turns out to be large with pit toilets, big trees, a dump point, and dumpsters at the entrance for rubbish disposal. We park in the dappled shade of a massive gum and take time to break out the camp chairs and have another coffee. We are booked into a park at Fitz-roy Crossing but decide to stay at Mary Pool on our next trip; not because it is free, but because it is beautiful.

Fitzroy River Lodge, where we *do* stay, is a combination of hotel, cabins, and caravan park, right on the banks of the massive Fitzroy River. The sites are large but grassless and unusually, the site number is set in the middle, not to one side. I trek up and down trying to decipher where the boundaries are and, keen to avoid setting up half on a neighbouring site, finally ask advice from a nearby camper.

His grunted reply is on the *leave me alone* end of the *chat-to-your-fellow-campers* spectrum. I might have caught him at a bad moment or even a bad life stage because we never really know what other people are dealing with. On the other hand, he might simply be grouchy. His curtness is unusual because travellers tend to be socia-ble, especially older travellers, who are free of job and time stressors and less concerned with trivial irritations.

I finally get us sorted and, as we are booked in for a couple of days, we have time to sit with drinks and nibbles and chat to those who pass by, many walking their dogs. I am very much a dog-person but have been dogless since our last dog died some years ago. We like to travel and while most van parks allow dogs, National Parks do not, so I take the opportunity to pat a few passing pooches.

The corellas wake us the next morning, which is nothing unusual; corellas like to hang about in packs and shout their arrival and de-parture, but the Fitzroy River means enjoying the cheerier chirps of lorikeets too and clouds of lime-green budgies (budgerigars). When we drive across the river later, I see egrets, storks and ducks on the still brown water; the egrets' snowy plumage brilliant against the Outback's dusty reds.

Birds have interested me more as I have grown older and I wonder if it is because, on an *unconscious* level, I recognise their flight symbolises transcendence. It makes sense on a *conscious* level too because, as death draws closer, we tend to spend more time thinking about what comes after. Of course, it may also be that when we quit the workforce, we simply have more time to think.

In a previous life on our 12.8 hectare (31 acre) property, I planted hundreds of trees and bushes with native bird habitat in mind and was rewarded with silvereyes, superb blue wrens, thrushes and willy wagtails.

In *Angel Caste*, Viv's love of birds symbolises her longing to transcend her violence-filled life that began as a child, with her abusive, alcoholic father, Jimmy Wright, but Jimmy Wright thwarts the child Viv's efforts to escape. Excerpt 6 begins with Thris showing Viv sumi: small, colourful mouse-like creatures.

Angel Caste: Excerpt 6

Viv laughed in delight. The sumi were like little gems, bright against the leaves, but she wondered how any survived. 'Don't they get eaten by the birds?' she asked, as they went on.

'Ezam has no birds.'

'But . . . don't you miss their music?' asked Viv, taken aback.

'Ezam is full of music. Everything that is, or ever was, has resonance, and resonance is music. We have no need of birds nor want of them.'

'Because they compete with you in the air?' asked Viv shrewdly.

'They can make transiting hazardous,' conceded Thris. 'Some rifts attract them and while they don't pass through, they can be disruptive.'

'I had a budgie once . . .' said Viv, and stopped as she recalled finding its bloodied wing in the driveway. Jimmy Wright had amused himself by bringing in the neighbor's cat.

I also wonder whether gardening, an activity popular amongst older people, serves the same purpose as birds. I have gardened since childhood and make gardens wherever I live (as do many people regardless of age) and while gardening obviously requires less exertion than running or competitive sports, gardens also have a symbolic regenerative aspect.

113

Dead matter returns to the soil to nourish new growth and continue the cycle of life and the over-arching cycle of the seasons also adds to the reassurance we are part of a grander scheme of things that continues after our death. I won't live to see many of the trees mature that I planted on our previous property but others will enjoy them, as I enjoy the glories of mature trees planted by those who have passed on.

We head out to Geikie Gorge the next morning, a short 20 km (12 miles) drive away. The map shows the road as bitumen but road-works create long rutted sections that slow us and finally bring us to a halt. It is strange to be sitting in the Outback with only birdsong for company, stopped by the most urban of objects: a red traffic light.

Imprisoned

The traffic light is red and we stop

Our lane is closed for roadworks
but there is no one in sight

Time passes and the light flickers to orange
then back to red

We wait

A car hurtles towards us on the closed-off lane
swerves back to its side of the road
and speeds off

We wait

Perhaps the light has malfunctioned, perhaps our turn
was stolen by the mad law-breaker
now happily on his way

Perhaps he has turned us into suckers
imprisoned by our inclination to
obey the law

Temptation grows to make our escape
but then the light turns green
and releases us

There is not much water in the gorge, which is surprising, given the
breadth of the Fitzroy River near the caravan park, and the signage
that tells us that, in the wet season (November to April), the water
rises over 16 metres (52 feet) up the gorge walls. All gorges have
their own particular beauty, with their combinations of soaring red
stone and silent pools of water, but my head is still full of the glories
of Cathedral Gorge and Geikie seems lesser.

The day is humid and it is not long before we drain our water bottles.
The heat and March flies (large flies with an appetite for blood)
encourage us back to the 4x4 and we spend a lazy afternoon at the
park. It is 18 days since we set out and we have covered a lot of
ground on our outer journey and, as I relax with a book, I hope I
have covered at least some on my inner one.

Want to explore further?
Mary Pool Free Camp: https://www.youtube.com/watch?v=4Iiotbon-hfQ
Fitzroy Crossing and Geike Gorge: http://www.aussietowns.com.au/town/fitzroy-crossing-wa

LARRADIY LARRGADI

Prisons come in many forms. Economic, where a lack of money keeps us confined; social, where class excludes us from liberating opportunities; physical, where ill health or disablement constrains our freedoms; or mental, where we lack the confidence to break free of imagined strictures. Or they might be of the more traditional *bricks and barred windows* variety.

The Big Boab tree we visit on the way to our next destination of Roebuck Plains owes its fame (or infamy) to the latter. It was *alleged* to have been used as a temporary prison, an allegation we later discover is false. This *wrongly-accused* Big Boab is at Camballin and one of several tourist-attracting *big boabs* in the Outback. Other well known ones are at Broome, Derby and Wyndham.

Boabs (*larradiy* or *larrgadi* in the local First Nation language) have spiritual significance as individual entities and, while I have limited understanding of First Nation spirituality, I sense this boab is more than just a massive hunk of splayed silver bark and ancient knobby limbs.

The boab is confined by a broad sweep of tarmac that bakes in the heat, and edged by rubbish spilled from skips in need of emptying. There are a couple of other vans pulled up and we grab the last patch of shade and have lunch before we wander over. A steel mesh fence has been hammered into the concrete-hard earth around the boab but is bent and broken, as if rammed by some vehicle. It seems to serve no purpose anyway. Even intact, it would not have stopped the people who scrambled over it to carve their initials into the boab's flesh.

Trees have a similar symbolism to angels and dragons (half physical, half spiritual) because their roots reach into the earth and their branches reach into the heavens, but this boab also has a grandeur that natural things acquire when they reach great age or size.

Had it been somewhere other than in a rubbish-strewn layby, the boab might have been venerated (it might still be by First Nation people) but its surrounds reduce it to a specimen to be gawked at, as if part of an old-style freak show. I gawk at it too but know enough to know how little I understand.

Big Boab

There is no sign to say how old it is
or how broad its girth
and if *it* knows
it is not saying

Maybe recording age and size
is a human thing
or at least a *woman* thing

The scales do not lie
and this tree is big
by any scale

It is fenced off
but whether to protect it
or us
I do not know

The fence is broken but
there is no escape
the boab confined by tarmac
that makes an easy turning circle
for RV's and vans who come
and go
none the wiser

ABSOLUTION

Broome is the key tourist town of the Kimberley region that, in the peak tourist months of June, July and August, grows its population from 14,500 to over 45,000, which is why we are booked into the Roebuck Plains Roadhouse caravan park, a twenty minute drive away.

Our friends join us again and we are relieved to hear they experienced no problems on the Gibb River Road (excluding a puncture and a microwave oven vibrated from its moorings to land undamaged on the caravan floor). Such things are barely worth mentioning given other friends broke a caravan axle on the Cape York Peninsula (in far north Queensland) and had to have their van retrieved by sea! Broome's cultural diversity, rich pearling history, and beautiful beaches give us plenty to do and I enjoy browsing shops, buying touristy things and eating at some lovely restaurants, including a special one to celebrate our friend's birthday. I also catch up on my swimming at the local pool but weeks of sitting in the 4x4 has done nothing for my fitness.

Broome Aquatic Centre

Is it an indoor pool? I ask the attendant
my mind still in Melbourne's winter

The attendant is from Melbourne too
which explains his lack of snort

He crisply recites the water temperatures
of a town that is either hot and dry
or hot and wet

The water (of the outdoor pool)
is cooler than the indoor pool at home
but I plough up and down

appalled by my clumsiness
and lack of ambition

I was better than this three weeks ago
and yet, despite the plod
something is washed away
and I emerge the better for it

Water serves as a symbol of the unconscious but it cleanses too, both symbolically and literally. The swimming my doctor prescribed for me (in a previous life) not only calmed me mentally but relaxed me physically by washing away my former, stressed self and I use this *transformative* aspect of water (in its various states) in several of my Deep Fantasy novels to illustrate its *cleansing* power in the soul-journeys of my heroes.

In *Messenger*, Jeph shucks off the last of his antagonism to Severine (and his old self) when they are caught in a violent snowstorm.

Messenger: Excerpt 1

Jeph ran on through the dying day. Snow filled his eyes, and ears, and throat; slicked the pastures; stole the light. Even Severine, who ran just ahead, appeared and disappeared, as if eaten by it. In Vishnu's name, how much further? The snow dulled to grey and he strained ahead as the ground began to rise. He hoped to God it meant the caves were near.

There was a deafening roar, as if the demons of Hell ran at his heels, and he was wrenched away from the ground, and then slammed back onto it. He clawed at the snow as the wind tried to lift him again and pressed his face to the ice. The wave of wind howled and shrieked about him, and then it was gone, and he struggled to his knees.

Severine? Silence. He scrabbled forward, panic like a mole-rat at his throat. The snow swirled chaotically, and he shook his head to clear his sight. 'Severine!' he screamed, but there was no answer. Where had she been? Where had he been? He ran back the way they'd come, searching the ground as he Sent to her frantically, and had gone nearly twenty lengths before he stopped.

*It was completely dark. The next wave of snow-laden wind
would bury her, then the freezing night would kill her. He stumbled to
his knees. 'Christ and Vishnu, I beg you. Let me find her and I pledge
to ask nothing more of you for all the days of my life.' He bowed his
head, his mind empty of everything but her, and slowly, in the deeper
darkness of his despair, an awareness grew. He struggled upright
and went forward blindly, and it wasn't until he stumbled over her in
the snow, that he saw her with his eyes.*

Likewise, in *Angel Caste*, it is only when Ataghan joins Viv in the
tempest-riven sacred lake of Astraal, that he relinquishes the last of
his hate (and so, his old self), something he explicitly acknowledges
later.

Angel Caste: Excerpt 7

*Viv sat on the stone seat and looked at the pool. It was skinned with
ice and she shivered, but she didn't want to return to the sett and,
after a while, footsteps crunched over the grass.*

'Can I sit with you?'

'It's your seat in your sett.'

He sat next to her and stared at the pool. 'It's not what you think.'

'And what is it I think?'

*'That my feelings for you are a lie, concocted to gain what I real-
ly want, namely the child of my dead lein. That anything I've offered
you is part of that lie; that my words of affection and our coupling
meant nothing to me; that they were a pretence which would end
once Sehereden's child was safely in my possession.'*

'And weren't they?'

*'When Ithreya offered me Sehereden's child, the gift was so
precious I was prepared to do anything to meet her conditions, right
up to the moment I saw you disappear beneath the waves in Astraal.
I thought I'd lost you, Ilris. It changed everything. What I've said or
done since has been without duplicity.'*

Earlier in the story (and in her soul-journey), Viv uses water to both
literally and metaphorically cleanse herself after Thris's attack. She

enters a jungle pool where she *consciously* rejects her angel part (represented by Thris) and embraces her human part. Her shedding of clothes (her old identity), musings on the Garden of Eden, and the pool's unspoiled beauty reinforce her determination to become something new and different.

Angel Caste: Excerpt 8

Viv continued warily until she reached the stream. It was scarcely more than a trickle under a mesh of undergrowth, but she followed it down to where the land gave way to a steep, rocky slope. The water fell in a silvery ribbon into a pool so clear she could see every pebble on the bottom.

Butterflies chased each other across its surface and a brilliant flotsam of crimson petals swirled as the water rippled and lapped. It was how Viv had always imagined the Garden of Eden to be and she scrambled down the slope and cupped the water to her lips, not because she was thirsty, but because she was determined to assert her human part.

Angels had abandoned her mother and attacked her and she'd have nothing more to do with them. But it was hard to shut Thris out, evidence of him plain on her breasts as she undressed: perfect bite marks made by his perfect teeth.

She slid into the water's cool embrace, the pebbles smooth under her feet and water-shadows masking her injuries. Tiny fish darted in shining shoals and as Moth Fold's filth washed away, Viv relaxed and floated. She felt outside time, a mote suspended between heaven and earth, and it was a long time before she swam back to the shore.

Viv had always avoided being naked but the water had washed away her fear along with the blood and grime. It was so peaceful at the pool that any threat seemed far away. She scrubbed her clothes and laid them out to dry, then wandered naked along the water's edge.

Viv's sense of being *outside time* hints at another of water's symbolic purposes, that of a medium of *dissolution*. Campbell's suggestion that heroes must *die* to their old selves, for their new selves to be born (that is, we cannot exist simultaneously in two life stages) is demonstrated multiple times by Chant (in *Heart Hunter*).

Chant cannot swim and comes close to drowning in a flooded river because she refuses the psychological change necessary to her next life stage.

Heart Hunter: Excerpt 2

Chant stepped into the flow. Leaves slapped against her legs and she tried not to think of what would happen if something bigger hit her. The water edged up to her thighs, chill and murky, and she wished there was more to cling to than cracks in the stone. She crept on, but her view ahead was blocked by a jut of stone. It sent the water into dizzying eddies and as sparks erupted on the edge of Chant's vision, she lost her grip on the wall.

A surge of icy water cut off Tanalan's shriek and Chant struck out with her feet, hoping to find the path again, but the path had gone. She was being pulled into the middle of the river, she realised in terror. She kicked with all her strength and managed to get her mouth clear but her pack dragged her under again. The current turned her over and over, and as the water pressed in, blacker than the void, the river carried her away.

Only later, when Chant's soul-journey has advanced, can she finally change. After being snatched by the Vulturi and retrieved by Tel, she engages in one last fight for her old self.

The fight is physical as well as psychological, and only when she plunges under the sea (into her unconscious) does she finally surrender her old self and emerge from the water able to continue her soul-journey as her new self (mature enough to give and receive romantic love).

Heart Hunter: Excerpt 3

Chant turned on Tel with fists, elbows and knees. She had always been close to him in strength and now her wildness made her impossible to subdue. Their fight ranged up and down the shore as he struggled to ward off her blows and then, as they stumbled into the shallows, he drove his hip and shoulder into her and threw her backwards.

The water was less than thigh deep, but cold and Tel gasped, and staggered upright. Chant remained limp under him and he wrenched her back to the surface and carried her up to the drier sand. Her eyes were shut and her hair plastered to her battered face and, as Tel crouched over her, blood from his mouth dripped onto the blood on her shirt. His blood had mixed with hers at the traps and they had inflicted more wounds on each other since, sometimes in spite but more often in ignorance.

At the traps, the full moon had lit Chant's face in all its alien beauty but now the moon was slight and Chant's features bathed in shadow. It didn't matter; he didn't need to see her face to know her.

'Chant?'

Her eyes opened and for a long moment, they regarded each other. Then she reached up and touched his bleeding mouth. 'It wasn't you,' she whispered. 'It wasn't . . .'

The *psychological* power of water can, in fact, be even greater than the power it exerts in visual or written stories. In a previous life, I was tasked with writing curriculum for a Creative Master's degree and researched the nature of beauty as part of the project. I had assumed that culture defined whether something was deemed beautiful but discovered there is a landscape that appears to be popular regardless of culture: an image that consists of forests with a lake, river or stream.

Researchers suggest this scene resonates because it contains trees and water, two things vital to early human survival. Trees provide wood for shelter and burning; food such as berries, nuts and seeds; and habitat for prey, such as foraging animals.

Water provides essential sustenance; contains food such as fish; and attracts prey-animals that must drink. Water's importance might also linger in the more primitive parts of our brains, given that life on earth began in the oceans and, as individuals, in amniotic fluid.

On a purely physical level, I enjoy my swim at the Broome pool and, given Broome's colourful European/Asian history, my next visit is to its cemeteries. There are three set side by side: the Japanese Cemetery, the Chinese Cemetery, and the Broome Cemetery. The heat is searing as I explore the Japanese Cemetery and, as usual, my only companions are crows.

They sing in a way I have never heard before and I search the tree branches, thinking there must be other birds there, but see only crows. The crows' song adds to the cemetery's strangeness. The Japanese graves are arranged with the exactness of a military cemetery but the ragged profiles of many of the marker stones are completely out of keeping with (my perception of) the orderliness of Japanese society.

Japanese Cemetery

The Japanese lie in precise rows
like the Emperor's obedient soldiers

but their headstones
are the opposite

of compliant

They thrust from the ground
rough-hewn and jag-edged

as if rebellion is only possible
in death

I later discover that many young Japanese divers (who worked in Broome's booming pearling industry) drowned or died from the bends (decompression sickness). A few days later while at the Night Markets, I come across a fourth cemetery: the Pioneer Cemetery.

Night Market

I doubt the dead enjoy the night market
despite being in its midst

Their graves are set between
the food stalls and
the photo op
across the ocean
and people wander over their feet
and heads

carrying take-away boxes
of Thai or Indonesian and
cans of soft drink

Some pause to read the tombstones
as they pause to read the ads
for hot coffee or doughnuts

and I wonder why
in a world criss-crossed by fences
this place is left
so open

SMASHED

We leave Roebuck Plains and start a series of short drives down the Western Australian coast. It is only 140 kms (87 miles) to our next stop, the Barn Hill Station turn off: a track of deep red sand complete with speed humps the sand disguises. We are in no hurry but the humps suggest other visitors are.

Barn Hill is a working cattle station that, like many Outback stations, has diversified into tourism by setting up a caravan park. We have sites right near the ocean and as the temperature zooms up, I go for a swim to cool off.

Untrustworthy Embrace

The water is as chill
as the southern oceans of home
and I creep in
slowed by cold and caution

I was raised inland with freshwater lakes
no stingers, sharks, or crocs there

Here I fear what lurks beneath
yet I let the water draw me deeper
into its untrustworthy
embrace

I take advantage of Barn Hill's showers: rough-made of curved corrugated iron and open to the sky. There is warm water but I do not linger. Fresh water (and bore water) is precious in these parts but especially so in drought. The station puts a lot of effort into making campers feel welcome and the manageress outlined the activities on offer when we booked in. Being a Sunday, a band will be playing tonight.

Just bring your chairs, drinks and snacks, she advises. There is a three-course meal on offer too and we buy our tickets and, as the afternoon draws on, settle in with the other campers around the band.

This singer is temporarily drowned out by corellas returning to roost but they quieten as the sun sets across the Indian Ocean. The horizon burns gold and, as the first cool stars wink into being, a cauldron of soup is carried around. We proffer our bowls and then afterwards, take our plates and queue for the roast and veggies, and then later, for the tinned fruit and custard.

It is good, honest fare, and the music has an honesty about it too, as live music often does. There is a timelessness in sitting around a musician, sharing food and goodwill and later, a restfulness in drifting to sleep to the sound of the sea.

We are back on the road again the next morning but less vigilant on the sandy track out and hit the last speed hump at speed. There is a jarring thud as the shock reverberates through the big 4x4 and then the van. A quick inspection reveals no obvious damage to the coupling but when we stop for a coffee later, I notice something dripping from the van door.

I am an inexperienced van packer and learn, as I survey the wreckage inside, that heavy items should *never* be stored high. Thanks to the speed hump, our back cupboards had burst open to create a mix of smashed glass jars of artichoke hearts in oil; pasta sauce; cordial; and split milk cartons.

Not only do I confront the *perfect* combination of slippery oil; staining red food colour; sticky cordial; and the potential rancidness of milk, all in a slurry of glass slivers, but the mess has splashed high up the walls and seeped under the cupboards to join the layer of red dust already there.

One of our friends wordlessly presents me with a large bag of jelly snakes (my favourite candy) but of all the things likely to upset, anger and distress me, messes aren't one of them and I decline all offers of help and methodically set to work.

Accidents like this seem too mundane to be part of a soul-journey but how we deal with such things can be instructive too. The level of upset they generate tells us a lot about whether we *sweat the small stuff*; our need for control; and our wish for order. They also offer us the opportunity to rank things according to their true importance, which helps us avoid wasting time and strength on things that are ultimately irrelevant to the richer, deeper lives we seek.

I spent my *paid* working life in education/academia and my *unpaid* working life in child-raising; food shopping, cooking and house-cleaning; washing, ironing and mending clothes; and keeping 12.8 hectares (31 acres) of land in order (mowing and poisoning). Society values and rewards these jobs very differently and, while it is hard to free ourselves from society's value system, part of our soul-journey is to decide for *ourselves* exactly what is valuable to *us* as individuals.

This struggle is real and can range from worries about being a *good* daughter (or son); sister (or brother); mother (or father), to anxieties about our *success* in the broader work/professional/public world.

I read of authors who are offered enormous sums by big publishing houses; have their work optioned for films or TV series; and win major literary prizes, and while this definition of success and the soul-journey are not mutually exclusive, what drives me to write is not the dream of commercial success but the need to explore something important to me. Deep Fantasy is not a well known genre and so I judge my success, not by fame and fortune, but by what a story reveals to me.

A brief search of the Internet details the many methods writers use to plan and write their novels but I am a *pantser*, that is, a writer who does not plan at all but writes by the (metaphorical) *seat of their pants*. As a pantser, I do not *consciously* know what the story is before I begin; my *unconscious* reveals it *as* I write.

This might sound odd, but even authors who meticulously plan their novels, speak of the wonderful moment when stories take off in unexpected (and unplanned) directions and/or when their characters develop lives of their own at odds with the lives the author envisaged.

My stories have been triggered by all sorts of things: phrases popping into my head; a song; an image in a magazine or on TV; a glimpse of something from a car window. My five book *Angel Caste* series was initiated by nine words of dialogue that came to me out of the blue: *So, this is the man you called your father.*

I Heard the Wolf Call My Name was written partly because, suffering from insomnia in late 2018, I got up and switched on the TV at midnight and, in a program reviewing past winners of the Eurovision Song Contest, I saw Mans Zelmerlow sing *Heroes* in 2015. The song (and Mans) gave me the hero Jax *and* his story.

The Emerald Serpent came about because I saw a TV ad. for a drama series, where a man on a beach looks up and sees someone or something that causes him shock, then dismay and then anger.

While a nine-word phrase started me writing *Angel Caste*, the actual series is around 300,000 words and so, as a pantser, I had to discover what those other 299,991 or so words were; what the story was; and crucially, why I *had* to write it.

To understand the beliefs/motivations/actions of my fictional heroes, I have to explore and consciously articulate my own beliefs, motivations and actions. For instance, in *Angel Caste*, I had thoughtlessly believed (like Thris), that good deeds advance a soul-journey (in his case, his journey to transcendence), but then he/I wondered whether *good* deeds motivated by *bad* intentions were, in fact, more destructive to the soul-journey than (inadvertent) *bad* deeds motivated by *good* intentions.

And like Thris, I began to wonder whether chance/the powers-that-be allow us multiple opportunities to get things right. Perhaps the soul-journey is not a singular journey at all, but parallel journeys weaving about each other; some carrying us on and others going nowhere (which is, in itself, instructive).

There comes a time in Viv's journey (in *Angel Caste*) when she must choose to continue to hate the perpetrator of her injuries or to forgive him. One road continues the cycle of destructive hatred, the other offers the potential to heal. But it is not an easy choice to make and the healing-road is not an easy one to travel (as I have discussed).

We make similar choices, sometimes multiple times a day (if we drive in peak hour traffic!): whether to honk at the motorist who cut us off; whether to let a queue-jumper merge in front; whether to hurl back the abuse hurled at us.

These seem trivial decisions and they are compared to the choices we make in dealing with life-threatening illnesses, or divorce proceedings, or navigating long-running family disputes, but they reflect our ability to identify what *we* value and, to hold true to those values to advance our soul-journeys.

Want to explore further?
Big Boab: https://www.fulltimecaravanning.com.au/boab-tree-wa/
Broome: https://en.wikipedia.org/wiki/Broome,_Western_Australia
Barnhill Station: http://www.barnhill.com.au
Mans Zelmerlow – Heroes (Eurovision 2015): https://www.youtube.com/watch?v=5sGOwFVUU0I

MANY MOONS

The moon rises over the ocean: huge and golden and, as it drifts into the night sky, a second moon rises, no less spectacular, and then a third. The sight is extraordinary even confined to my imagination but what if multiple moons *did* orbit the Earth? I remember how thrillingly strange the cover of *The Third Moon* became when the cover designer added the extra moons and oddly, our next destination, Eighty Mile Beach, is known for its many moons.

Eighty Mile Beach should, in fact, be called One Hundred and Thirty-six Mile Beach (its actual length). Long sandy beaches are nothing unusual in Australia but this one has a big tidal range and I join friends in a seaward stroll that extends over 100 metres.

The sand is pale grey, covered in a warm slip of water and rippled with runnels that run parallel with the shore. The great sweep is scattered with shells, the occasional jellyfish, and odd creatures that cling to masts of their own making.

The beach is even more popular at night when it claims its clutch of extra moons. At certain times of year, the rising of the full moon is reflected in myriad images across the exposed sand to create a phenomenon known as *The Staircase to the Moon*.

We happen to be here at the right time of year (and moon) and enjoy the spectacle with others who take up vantage points along the dunes.

Landward Run

The tidal range is 100 metres and counting
the grey sand strewn with creatures
attuned to salt

Chinaman's fingernails, bivalves, whelks
and a jellyfish bright as the sun

creatures that have other ways of living
and thinking and knowing
unknown to me

Later the sand glows gold as the jellyfish
lit by the setting sun until
the moon's cool gaze
turns it back to silver to welcome
the ocean's landward run

OUTSIDERS

We are on the road again the next day, the glorious azure of the Indian Ocean stretching to our right and the usual reds and dull sages of the desert to our left, both lit by a cloudless sky. This is cattle country with some stations thousands of hectares in size. The one we head to, is over 200,000 hectares (494,210 acres), although stations in Australia's Outback are often measured in kilometres. Like Barn Hill, it is a working station that has diversified into the tourist industry to buffer against the vagaries of drought and international beef markets.

We reach the park via the usual sandy road but get no further than the carpark. Entry requires a code and the office is unmanned. Shade is scarce and the temperature and humidity high. Our friends who travelled faster share their code so we can get in out of the sun, and we set up and once the office opens, return to pay.

There is a queue (given the limited opening hours) and we are still there when a couple attempt to pay for a cabin they booked weeks prior. They are told the cabins are presently closed. The couple politely point out they were not told that when they booked and that alternative accommodation is several hours drive away. No explanation, apology or alternatives are offered. The person behind the counter simply turns to serve the next customer.

The couple leave but I am taken aback by their treatment. Poor service happens in any industry and is often inadvertent but it jars after Barn Hill's friendliness. The couples' exclusion resonates with me on a deeper level too. It is Joseph and Mary turned away from the inn; it is Jews denied entry to other countries then murdered in the Holocaust; it is refugees pressed against mesh fences in Australia's off-shore detention centres.

Human society has complex overlays of conventions/laws about rights to territory, movement, settlement and so on, but at the root of so many cultures (often expressed overtly in religions) is the shelter owed to the stranger/outsider.

In this way, the historical suspicion of strangers/outsiders is countered by a sense of shared humanity; of having sufficient empathy to put ourselves in the stranger's shoes; of understanding that, next time, *we* might be the stranger/outsider in need of shelter.

Heroes in fantasy narratives are always the stranger because they leave the familiar (landscape/community) behind and set out on a journey through alien lands and peoples. Their journeys are a physical and psychological search for place, and their efforts aid the reader/viewer to navigate their own psychological journey (soul-journey) in search of *place* (a state of centredness/peace/belonging; eloquently summed up in T.S. Eliot's poem *Burnt Norton*).

Heroes are changed by being *the stranger* and, in turn, change those they meet. In *The Kira Chronicles*, Kira brings healing to Sarnia when she puts aside her antagonism to the Terak's warrior ways and to the city's stone; the antithesis of her healer heritage. By accommodating the ways of strangers, she enlarges her understanding and becomes a more complete human being, as Tierken finally does.

In Extract 1, Kira's greater understanding (progress in her soul-journey) is contrasted with that of her clanmate Tresen, whose soul-journey is less advanced due to his lack of contact with strangers such as the Northern Leader Tierken.

The Kira Chronicles: Extract 1

'I don't have time to sleep,' muttered Kira. 'Tierken's only granted me three days and then I have to go north again.'

'You let the leader of the Terak Kutan dictate when you come and go?' asked Tresen in astonishment. 'What right has he?'

'They're the Terak Kirillian. Kutan is an insult they don't take kindly to.'

'Whatever they call themselves, they have no rights over the Tremen leader!'

'Tierken wanted me to stay safely in Sarnia so I pledged to spend no more than three days here,' said Kira thickly, struggling with the residual effects of sickleseed. 'Breaking my pledges isn't

going to help us fight together.'

'So, Caledon was wrong?'

'Wrong?'

'He said the Terak Ku—Kirillian wouldn't accept the kin-link.'

'No, he wasn't wrong. The Terak Kirillian claim Kasheron and his followers went north, over the seas.'

'So, this . . . this Northerner calls us liars, does he?'

'He calls our histories lies.'

'He came here, you know, with Caledon, while you slept. Caledon led us to believe he was to bond with you but it looked more like the Northerner was.'

Kira said nothing and Tresen leaned across the pallet. 'Well?'

'Well what?' she asked, struggling to focus. Curse the slow-headedness of sickleseed.

'Did Caledon lie to us? Did he pretend love for you to convince us to send men? Or in Caledon's absence, did you turn to the leader of the Northern swordsmen?'

'It's not as simple as that.'

'Whether you bow before a man who denies our very existence is simple, Kira!'

'He refused to bond with me, if that's any comfort,' she mumbled.

Tresen stared at her aghast. 'You wanted to bond with that man? Stinking heartrot! You're the Tremen leader, Kira. To stay with him would mean to leave Allogrenia, to leave us, forever! Does Allogrenia mean so little to you that you would give it all away for the scion of the brute Kasheron fled?'

Tierken flicked back the curtain and Tresen froze, then strode past him out of the alcove. 'So, would you give Allogrenia away for the scion of the brute Kasheron fled?' demanded Tierken.

'Tresen thinks like I once did. Our tales lie about you, as yours lie about us,' said Kira.

'You haven't answered the question.'

'I traded Allogrenia away for just three days here, remember, and I've already wasted one in sleep.' Even keeping her eyes open was an effort and she let them close.

'For three days here but not for me?'

'It was you who refused the bonding, Tierken,' she whispered, as she started to drift.

'I didn't understand what it meant,' he murmured. 'I still don't.' He bent and kissed her, but she was asleep.

It is an even longer journey for Tierken to reach Kira's level of understanding and advance his own soul-journey.

The Kira Chronicles: Excerpt 2

'It wasn't you who was faithless, Kira, it was me,' said Tierken. 'When you left, all I wanted was to gallop after you and force you back. But to what? All the hard seasons of training with Poerin and the moons of fighting the Shargh, had taught me how to hunt enemies and to kill well, but they hadn't taught me to be patient, or to understand and accept Tremen ways.

'So this time I forced myself to wait, to have patience, to try to comprehend how it must have been for you, and how I could make it better. I've had hand-workers from Kessom make Queen Kiraon's garden lush with herbs again, and to replace the allogrenia stump with a strong young sapling. Trees have been planted throughout Kasheron's Quarter too, and Tremen already live there with their Terak wives and bondmates. Plantings along the Domain path were begun before I left and should be complete now.

'Sarnia will be a green city instead of a stone one, and the Tremen who live there will share your ways of thinking and seeing and bring you comfort.'

The station's lack of welcome (of two of its guests) is exacerbated by the longest list of rules I have ever seen. Caravan parks and free camps all have rules which are mostly reasonable, such as keeping noise low (especially after 10 p.m.), controlling pets and, (with free camps) limiting a stay to 24 hours (free camps are designed as overnighters for travellers, not holiday sites).

We head off to explore and I am struck again by how different Western Australian beaches are to those of my home state. They seem older and, like the landscape, more extreme.

Broken

The sea throws up broken things:
half a shell, sponges torn from moorings
smashed coral

We search along the shore for something intact
or still shining, or different from the sweep
of wreckage

These things once lived but we care nothing
for their histories as we trawl
the salty cemetery
for something that makes
us feel whole

We follow the station's *designated* tracks over the hard, pale earth
with its scatter of pebbles and animal bones to the detritus-filled river
mouth. The cries of plovers join those of gulls and (edible) samphire
(also known as glasswort) crouches in clumps amongst the spinifex.

Our next stop is a beach where stone juts from the sand like a ragged
city of stalagmites and we pick our way over and through them to
the water. There is little familiar in this region of the Pilbara (except
its vast iron ore mines frequently shown on TV), and we continue to
be awed by its ancient land forms and magnificent sunsets.

Sunset

The sunset is to die for but we do not die
or drive back to the viewing platform
as we pledged to yesterday

We stay at the park and watch the clouds blaze
crimson across the heavens
as sunsets do when horizons are broad
and the land as big
as the sky

CHAINS

We leave the station in a convoy that breaks 47 kms shy of Port Headland. We are to go straight to Marble Bar but our friends need to visit Port Headland to sort out things in the facilities only bigger towns offer. We will meet up again in a couple of days.

Marble Bar claims to be the hottest place in Australia (or the second hottest after Wyndham - also in Western Australia) but regardless of which settlement holds the record, I am glad to be here in winter when temperatures are in the high 20's C (around 82 F) rather than high 40's C (118 F).

Apart from heat, Marble Bar's claim to fame is a large jasper deposit, originally thought to be marble, hence the town's name. But despite the jasper, it was another gold rush that put Marble Bar on the map.

We stroll along the main street and see the Iron Clad Hotel which opened in 1893. As the name suggests, it is clad in corrugated iron, historically a popular building material in Australia and still commonly used in farm buildings (and increasingly, in up-market housing). The hotel looks like a great place for a pub meal, which is confirmed by the young woman at the local Tourist Information Office, who also tells us there is no need to book. Sadly, this last piece of information turns out to be wrong and we never do get that meal.

The same young woman provides us with a map of *points of interest* and we set out in search of the Marble Bar Old Cemetery also known as the Marble Bar Pioneer Cemetery. We reach it down a broad dirt road and the usual crow-song adds to the sense of desolation created by a dry creek bed, bleached grass, scraggly spinifex, and stone-hard ground.

Many of the graves are decorated with shells but several have heavy chains laid across them that form a lengthwise X. They do not seem to be religious markers and I wonder whether they serve the same purpose as gravestones once did: to ensure the dead stay buried, both physically and in wraith/ghost/spirit/shade form. The chains cross multiple times on some graves and as these plots have no headstones, just boulders around their perimeters, I wonder if the chains delineate the burial site too.

I am again reminded of the randomness of my place in time and space *and* of the power of ritual to mark changes relevant to both physical and psychological journeys. These (Christian) burials I wander among were preceded by sermons and prayers in a church; a measured procession down the aisle, the coffin carried feet first on the shoulders of chosen pall bearers; a second procession on foot, horse, carriage or motorised hearse to the cemetery, led by the deceased's closest relatives; a lowering into a grave dug six feet deep and often facing east; the delivery of more ritual words, sprinklings of water and earth; and the final setting of a marker stone, adorned with sacred symbols.

The ritual *words* in a Christian funeral service confirm the death of the person's physical self and the transition to ever-lasting life of their spiritual self, while the ritual *actions* of burial (or burning) confirm (in a very concrete way) the cessation of the person's *physical* form. In contrast, the transitions *within* the soul-journey are psychological and death (of the old self) metaphorical rather than literal.

This is powerfully illustrated in Peter Jackson's film versions of J.R.R. Tolkien's *Lord of the Rings* by Gandalf the Grey's transformation to Gandalf the White. This is a complex and richly symbolic episode in the films but at its simplest, Gandalf descends in the Mines of Moria (symbolising the unconscious) where he encounters the Balrog, a demon that broadly represents what we must confront/overcome to advance to our next life stage. In a battle that encompasses the primal elements of earth, fire, water and air, Gandalf defeats the Balrog to wake high on a mountain (symbolising consciousness), reborn as Gandalf the White.

Gandalf's transformation fits neatly into Joseph Campbell's three broad stages of the hero journey:

- Separation/Departure – Gandalf the Grey leaves the daylight world behind and descends into the Mines of Moria
- Trials of Initiation – Gandalf the Grey endures many tests including navigating the dark; fighting orcs, goblins and a cave troll; to finally defeat the Balrog
- Return – Gandalf emerges from the darkness and re-joins his comrades as Gandalf the White

The heroes of my Deep Fantasy stories complete their journeys of psychological transformation within this structure, although I had never heard of it when I wrote my first series *The Kira Chronicles* and was shocked to later discover how perfectly the series fitted. Joseph Campbell calls the structure he identified *the universal hero journey* and suggests the structure lies deep in the human psyche and so manifests in myth and story regardless of time and place.

My *unknowing* adoption of the structure in my first books and since (as a pantser, I do not *deliberately* follow any plan including Campbell's hero quest structure), may well have flowed from my psyche but I might have also unwittingly acquired it through Tolkien's *The Lord of the Rings* (which also uses the structure).

I fell in love with *The Lord of the Rings* in my late teens and read the series multiple times before starting my own writing career. In turn, *The Lord of the Rings* probably uses Campbell's hero structure because Tolkien acquired it *unknowingly* through his studies of Scandinavian myths (which conform to the same structure).

In *The Kira Chronicles*, Kira's entire family is murdered by the Shargh. Losing everyone she loves loosens her ties to her homeland (Allogrenia) and initiates the process of *Separation/Departure*.

There are two rituals that mark the death of Kira's old self. The first is cutting her long hair to disguise her escape from the enemy. (Making radical hairstyle changes is surprisingly common for women exiting relationships as if by literally cutting their hair, they metaphorically cut off their past) The second ritual is more obvious when Kira conducts a funeral for the pipe that belonged to Kandor, her beloved younger brother. In burying his pipe, she symbolically buries him, and her past life/former self.

The Kira Chronicles: Excerpt 3

Kira knew she should go, but something held her there beneath the alwaysgreen, and it came to her that she was the first Tremen to ever leave Allogrenia.

It was akin to dying, except there would be no slow procession through the trees, no songs, no one to mourn her as she had mourned no one: not her father, or Merek, or Lern, or—

Without really knowing why, she slipped off her pack and retrieved a cloth-wrapped bundle. Then she knelt and using her herbing sickle, cut out a neat patchwork of sods from between the roots.

The soil was rich and dark, and she used her hands to gouge out a hole and then unwrapped the bundle. For a long moment she simply held it, eyes shut, head bowed, then she gently laid Kandor's pipe in the narrow grave.

'The roots have taken you, the tree grown strong from you, the leaves been spun from you, the wind sung songs of you—' she choked to a stop, scooped up the earth and let it sift through her fingers until the pipe's pale wood was hidden by the fragrant soil. Then she firmed the sods back into place and rose.

Beyond the alwaysgreen, the first stars glimmered in the sky. 'Kashclan thanks Renclan,' she said softly, hefted on her pack, and turned northwards.

And so Kira departs from everything and everyone she has ever known, leaving her former life behind. The middle stage of the quest for a new self (*Trials of Initiation*) is perilous because the hero is neither in the safe familiarity of their old life nor within the structures/bounds of their new. Instead, they are in the amorphous space *between* (called the liminal) where anything (both good and evil, but always disruptive) can intrude.

This is the equivalent of *mid*night; the time *between* beloved of fairy stories; because *mid*night is neither one day nor the next. It is the *witching hour* when Cinderella must leave the ball. Likewise, the liminal is central to Shakespeare's *A Midsummer Night's Dream* because *Mid*summer's Day is the day when the hours of daylight cease to grow and begin to shorten again, a pivot-point into which the other-worldly demons and Fae might enter. It is the gibbet at the crossroads too: a place that is neither east, west, north or south, and so prevents the vengeful spirit of the executed person hunting its murderers down.

Campbell's *Trials of Initiation* are exactly that: tests and trials that force the changes necessary to transform the hero in readiness for their next life stage. Kira's strength, courage and determination are challenged, but it is her attitudes and beliefs that face the greatest test, and her ability to change and/or enlarge them that allows her soul-journey to progress.

She begins to see her enemies the Shargh as victims, especially the women and children, and resolves to risk her life to help them and, if worse comes to worse, take the lethal herb everest to avoid a more painful death. At the last moment, she overcomes this destructive impulse and embraces life instead.

The Kira Chronicles: Excerpt 4

They were going to the highest hut! Kira's breathing quickened until she panted. Arkendrin probably waited inside with his rotted eye, his hatred, and his sword! Her feet dragged but Ormadon hauled her along behind him. And then they were at the hut!

Take the everest before it's too late! the voice in her head ordered. Ormadon thrust her through the door flap, and Kira dipped her chin and tore a leaf free as she stumbled onto the soft pelts, but she didn't swallow. Her knees had come up under her belly and within, something had flickered.

Kira let the everest fall from her mouth as the terrible realization washed over her and then a knobby hand wrenched her upright, and she was dazzled by light.

Embracing life (saving herself to save her unborn child) allows Kira to *Return* to her community as a mature woman, confident in her impending motherhood and in her leadership of the Tremen. The change is evident in Kira's dealings with the Clancouncil. Her very first meeting with them as leader was marked by nervous uncertainty but certainly not her last.

The Kira Chronicles: Excerpt 5

In the meeting room, there was a jumble of speech as the other councilors offered contradictory opinions and their volume increased as they fought to be heard. Outside, Tierken sprang from his seat and strode to the meeting room door, Kest and Tresen hastening after him. 'You can't break protocol by entering,' warned Tresen.

Tierken's face was like thunder. 'If they distress Kira . . .'

'Kira's dealt with the council before,' said Kest, exchanging quick glances with Tresen. 'The worst they can do is reprimand her.'

'Reprimand her? What in Irid's name for?'

'The Tremen Leader isn't free to do exactly what he or she wants,' said Tresen. 'They are required to take advice from the council and to keep the council informed of their intentions.'

'And that's what her father Maxen did?'

'You underestimate Kira's ability to look after herself,' interrupted Kest, ignoring Tierken's challenge.

Tierken's brows lowered and then Kira's bellow for quiet sounded from beyond the door. 'See?' said Tresen with a smile.

The councilors paused, and Kira seized the moment to order an end to their argument, gratified to see them obey.

Kira's newfound maturity as a woman is also evident in her relationship with Tierken.

The Kira Chronicles: Excerpt 6

As the day's passed, Kira grew more dismayed at having broken her pledge to herself to remain in Allogrenia. Tierken had made many concessions to tempt her back to Sarnia, and his admissions about his behaviour had been painful in their honesty, but in the end, none of these things had been the reason she had agreed to return to Sarnia, if he still wanted her by Thanking.

As she lay in bed each night, wondering if she had made a terrible mistake, Palansa and Ersalan's plight came back to her. Ersalan would grow without his father, and Palansa endure a future without her bondmate, but Kira still had a chance for happiness, and in Sogren's shade, where the happiness of so many others had ended, she had snatched the chance, for her own sake and the babe's.

However, the clearest evidence that Kira's former life has ended is when she finally visits Kandor's burial place. Kandor was the most precious person in the world to Kira, and his death haunts her, but when she tries to mourn him (in essence, mourn a part of her former life), the babe, which is part of Tierken and her future life, draws her back.

The Kira Chronicles: Excerpt 7

Kira circled the alwaysgreen, nerves taut, the babe prodding and punching inside her as if it sensed her turmoil. It wasn't supposed to be like this. Kandor lay beneath her feet, along with the mother she had scarcely known, and the bones of countless Sarclan dead, but she felt no more connection with her younger brother than she had with Maxen and Merek. She laid her palms against Sogren's trunk and struggled to think of their happy times together, but the babe seemed determined to drag her back to the present.

The three broad stages Campbell identified in the hero journey (and the 17 elements associated with the stages) have been popularised by Christopher Vogler in *The Writer's Journey: Mythic Structure for Writers* and widely used in written and film narratives. As a result, they are likely to be familiar to readers and viewers at an *uncon-*

scious level, even if readers and viewers do not recognise them *consciously.*

It is one of the reasons certain written and visual works resonate so strongly *unconsciously.* Yet *consciously* knowing this structure is useful in identifying the *stage* we have reached in our own soul-journeys. We do not need to be the hero in a fictional, fantastical world because the structure and its elements can play out in the most mundane of ways.

For instance, shifting house can be a confronting mix of getting rid of possessions (where has all this *stuff* come from?); dealing with unfamiliar matters (sale and mortgage documents; taxes and fees; titles and legal requirements); packing and moving possessions; settling in and orientating ourselves to our new environment (where did I put the frypan; how do I get to work from here?)

Separation/Departure starts when we decide to move; *Trials of Initiation* involves the processes of selling our property and acquiring a new one; and *Return* involves feeling comfortable in our new property due to our increased confidence and autonomy.

The daily routine of my Outback journey has grown familiar but at each stop we embark on excursions to rediscover the unfamiliar. This time, we head out to Glenn Herring Gorge via a scenic drive that takes in an abandoned jasper quarry; the old Comet Gold Mine; and the Flying Fox Lookout, which has nothing to do with flying foxes (fruit bats).

The views from the Lookout are sweeping and include the pale swathes of gravel and the still, silvery water of the Coongan River, unlike the confined views from the Marble Bar Road where we search in vain for the gorge turn off.

Glenn Herring Gorge is not well sign-posted from the road or from the track that takes us in but we keep going until the track ends on the banks of a steep-sided and waterless creek bed. A walking trail leads us on but soon disappears into thick, scratchy bushes, fallen logs, and unstable stone and we abandon it in favour of the boulder-strewn riverbed. This is a far easier walk and, as the red walls of the gorge rise around us and water fills the riverbed, we continue our trek along the coarse sand at its edge.

The sky is adrift with clouds that shift to shift the colours of the gorge. The usual blood-rust reds and pinks contrast with emerald-tipped reeds with bright lime stems that grow twice: once into the air and once downward in reflection, and the dark grey river stones deepen and lighten around pools of tannin-stained water. Pale-barked gums lean over the still waters to add to the glorious palette.

Glenn Herring Gorge

The signpost has seen better days and
remains unseen
as we drive past, turn
and all but miss it again

The rutted track dips and rolls
then forks with no sign at all

We gamble on the right
and rumble on until it ends
in rocks and bushes

Our feet take us further
along a riverbed

stone-cobbled

that rewards us with still water
bright with reflections
and birdsong

Glenn Herring is one of many gorges we visit but the most poorly sign-posted to date. Likewise, the hero who leaves his familiar world behind must navigate *alien* landscapes; a physical journey that is rarely without help (or hindrance) that impacts on the hero's inner psychological journey as well.

When Kira leaves her war-torn home of Allogrenia, her only plan is to gain aid from her long-sundered warrior kin in the north. She comes across Caledon early in her journey and accepts his offer to guide her north.

Caledon *does* guide her but he is also a servant of the stars and their dictates soon override his pledges and later, his feelings for Kira. His manipulation of *her* feelings for him result in Kira meeting Tierken, who also aids her but, like Caledon, seeks to guide her in the direction *he* desires.

Kira's gradual understanding of her helpers' motives is an important part of her evolving soul-journey and she needs no guidance to remove herself from both. It is Tierken who needs guidance to win her back and who, in turn, is guided by his grandmother and close friend in the task. As noted, Tierken's soul-journey requires him to accept Kira's healer aspect (as she accepts his warrior aspect) and the greening of the city of his rulership and public acknowledgement of her as his bondmate is evidence of his acceptance.

But guides do not have to be human. In *Heart Hunter*, Fleet/Chant is close to death in a blizzard when a berian (bear) appears.

Heart Hunter: Excerpt 4

Something moved on the slope ahead and Fleet dashed the snow from her eyes and strained into the gloom. Within the darkness was a deeper darkness. Fleet gasped. It was a massive she-berian! Had the void sent her to take Fleet into death? The berian turned and for a moment outside time, each regarded the other, and then the berian moved off and, desperate not to be alone, Fleet struggled after it.

The wind moaned and the snow eddied and whirled, so thick it seemed that the berian walked upon air and that Fleet did too. Earth and sky became one and the ice a deadly embrace. A delicious languor invaded her body and she swayed, staggered and pitched forward. Her face hit the snow and the shock thrust Fleet back into awareness. She struggled to her knees and stared about. The berian had gone.

Fleet clawed her way upright and staggered on. One step, two steps and then the snow collapsed in upon itself and, with a terrified scream, she was plunged into oblivion.

Fleet/Chant survives the fall into a cavern and uses bear scent to navigate the tunnels' utter darkness. Bears guide her twice but are tied to her old life and cannot guide her in her new life stage. As she nears the river she must cross to continue both her outer *and* inner journey, she discovers a dying bear in a trap and then steps in a trap herself. The injury ends her old life as a hunter and forces her to accept her new name (Chant) and role (*and* life stage) bestowed by her people's shamanic leader.

Warrain's guide (in *The Third Moon*) is also nonhuman as is Etaine's (in *The Emerald Serpent*) and both stories highlight the importance of the nonhuman creature in the outer and inner journeys.

Animals teach us much about what it means to be human and the human impact on the broader animal world goes to the core of our individual and society's values. What constitutes humane treatment of food animals (or should there even be such a thing?); of animals used in research; of animals used for racing or entertainment? What are our rights *and* obligations, as *part* of the animal world, to other animals?

The role of helpers such as guides (in the middle part of the hero journey) is to orientate the hero to new lands/systems, not to take responsibility for the hero's journey. To move to the next life stage, heroes must change/grow to the point where they can survive and even thrive without guidance in their new environment.

In *The Third Moon*, Warrain assumes an important role in his community *after* the planet's sentient life-form helps him understand his place; and in *The Emerald Serpent*, the bear-shifter Arturo guides

Etaine back to Cormac which allows her to access the Emerald and Serpent Ways and defeat the enemy.

Want to explore further?
The Kira Chronicles – Complete 6 Book Series: https://www.amazon.com/Kira-Chronicles-Complete-Book-ebook/dp/B082QK4X36/
Eighty Mile Beach: https://parks.dpaw.wa.gov.au/park/eighty-mile-beach
Ironclad Hotel: http://www.marblebar.org.au/destination/marble-bar/ironclad-hotel/
Marble Bar Pioneer Cemetery: http://inherit.stateheritage.wa.gov.au/Public/Inventory/Details/728af36e-144e-47f6-b9e8-d0e18b134d18

LONG-BURIED BEAST

Australia is home to some of the oldest exposed rocks on earth and the worn red lands outside the 4x4 window look ancient. We are back in our convoy of three as we head south-west to Karijini National Park which at 627,422 hectares (1,550,393.53 acres), is both one of Australia's largest national parks and one of its more popular. We take the precaution of booking but are in no hurry to reach it; planning to free camp tonight in the Hamersley Ranges.

We retrace the previous day's route along the Marble Bar Road and pass the Comet Gold Mine and the much missed turn off to Glenn Herring Gorge. We could go directly west and join the sealed Great Northern Highway sooner but the Marble Bar Road promises new landscapes and we are assured the road is in good condition, which it is. The Chichester Ranges emerge from the west and as I gape at them, I am glad we chose this route.

The ranges run parallel with the road for kilometres: zebra striped in astonishing symmetry with pale green spinifex and chocolaty stone. The patterns fill me with delighted wonder but I forget them when we turn west onto the Munjina Roy Hill Road and the Hamersley Ranges hove into view: blunt-browed and hulking. If the Pilbara's landscape were architecture, the Hamersley Ranges would be Brutalist.

Old

The mountains rear from the land
like the backbone of some long-buried beast
wrenched back to the surface
for our amusement

They are fixed while we are as transitory as flies
as we zip past
snap, snap, snapping with our smartphones
as if we can capture Time

An escort vehicle appears ahead, orange light flashing, and we move to the side. Escort vehicles are common in the Outback and precede the transportation of enormous pieces of mining equipment. We are more than happy to give them space but a police car follows and orders us completely off the road. We park and get out to stretch our legs.

The equipment turns out to be a massive dump truck that dwarfs the equally massive truck that carries it. We watch it pass but there are times on this trip when *we* must pass massive vehicles; a manoeuvre not without risk. We tune our CB radios to the vehicles' channel and know when their drivers are aware of us and acknowledge their instructions about speed, when to sit behind, and when to go.

I have described the broader importance of helpers/guides on the hero's journey in alien lands, but the stakes are higher when danger is present and the guidance comes from strangers. On the night Kira meets Caledon (in *The Kira Chronicles*), they must scale a treacherous mountain, a danger exacerbated by Kira's fear of heights.

The Kira Chronicles: Excerpt 8

A cluster of large broken boulders loomed ahead. They jutted into space and Kira stopped. There was nothing but air between them and the Dendora Plain but the man simply edged around them and back onto the mountain's slope. He made it look easy, as if he had done it a hundred times before. She expected him to keep going but he stopped and turned. 'Come,' he said, in the same gentle tone he had used before.

Kira willed her feet to move, but nothing happened. 'I can't,' she said hoarsely.

He stretched his hand out to her. 'I will keep you safe.'

It was still too dark to see his face; all she knew was that he killed well and that his spicy scent reminded her of the alwaysgreen. She crept forward and her breathing quickened as she struggled to remember where he had placed his feet.

'Almost there,' he said, and then the stone under her feet skewed sideways and she clutched frantically at the boulder and missed.

There was a sickening moment of knowing she was going to fall and then his hand clamped about her wrist. He held her but she had no idea how he anchored himself, only that he couldn't do so for long.

His calm voice came to her again. 'There's a ledge just above your left hand. Reach for it.' Blood roared in her ears, blocking all thought. 'Reach for it,' he repeated. Kira numbly obeyed and managed to grip it. 'Good. Now bring your right knee up onto the slope. That's good. Rest a moment. Calm your breathing. Good. Now, keeping your weight forward, slowly stand.'

Kira obeyed. 'Keep your face to the boulder and step sideways.' She froze again and he calmly repeated the instruction, and as she moved sideways, he slowly spoke her back to his side.

The urgency of the incident builds Kira's trust in Caledon and similarly, we must trust the experienced and skilled truck drivers who guide us safely on our way. These guides are in the outer world and relatively easy to recognise but it is harder to recognise and trust the feelings, hunches, intuition and odd dreams the unconscious provides as guides.

The first part of Campbell's hero journey (*Separation/Departure*) includes elements known as the *Call to Adventure* and the *Refusal of the Call*. In the former, an event triggers the hero's abrupt departure from their former life. In *The Kira Chronicles*, the event is the Shargh's attack while in *Messenger*, it is Jeph's drunken assault of Severine, but the wrench to leave the familiar behind is hard however it comes.

Messenger: Excerpt 2

Jeph's gaze jerked between Acran's rim and Severine's rapidly disappearing back. Every fibre of his being yearned to fight with his friends but she was all but hidden by the bushes and he swore savagely and followed. He was deserting now, whichever way he looked at it.

Deserting everything Abram had fought for and Caleb had trained him to defend: the women and children of the Mob; the old; the entire Enclaves. He stormed down the gully, risking a twisted ankle with every stride, and hadn't gone far when a storm of gunfire erupted above. 'They're in the Enclaves!' he cried, and half turned back. Severine kept going. 'What the Hell's happening?' he demanded.

'Caleb hasn't Sent,' she tossed over her shoulder.

'For Christ's sake, ask him!'

'It would be dangerous to distract him,' she replied, without stopping.

Jeph raged as he followed her. Had she no feelings? No loyalties? She had lived with those of the Enclaves for months, and now she walked away. But that was the way of Gelds! No commitment to anything except themselves! No planning, no building, no wanting of a better tomorrow. What else could he expect? And she was Abram's blood! Abram, who'd spent his entire life building the Enclaves, had spawned this feckless, faithless Half-Geld, Half-Silverskin.

Severine turned on him furiously. 'I didn't ask you to come with me! I didn't ask you to get drunk and desert. Get the Hell away from me! I don't want you!'

'And I didn't ask you to read my stinking thoughts!'

'How in Christ's name can I not read them when you throw them all over the place?! If I could bloody well shut them out, believe me I would! And what have Travelers ever done to you, man, that you hate them so much? Have they murdered your family? Destroyed everything you loved?'

Jeph struggled to cool his temper. He needed her with him and away from any stinking caves that opened near the gully. 'We need to keep moving,' he said, keeping his gaze on the way ahead.

Kira and Jeph heed the *Call to Adventure* but sometimes heroes resist (*Refusal of the Call*) until events build to a crisis that gives them no choice. In *I Heard the Wolf Call My Name*, Jax lives in a space he creates for himself between a past too painful to acknowledge and a future he cannot face. When the pressure to acknowledge his past and accept the future becomes unbearable, he flees, with disastrous results.

I Heard the Wolf Call My Name: Excerpt 1

Briggs' bawled numbers to divide them into teams and Jax shuffled into place and feigned attentiveness as Briggs yelled instructions on how the obstacle course was to be completed. It consisted of the usual low pole-jumps, logs in ladder-form and laid end to end, towering walls, bridges and climbing-nets of rope, and a tunnel of barbed wire, but it was longer and its walls higher than those at Nakoda and Arozi.

Briggs shouted an order and the first two men set off, their comrades urging them on. Jax knew he should study the men's techniques but even if he survived the course, Briggs would devise something worse, and Jax stared beyond the perimeter fence instead. Forests clothed the valley's sides enclosing places that were quiet and dark and hidden, and he kept his gaze on them.

The men around him dwindled but he was barely aware of it and then it was his turn. The shouting was so loud he had no idea which team led; he simply ran for his life. He sensed the men's surprise at his speed, and Briggs', as he vaulted the lower walls without breaking stride, sprinted along the logs and threw himself at the wall. His speed gave him the momentum to get a grip halfway up and he clawed his way to the top, taking the skin from his hands and knees, half slid down the rope designed for descent and let go to land with a jarring thud.

He scarcely registered the pain as he navigated the net, aware of cheering as he ran on over the rope bridge, and then he was at the final obstacle, the tunnel. The other man was hard on his heels and Jax used his hands and knees, not elbows and belly. The barbs tore through his shirt and back but the pain was far away too, his head empty of everything but the sanctuary beyond the fence.

He exited the tunnel and ran on past the end of the course, heard the cheering give way to stunned silence, and then to the boom of Briggs' bawled orders. He didn't stop, just hurled himself at the fence as he had hurled himself at the wall. He reached the top and scrambled into the razor-wire.

It trapped him like a bird in a net, and his body burned with searing slashes as he struggled to break free, and then his blood-soaked shirt tore loose, and he fell to the grass on the other side, struggled to his feet and ran, aware of nothing more than the need to escape.

Jax's past is so traumatic it robs him of hope for the future and, even as death nears, he continues to *Refuse the Call*.

I Heard the Wolf Call My Name: Excerpt 2

Jax ran, his breath torn from his throat in scalding sobs, his body afire with pain. There was no easy lope like his runs in Arozi's arid emptiness, just a shambling stagger driven by a desperate need to escape. He stumbled down slopes into shallow valleys and clawed his way up their sides. The trees wavered as if under water and when he wiped the sweat from his face he found it was blood. His arms wept blood too, and his torso, and legs, and in the reaches of his brain that still functioned, he knew he must rest if he were to survive.

Survive Briggs, survive Keli, survive Arozi, survive Nakoda, survive Sawquorn Training-home for Boys, survive moana's icy embrace; survive the blast that had torn his old self apart. His mind ran backwards in a bizarre inversion of time he was powerless to stop, and he wondered if it were because he had no future.

But he had no past either, not beyond the blast; he existed only here in this time of pain and endless running. He came to a stream and stumbled to a stop on its banks. He knew its rush, its glassy slide over river-stones, the smell of its moss and wet reeds, and he knew where it came from: its silent seep, its silver stream, its shining waterfall.

It lived in his memory, before the blast, when there had been songs and Kawai Alanui he had loved and who had loved him. The stream's birth lived there too in a quiet place, where leaf-fall and bark-fall, flesh and feather and bone, rotted down to a soil that fed new life.

He lurched into the stream and fell to his knees. He had swum in pools and lagoons; felt waterfalls pound his shoulders; watched their rainbows arc into space. The stream swirled around him, tugged at him, pulled him apart, and he collapsed forwards, face down, and let himself go.

Water (again serving as a symbol of the unconscious) frees Jax from the past but he remains in limbo, unable to commence his future. This hiatus continues in the white, featureless Military Infirmary where he is rendered impotent by medication and straps that tether him to the bed. It is Matiu's love and urgent news that finally frees Jax to start his next life stage.

I Heard the Wolf Call My Name: Excerpt 3

Saliva flooded Jax's mouth and as he fought the straps, bile surged. He tried to swallow but being flat on his back, choked, struggled to drag in air, and choked again. The door was flung open, which told him the room had mics, and then medics were all around him. Matiu was there too. 'He can't breathe,' he cried. 'You need to sit him up!'

The straps were loosened and he was hauled upright and his head held over an instrument tray. He spat and sucked in air, the relief of being free, even briefly, overwhelming. The medics were muscular and straps still tethered most of him to the bed, but they hurriedly fastened the straps again as if they expected him to flee. Matiu hovered anxiously but didn't speak again until they were alone, and then only to ask if Jax still felt nauseous.

Jax made no reply. It was pointless explaining the toll it took to suppress memories and he pushed at the straps again. The constriction might have been bearable had he not been horizontal. All he could see was the endless white of the ceiling, the shadow bars on the wall, and Matiu.

He turned his head and looked at him properly, the dream-image of Matiu's unscarred younger self still clear in his mind. 'Let me go, Mati,' he said softly.

Matiu took his hand again. 'I can't.'

'No. It would be a massive black mark against your exemplary military record, wouldn't it?' sneered Jax, and stared at the ceiling again.

'You are all I have.' The words were Kawai Alanui and Jax shut his eyes. 'If I took the straps off, where would you go?' continued Matiu softly, in English. 'Through the razor-wire again? And if you survived that, what life would you have? You were always a fast runner, Jax, and still are according to my friend, but you can't run

156

forever, and when the military caught up with you, as they inevitably would, there would be more cells, and more of this,' he added, gesturing to the room.

Jax had concluded the same thing during Briggs' training course but hearing Matiu voice it woke his anger. 'So, you want me to build a nice shiny career with the opala like you.'

'I want you to help Commander Keli stop Iolana suffering the same fate as Rua.'

'Why should I?' demanded Jax.

'Because you are Kawai Alanui like me, and they are our people.'

'I am not Kawai Alanui!'

Matiu stood and Jax thought he was going to storm out but he caught Jax's jaw and forced Jax's face to his. 'It isn't your fault Rua blew up. It isn't your fault I was scarred. It isn't your fault you lost everything you loved. We were racing because it was something we always did. We were far from Rua because we competed, as all younger Ahi males compete. You aren't responsible for anything that happened!'

'Let go of me,' gritted Jax.

'No! The time for running is over, Jax. You aren't responsible for the past, but you are responsible for the future, for Iolana's future. Ahi become the guardians of everyone's future when they die and are born again as Ikaika. You have to go back! You have to go back and die so you can stop what happened to Rua happening to Iolana. It isn't a choice, Jax! It's your responsibility.'

Jax's chest heaved but he didn't wrench his face free even when Matiu loosened his grip. He simply stared into Matiu's green eyes, as he had so many times before, but this time he saw Rua's verdant valleys and the deep emerald of its lagoons.

Tears seeped from his own eyes but he let them come and then Matiu's mouth came to his, his lips soft, the kiss fleeting. 'I love you, Jax,' he whispered in Kawai Alanui. 'But I can't do this for you. You have to do it for all of us.'

In the outer world, the sudden acceptance of the *Call to Adventure*/ the next life stage can be triggered by the urgency of a health scare when half-hearted attempts to stop smoking or lose weight can become super-charged (and successful) attempts to create a healthier next life stage.

Likewise, redundancy can transform people trudging along in unful-filling jobs into highly committed job-seekers/small business owners in the area they had only fantasised about. These changes take place in the outer world but result in changes in the inner world too. Where individuals take back power over their circumstances/lives in the outer world, their new life stage in the inner world is more autono-mous and contented too.

We see no more mining equipment as we cross the Great Northern Highway at the Auski Roadhouse and continue along the Nanutarra Wittenoom Road to the Hamersley Gorge turn off. The gorge sits in the northern most part of Karijini National Park and the usual sweep-ing vistas are hidden by boulders and bushland.

The descent to the gorge carpark is steep and halfway down we notice signs that prohibit camping. The prohibition is a surprise and ends our plans to spend the night near the gorge. Steps lead down the cliff face from the carpark to the Fortescue River but I am content to look down from the above while the others explore. Silver-limbed trees stir in the breeze, sending shadows over the water, and I perch on a step, breathe in the fragrant air and birdsong, and let the sun-shine warm my skin.

We reconvene in the carpark to discuss where to camp that night. Our wiki's and camp books tell of a nearby campground and we set off on what proves to be a fruitless search, give up, and head west again, alert for camping spots near the road. We find one sheltered from the sparse passing traffic, form a circle with the vans, and get the fire going. Being self-sufficient has many advantages, and we spend another evening enjoying simple food and superb stars.

TWO TALES

The pretty, purpose-built mining town of Tom Price shares its name
with the iron ore mine, the mountain that initiated mining in the
area and, of course, the owner of the name: Thomas Moore Price,
vice-president of the US steel company Kaiser Steel in the 1960's.
Tom Price is the neatest Outback town I have been in with pristine
concrete footpaths, immaculate emerald-green lawns and rub-
bish-less roads. It also has a great supermarket where we stock up on
food before we settle at a café for coffee and to watch the galahs at
play.

Flockless

The town has a very Anglo-Saxon name
but this is no green and pleasant land

and those who later named
Mt Bruce and Mt Nameless had no ear (or care)

for the poetry of
Punurrunha and Jarndunmunha

Nor do the galahs
who hang upside down on taps

flockless for a moment
as they drink

We fuel up because Karijini National Park has no fuel (or water or
food) and is a 210 kms (130 miles) round trip from Tom Price. The
drive out is so spectacular we stop several times for my husband to
set up his tripod and take *proper* photographs with his Canon. All the
Pilbara is magnificent but there is something special about this area.

The Scottish Highlands has a similar sense, as does much of Iceland, but Iceland is a new landscape and the Pilbara groans with age. Mt Bruce (Punurrunha in the local First Nation tongue) crouches like a prehistoric beast and the Karijini campground is creased by ancient gorges.

The sites are enormous and resemble inlets off the winding river of the road. We can see our neighbours but not hear them which allows the quiet that sustains me. We will be here for a few days and we set up a second solar panel (the first is on the van's roof) to top up our batteries.

When we set out, I worried about axles and tyres but I soon discovered it is battery systems that cause the problems. We can run the fridge and cooker off gas but not the lights, toilet and water pump and it reminds me of the decluttering necessary to travelling.

Despite the luxuries of a 4x4 and van, we have indeed simplified our lifestyle and those who hike know how quickly and ruthlessly unnecessary baggage is discarded. I miss nothing of our former luxuries although I admit to enjoying the convenience of washing-machines and the bliss of hot showers in parks.

The everyday luxuries many of us take for granted came with relinquishing a life of roaming. Nomadic peoples carry their belongings with them and so accumulate few goods. Life on the move impacts cultural practices too including rituals associated with death.

In *The Kira Chronicles*, Kira's sedentary people bury their dead among the trees and believe their voices live on in the whisper of leaves. The practice keeps the dead close but the Terak Kirillian, some of whom are still nomadic, keep their dead close by using fire to release the spirit into the ether.

The Kira Chronicles: Excerpt 9

'After Pekrash died, we combined forces, and when the fighting came North, Lord Caledon led the Tremen,' said Tierken.

'So, Caledon would know who was killed and where they're buried?' asked Kira.

'He would know who was killed but we followed Terak funeral practices.'

Kira's mouth dried. 'Which are?' she asked hoarsely.

'Burning.'

Kira had to grip the chair. 'But that means their voices have been silenced forever,' she whispered.

'The flames loose the spirit to the sky and so the spirits of the dead are all around us. We couldn't risk more lives by seeking groves and digging graves.'

Regardless of a culture's funeral practices, the rituals that surround physical death belong to the *outer* world. I have noted Campbell's claim we must die to our old selves to embrace our next life stage and the symbolism of women cutting their hair after ending a relationship, but it is easier to cut off hair than to cut off negative experiences, and the latter *baggage* has the power to impede our soul-journeys.

Each book I write is the best book I can write *at the time* and knowing this allows me to move forward to the next book. Yet each time I re-read one of my books, I see a multitude of ways I can improve it. Some authors rewrite their first book over and over again and some never write another book because they simply cannot move on.

Similarly, if we continue to churn over what we *could* have done better in the past, we risk becoming stuck (and often frustrated, angry, and unhappy). It is one of the reasons I see my life as a *series* of discrete lives. I did my best in each of my former lives, given my human flaws and the circumstances *at the time*, but that particular time has passed and I am in a new and exciting one.

Our first foray in Karijini is to the Gorge Rim Walk where we peer down into the shadowed cherry-red stone and silver rush of the Fortescue and Circular Falls before descending a series of metal steps, turning left and setting out on the Dales Gorge Walk. The gorges were formed when sedimentary rock, laid down under the oceans, was uplifted and cracked to create crevices that were later down-cut by rivers.

Pools of shade transform the Fortescue River's inlets into muted mirrors of the gorge's red-cragged walls, snowy-trunked gums, and lime-green figs while elsewhere, sunlight pierces the water's sliding layers to reveal their deep rust-brown. The riverbed's smooth stone makes for easy walking and overhead, the gorge's upper edges create a sky-path that runs parallel with the earth-bound path we tread. Sulphur-crested cockatoos and corellas flash along it, their white plumage translucent in the sun, and smaller, darker birds flutter at its margins.

Later that day, we take the same metal steps into the gorge and turn right this time to Fern Pool. My husband takes a dip and enjoys the pound of the pool's waterfalls on his shoulders. The water provides a second mirror, broader than the first and rippled, so that the gorge's reflections of red, green and bright white form abstract patterns on its surface.

I later discover a third metaphorical mirror that reflects a different story to the one I have related. In this story we are still camped at Karijini – a First Nation Banyjima word meaning hilly place, but the river is called Manggurdu. Along with Karijini's other waterways, Manggurdu was formed by the Creation Serpent as it made its way from the coast through Karijini before taking up residence in Jubara (the Fern Pool); a place sacred to women.

Karijini Gorges

We stand on the metal viewing platform
where the four gorges meet
and peer down

Well-kept paths give way to rough-hewn rock
and sunshine to shadow

We cannot see the bottom and leave
thinking we have learned the answer to a question
we did not think
to ask

My husband would have swum elsewhere had we known Jubara was
sacred to women and, as I consider the two stories of Karijini, I hope
there is a point of connection such as beauty or a sense of the sacred,
neither of which can be fully explained by the earth's ructions or
those of the Dreamtime Serpent.

There is no phone coverage at the campground but occasional
coverage at the Visitors' Centre, a ten-minute drive away and we are
there sorting bookings for later in the trip, when my phone picks up a
video of polar bears scavenging in a Russian rubbish dump.

The images of scrawny, dirt-stained bears resonate when later that
day, I see a malnourished dingo nosing around our campsite. Both
remind me of a poem I wrote in a previous life, when we still lived
on our country property.

Fox

I know I am a traitor to my neighbours
who farm
the land does not feed my family
only my soul

But when I saw you run
across the grey sky
your brush painting the morning
red
my heart sang

As a child I saw eagles
strung out along a fence
and twisted a claw free
as a keepsake

I am ashamed now of
my desecration

They kill the lambs, the farmers said
and they say the same
about the fox

Yet how can we grudge them food
when we have eaten their
entire world

SACRED SONGS

Gradations of colour on fibrous stems; the riffle of water under gentle winds; the shadow-throws of insects on their own journeys over
stony ground; I have time to enjoy many instances of subtle beauty
as we explore Karijini's gorges over the following days. And then we
are off again, out along Karijini Drive to Mt Bruce.

The great hulk of the mountain watches our approach as a cat
watches a mouse and signage tells us it is Western Australia's second
highest peak. Other signs deliver stern warnings about fitness levels,
walking in hot weather, and carrying sufficient water for those in-
tending to climb.

We choose the short Marandoo View Walk that provides a panorama
inclusive of the Marandoo Iron Ore mine. A railway line stretches
into the distance complete with a stationary ore train with so many
trucks, I give up counting them.

There is a *parallel* story here too, where I do not stand on the slopes
of Mt Bruce but on the slopes of Punurunha (Punurrunha/Bunur-
runha), a mountain sacred to the First Nation Kurruma, Banyjima
and Innawonga people. There is no mine in this story, and no railway
trucks, just Dreamtime animals and birds busy coming and going as
they store their songs at Punurunha for safe-keeping.

I hear and see no animals but as I slowly turn, enjoying the blue-sky-
sunshine and 360-degree vista, a small breeze wakes the mulgas'
song and my breath slowly empties. I am not the first person to suggest we are happy when we are not consciously *un*happy, and when
we are *consciously* happy we are in a joyous state and I am definitely
in a joyous state as I stand on Punurunha's slopes surrounded by
tree-song and the Outback's glorious sweep.

That night we camp at a park on the edge of Tom Price, the neat
little town we visited on the way to Karijini. The park is at the foot
of Mount Nameless, a mountain that would have been better left
with the poetry of its First Nation name of Jarndunmunha. There is a

4x4 drive track to the summit that claims to be amongst the highest tracks in Western Australia but as the sun sets, I find Jarndunmunha's changing hues more than enough to entertain me.

OUTRUN DEATH

It seems that everything has a price and the spectacular sprawl of the Hammersley Ranges extracts its the next morning when our friends lose their back windscreen to a stone. We pull over and pool our supplies of duct/gorilla tape to weave a new one.

Duct tape already seals our broken external tap and keeps our broken-latched van window secured but I had barely heard of it before this trip. It has proved indispensable, along with WD-40: an all-purpose lubricant that stops the hitch from seizing up with dust.

A little later we see our first snake on the road and stop to let it pass. Its girth tells me it is some sort of python but I am only familiar with the deadlier tigers and browns of Victoria. Our drive is slowed by euros (whippet-thin, pale-coloured wallabies) that make suicidal dashes across the road in front of us, and it is late afternoon before we reach our destination of Old Onslow's ruins.

The wind whistles between the derelict buildings as we circle the blackened and broken machinery and rubbish-strewn fire pits in search of somewhere to camp. The trash and wind make the ruins desolate and we head for the Ashburton River instead.

A series of broad compacted dirt roads take us through a surprisingly green landscape until, as dusk falls, the river sheens in the distance. Vans dot its banks and we continue until we reach a clear stretch and bring the vans in nose to tail.

The river is broad with reeds that bow to its ripple, and slender gums that dip their leaves into its flow. Ducks make bow waves to add to the river's lap that shines silver in the dying light and gold as the sun sets. We gather wood and soon the spicy scent of eucalyptus smoke joins the throw of stars. As we eat around the fire, we debate the origin of the glow in the distance and, after checking our maps, decide is either a mining camp or the town of Onslow.

Another van pulls in ahead and we invite them over. Wine and nibbles are produced and we settle in for a chat.

On the Road

The couple who join us
at the fire have been on the road
nine years and he asks us half in jest
whether we work for the
Tax Office

before he tells us of *their* work:
cashier, camp guide, truck-driver
and the pay they sometimes get
in cash
great wads of it
not worth the counting

As they speak, I wonder if I could
be on the move so long
although in truth
they have stayed put for months:
working, volunteering, enjoying
some special place

I wonder too whether when
we are needed less
(kids grown up, scattered over the earth
as this generation is)
we revert to type

hunters, gatherers, wanderers
not content to sit
because only nursing homes await
or the long grey trudge
of dementia

and so we keep on moving
as if to outrun
death

Want to explore further?

Hamersley Range: https://www.australias.guide/wa/location/hamersley-range

Tom Price: http://www.aussietowns.com.au/town/tom-price-wa

Mt Bruce: https://parks.dpaw.wa.gov.au/site/mount-bruce

Dales Gorge: https://parks.dpaw.wa.gov.au/site/dales-recreation-area

Fox: first published in Poetrix, #16, May 2001

Mt Nameless: http://trailswa.com.au/trails/mt_nameless_tom_price/print

Old Onslow: https://www.prc.wa.gov.au/project/old-onslow-conservation/

DEMONS

Dawn delivers a river swathed in mist; one of the many jewels we encounter on this trip. I pause to watch the silver streamers adrift above the water; feel the air's moistness against my skin; breathe the scents of grass and earth and trees and am reminded of the power of small things to centre us, and how easily these things are swept aside by the busy-ness of our lives, even when we journey.

We detour an hour north to explore Onslow, a settlement that owes its existence to pearling, farming and gold mining. It also bears the ominous nickname of *Cyclone City* thanks to the 12 cyclones (hurricanes/ typhoons) it has survived since 1883. We arrive in time to enjoy the local market and wander through the half dozen stalls set in the main street.

They include the usual collection of self-propagated plants; baby clothes; and home-made jams and chutneys, the latter a favourite of my husband, so we stock up. The market is set in front of the local museum and we pay our small donation and peruse the aisles of farming bits and pieces and domestic paraphernalia such as washing-boards, coppers for boiling clothes and mangles for squeezing out water, all of which make me grateful for being born a century later.

I complete my round of the museum in a few minutes and am on my way out, when I pause at a table of books written by local historians. One of them details the life of Onslow's women and I settle on a stool to read and am still there twenty minutes later.

Onslow's Women

They have their own small section in the local museum
between the farm equipment and the kerosene lamps
Onslow's women

and I read of Japanese women
who came with their pearl-diver husbands
and Japanese women who came
to work in brothels

I read of respectable women who came
with respectable husbands
and independent women who came
to run a business

I read of women who nursed and taught
and women who lived poor
and I read of black women raped,
enslaved

I read of a woman whose child died of diphtheria
whose new-born died a week later
and whose husband died
when she was thirty

and I think of her lifetime of grief
as cold and hard
as the pearls that drew so many here

and I think of the heat and dirt
and the weight of women's petticoats
but mostly I think of menstruation

of trying to stay clean
of trying to stay dignified
of trying to stay alive

Life in the Outback was harsh for pioneer women who must ac-
commodate European notions of respectability while managing
menstruation, contraception, childbirth, child-rearing and of course,
clothing totally inappropriate for Outback conditions. There is little
written about them (compared to men) unless they were notorious or

wealthy in traditional male pursuits such as managing businesses or cattle stations.

There is a barely questioned assumption their lives were similar to their fellow *male* pioneers, an assumption applied more broadly to the female heroes of book and film. Often described as *kick-arse/ ass*, these female heroes are presented as beautiful clones of the male heroes, with the same fighting skills, sensibilities and motivations.

Joseph Campbell claimed the hero journey was applicable to both male and female heroes but his definitive work *The Hero with a Thousand Faces* discusses very few female heroes and, despite being a huge Campbell fan, I wondered whether it really was. It was the reason I undertook a Ph.D. in the area and one of the reasons I write Deep Fantasy. The nature of the female hero journey is also important to our own soul-journeys, whether we identify as male or female.

Writers must decide early in their narratives which of their female (or male) heroes' bodily functions to ignore. While there is a joke that no fantasy hero ever needs to visit the bathroom or owns a pair of socks, narratives are stronger when they include physical functions *relevant* to the hero's soul-journey.

Females menstruate but, until relatively recently, even acknowledging menstruation in *polite* society was taboo in the West and still is in many parts of the world. Females can also conceive, and to ignore these things, risks creating a male hero in drag. Menstruation and/or pregnancy is part of a female's life and is explicit in the female hero journeys of *The Kira Chronicles*, *Messenger*, the *Angel Caste* series and *The Emerald Serpent*.

The Kira Chronicles: Excerpt 10

Kira sat on her sleeping-sheet next to the fire, an ache in her belly she hadn't felt for many moons. Put some flesh on your bones or you'll never carry, Sendra had admonished, shortly before her father had sent her back to her own longhouse. Of all the helpers who had come and gone from the Bough, Sendra had been the only one who had commented on how rarely Kira bled. It had never worried Kira; mothering was the last thing on her mind.

She drew her knees up to ease the ache and thought of what she carried in her pack. 'I need some time alone,' she said to Jonred, when he returned with windfall.

'The Feailner orders you're to remain here until he returns.'

The guards kept a constant patrol beyond the circle of fires and Kira rested her head on her knees and must have drowsed, starting as grass crunched underfoot. 'Jonred says you request time alone,' said Tierken. 'Come.' She struggled to her feet and followed him into the trees. 'Here will do,' said Tierken. 'I'll turn my back.'

'I need to go to the spring to wash.'

He shook his head. 'You'll have to accept being grimy for a while.'

'It's not because I'm grimy . . .' Stinking heartrot! Must she beg his permission for everything?

'No further,' he said, hands coming to his hips. Kira sat on the grass and pulled off her boots.

'What in Irid's name are you doing?'

'I need to change my underclothes. To do that, I have to take off my boots and trousers.'

'There's no reason—'

'I bleed, Tierken.'

Comprehension dawned and for the first time since they had set out, he looked other than angry. 'Kira, I—'

'Just turn your back.'

Messenger: Excerpt 3

Severine set off down the slope but Jeph hurried after her. 'Where are you going?'

'That's no concern of yours,' she snapped.

He was to her in a stride and caught her arm. 'Unfortunately, it is.'

The wash of firelight caught the angry flash of her eyes. 'Can't I even relieve myself without you spying on me?'

'It's not safe on your own.'

Her chin was up, and the wash of firelight exposed the curve

*of her neck and the bruises that mottled her throat. Repugnance at
Daniel's attack mixed with a surge of attraction. 'I'll look away,' he
said gruffly, taken aback by his jumble of emotions.*

'Do what you like,' she said, and strode off into the night.

*'Don't go too far,' he called after her. 'The land drops away.'
There was no reply. 'Girl?'*

'I heard you, man!

*Jeph grimaced. He deserved the retort. She had a name and
would soon have a place amongst the Enclaves' women. At least
then, she'd no longer be his problem, and he could resume his previous, uncomplicated, life. He stared back up at the campfires as he
paced up and down, waiting for her. The fires showed the silhouettes
of men but not of women. Stinking Hell! He wished he was staying at
the Enclaves. Even one night with Sarah was better than another six
months of nothing! He chaffed his hands. What in Vishnu's name was
keeping the Half-Geld?*

*'Severine?' There was no answer and he took several steps in
the direction she'd gone. Then she appeared out the gloom, pushing
a bloodied cloth into her jacket pocket. 'Have you hurt yourself?'*

*'No.' She went to pass him, but he barred her way. 'Do you
know nothing of women?' she demanded angrily.*

*'Jeph?' It was Caleb's voice, checking on their whereabouts
and she pushed past him and went on up. Jeph followed. Of course,
he stinking-well knew of women, of the way they bled, it was just
that until a moment ago, he'd thought of her only as something that
curtailed his more enjoyable activities with Adam and David.*

Angel Caste: Excerpt 9

*Viv had had plenty of time growing up and later in jail to wonder
why Lettie O'Brien had married such an arsehole. Now she guessed
it was because she was pregnant by Kald. Well, she'd paid a high
price for her respectability and Viv was glad she'd never find herself
in the same predicament.*

*Viv had never menstruated and Jimmy Wright's interest in his
only daughter had been so low he had never sought medical advice.
All that had changed when Viv had come to the notice of the author-
ities. They had been obsessed by her lack of periods. The State's ne-*

glect of a minor in moral danger wasn't an issue but their neglect of a pregnant minor apparently was. Every time she had been dragged through this or that welfare agency she had been pregnancy tested, but she had been sixteen before she had discovered why so much unprotected sex had left her so thoroughly unpregnant.

Most of those who had processed her had blurred in Viv's memory, but not this particular doctor. She had worn her gleaming blond hair in a perfect French roll and her perfect body in a pristine white coat. Viv had noted both as the doctor had settled behind her leather-bound desk and flipped open a folder.

'Extraordinarily low levels of estrogen,' she had murmured, before her ice-blue eyes had flicked up. 'Most unusual, given the feminine characteristics you exhibit, but probably for the best, considering your life choices.'

Kira (in *The Kira Chronicles*) and Etaine (in *The Emerald Serpent*) also become pregnant. Etaine makes a conscious decision to conceive; something necessary to her entry into the Serpent Way but for them both, motherhood is a major life-altering event, as it always is. It stops Kira sacrificing her life and allows Etaine to save her *people* (the elf-like Eadar).

It is also the harsh reality that females in conflict situations risk rape and that fantasy narratives are full of conflict situations. Chant (in *Heart Hunter*) and Severine (in *Messenger*) narrowly escape rape and Viv *is* raped in *Angel Caste*. Viv's long history of sexual abuse forms part of her back-story but her hero journey demanded I write a rape scene, something I had hoped to avoid.

Even writing the scene was distressing and reinforced how damaging rape is to its victims, both female and male, and that rape's consequences are far more profound than a sword slash or cudgel blow. Viv is terribly damaged by her life of sexual violence and only begins her healing journey when she reaches the Iahhel, the female-aspected angels in Erath Fold.

Males and females also fight differently. While both sexes can be trained to fight, the *average* male tends to be bigger and physically stronger than the *average* female. Kira fights only once: a clumsy sword attack on a Shargh distracted by attacking Caledon and is only saved by Caledon's sword skills. Etaine picks off her victims with knife-throws from a distance and when she must fight up close, survives because she cares nothing for her own safety.

Brute strength and weaponry like swords and arrows are not the only weapons available to heroes. Verbal and nonverbal language can be weapons too and research suggests females are more skilled in both. In *Heart Hunter*, Chant is taken prisoner after she goes out weaponless. Knowing she cannot overcome an armed man, she firstly uses nonverbal language and then later verbal skills (lying) to protect herself.

Heart Hunter: Excerpt 5

The man's aggression was as sour as his breath and Chant wanted to spit in his gloating face but she daren't risk the beating that would follow. She forced her shoulders down and dropped her eyes and didn't retaliate even when he dealt her a stinging blow that split her lip. The man enjoyed inflicting pain but the greater her injuries, the lesser her chances of ever returning to Berian-tur.

Heart Hunter: Excerpt 6

The older man seemed to be losing interest in his sons' quarrels. Perhaps he would let them fight it out—or share her.

Chant gulped down air. 'My husband will be angry I've been taken,' she said wildly.

The man's eyes narrowed. 'Your husband's Okianos?'

'He's Sunnen but kin to the wife of Septim.' The man's jaw tightened at the mention of Septim, but Chant didn't know whether his animosity boded well or ill.

'Your husband's a careless man to leave you loose.'

'He's ill and forced to his bed. I . . . I like to wander. It makes him angry. I cost him a lot of . . . taka when he . . . traded for me. I come from beyond the mountains and have caused him trouble before. He'll be very angry,' she repeated.

The older Vulturi would understand a man's wrath at losing a possession and she wanted to plant the idea that, having traded for her once, her husband might trade for her again. The Vulturi wore a small disk of taka and Chant knew it was greatly valued amongst the Okianos, and here, she hoped.

Presenting female heroes in the same way as male heroes makes them less useful as vicarious hero journey guides to both women *and* men because it ignores the *full* breadth of what it means to be human, as does pigeon-holing heroes according to their sex and/or sexuality and/or gender (or gender fluidity).

I counter such pigeon-holing in a variety of ways in my Deep Fantasy narratives. In *Heart Hunter*, I reverse traditional male/female roles. The female hero, Chant, is a Sceadu *hunter*; the Sceadu leader is a *female* Shaman who leads via *dreams* and *intuition*; the Sceadu live by *hunting* and *gathering*. The settlement is on the rain-shadow side of the mountains (s*ceadu* is the archaic form of the word *shadow*). Chant feels she is socially mature and ready to marry; the Shaman disagrees.

The male hero, Tel, is a Sunnen *farmer/gardener*. The Sunnen are led by a *rational male* Council. The Sunnen live mainly by cultivating fruit and vegetables. They live on the ocean-facing side of the mountains. *Sunnen* is the archaic form of the word *sun*. Tel does not feel ready for marriage but the Sunnen women with marriageable daughters disagree.

Heart Hunter also challenges the divisions between different types of love: that of friends; of mentor and mentee; of hetero and homosexual couples. After Snowhawk is injured, both Tor (his friend) and Mist (his male lover) fight to save him.

Heart Hunter: Excerpt 7

Tor built a fire while Mist hurriedly collected an enormous pile of windfall so the fire would burn hot all night, and then Mist supported Snowhawk's head while Tor tried to coax water down his throat.

But no matter how they held him, the water trickled from his mouth.

'He's going to die, isn't he?' said Mist.

Tor remained silent, gripped by the same dread. Snowhawk reminded him of the tinsel-flies caught in snowcome's ice; their glittering beauty preserved until snowmelt released them to decay.

'He's going to die!' shrieked Mist, and Tor's head snapped up.

'Don't—' he growled, and grabbed Mist by the arm. In his own weariness and fear, all Tor wanted was quiet, but in the next moment, Mist was sobbing in his arms and Tor muttering words of comfort. Mist felt different to Serest, harder but somehow more fragile—the type of body Snowhawk liked, no, the type he loved. And Mist's kisses had roused Snowhawk before!

'We need to give Snowhawk reason to come back to us,' he said urgently.

'I don't understand,' said Mist, sleeving his eyes.

'The child's first warmth is skin to skin with its mother, but it's not just warmth, Mist, it's scent and heartbeat, breath and love. We'll put Snowhawk between us, skin to skin, heart to heart. We both love him. If our warmth doesn't draw him back, perhaps our love will.'

Mist smiled tremulously. 'And if he leaves . . . if he returns to the void, I'll go with him. He'll go safely with my love.'

'Snowhawk wouldn't want you to give up your life,' said Tor, but his thoughts were on Serest, who wouldn't even give up a few days for him.

Mist's slender fingers caressed Snowhawk's cheek. 'We both know what it is to be alone, Snowhawk and I, and what it is to be as one. The void holds no fear for us after that.'

I delve deeper into what it means to be human in *I Heard the Wolf Call My Name*, where the fluidity of *our* physical forms *and* of our sexuality is explored explicitly via a narrative about *shifters* because, in a sense, we are all shifters.

We start as babies who are different to children; who in turn are different to adolescents; who in turn are different to adults. We come in different colours and sizes too and, despite sometimes lethal prohibitions on the expression of humanity's full range of sexuality, we have never divided neatly into female or male, homosexual or heterosexual or, in terms of gender, woman or man.

The following excerpts from *I Heard the Wolf Call My Name* explore the relationships between the male Jax and female Anahera; the males Tamati and Malo, and between Tamati and Anahera.

I Heard the Wolf Call My Name: Excerpt 4

Keli's attention swung to Jax. 'Your shifter heritage has been dis-cussed at the earlier briefing, Airman, but it is important those of Operation V understand fully what a shifter heritage means. I would like you to demonstrate shifting.'

'Yes, Commander Keli.' Jax pushed back his chair and took up position at the side of the room where there was more space. The men present had last seen him tear himself to pieces on the perimeter fence, which was hardly the sign of a dependable person they might have to risk their lives for, and he wondered how they would react to him shifting.

'With your permission, I will summon Professor Connel, who wishes to see a shift for research purposes,' said Keli. Jax nodded though they both knew Keli didn't need his permission for anything. The men's feet shuffled under the table as if nervous they were about to witness an embarrassingly poor party trick, but Jax kept his atten-tion on Anahera's rigid face.

The Kawai Alanui had never hidden their ability to shift but nor had they used it to sate Off-islander curiosity or appetite for the bi-zarre. Connel came in and Jax stripped down to his underwear and sensed the men's distrust increase as his part-healed gashes were revealed.

The men showered together so being naked was less of an issue than Anahera's presence. Her body reeked of anger at her predica-ment and she glared at Keli.

'Anahera?' he prompted.

She rose and the men's heads swivelled in her direction. They probably thought they were in for a double party trick, but she turned her back.

'We are both older Ahi,' explained Jax evenly, 'and older Ahi do

*not look upon each other naked.' He enjoyed a moment of grim satis-
faction as the men struggled to reconcile the news with the rumours
of sexual hijinks at his quarters last night, then considered which
shift-form to take as he removed his underwear.*

*He resisted the urge to choose a snake to test their mental
strength by slithering around the room with tongue flickering and
chose a white-wolf instead. Off-islanders admired what they saw as
a wolf's noble savagery, but he mainly wanted to reassure Anahera
he hadn't changed into an Off-islander.*

*He shifted and remained motionless for a long moment to allow
the shocked men to make sense of what they had seen, then padded
around the table to Anahera. She still stood but had turned again
and he put his front paws on the table beside her, so his head was
level with hers, and faced the men as she did.*

*Jax had intended it to be a declaration of oneness with her but
as she brought her arm around him and stroked his pelt, Carter's
gaze sharpened. The message could be read two ways, Jax realized,
as he continued his circuit back to his neat pile of clothes. Anahera
turned away again and he shifted back. His gashes burned but he
masked the pain, requested permission to dress and was granted it.*

I Heard the Wolf Call My Name: Excerpt 5

*Tamati emerged from the water, donned his whitiki, and watched
Malo don his. Malo's water-sleeked body gleamed and Tamati's
blood fired again, but then his gaze was drawn to Tihi. 'Not long
now,' he said hoarsely.*

*Malo kissed him tenderly but Tamati returned the kisses hungri-
ly. 'Sometimes I want nothing to change,' he growled, 'and sometimes I can't bear the sameness a moment longer.'*

*'Your beauty won't change,' said Malo, as he stroked Tamati's
cheek. 'Whatever ohaku brings, that will be the same.'*

I Heard the Wolf Call My Name: Excerpt 6

*'I wanted to farewell you properly,' said Tamati, 'and remind you to
be careful. There is no need to delay in the Cloud Crown once you*

discover your skin-spirit, or at Huna, especially given the coming weather.'

Tamati echoed Shenrin's warning but it was sensible advice the Kuwaini probably gave to everyone after the four had died. Anahera felt like flinging back that he should be careful too, but his face was tender. 'I have a gift for you,' he said, and slipped something over her head. It was cool against her skin and she peered down. It was a wolf's head skilfully carved out of pearl shell. 'I don't know your skin-spirit or mine,' said Tamati, 'but the white-wolf is beautiful like you.'

Gift-giving was part of Ikaika courtships not Ahi friendships and she had trouble meeting his eyes. 'I don't know what is to come, Tami. Neither of us do,' she muttered.

'It is a gift, Anahera, nothing more.'

It would be churlish to refuse it and Anahera nodded but she doubted even Tamati believed his own words.

Recognising and accepting humanity's rich complexity aids our inner journey by removing the constraining dividing, divisive and ultimately meaningless segmentation of our outer lives and by doing so, allows us to achieve the wholeness described by Carl Jung.

Put *very* simplistically, Jung suggests the human psyche has two elements: a male element (the animus) and a female element (the anima) and that when peoples' respective cultures gender them according to their sex (teaching males how to present/behave to be *accepted* as men and teaching females how to present/behave to be *accepted* as women) males and females suppress the elements that are *unacceptable* (do not conform to their culture's requirements) into a part of their unconscious Jung calls the *shadow*.

To be *whole*, we must recognise, embrace, and re-integrate the parts of us that reside in the shadow. These spurned elements whether deemed beautiful, ugly or detested, are the riches that form part of all of us. This process (of re-integrating the shadow part of ourselves) is powerfully illustrated in Ursula Le Guin's fantasy narrative *The Wizard of Earth Sea*.

In the story, the young wizard Ged, in an act of immature arrogance, releases a demon into the world, which then relentlessly pursues him. True names are powerful in the story *and* secret (Ged is known by his public name of Sparrowhawk) and after a time, Ged realises that if he can discover the demon's *true* name, he might be able to banish it.

The understanding causes him to turn and pursue *it* and the chase ends in a shallow sea, where Ged calls it by name (Ged) and embraces it. The demon vanishes for, in embracing it (acknowledging and accepting his *own* destructive elements) Ged controls those elements and becomes whole.

This is also Gandalf and the Balrog (in Peter Jackson's film version of *The Lord of the Rings*) where Gandalf the Grey confronts the demon that prevents him from being his fully-realised self (Gandalf the White); and it is all of *us* when we confront, with brutal honesty, the things we are least proud of about our traits, motivations and actions. Doing so is hard but liberating, because knowing ourselves, warts and all, allows us to progress our inner (and outer) journeys in more fruitful and fulfilling ways.

The small settlement of Onslow turns out to be a strange combination of an Outback settlement and a beach resort. We leave the market and museum and turn the corner to see fashionable beachfront apartments and chic restaurants. We have a coffee and wander along the boardwalk to enjoy the sunshine and the deep azure glitter of the sea before we hit the road again.

Our eventual destination is Exmouth, but we won't make it tonight and pull off into a broad rest area, set camp, and are treated to another glorious 360-degree sunset. The night is perfectly still; the vehicles along the nearby highway few and far between; and we enjoy a quiet night before turning in.

Strangers

They arrive after we have
doused the fire and
gone to bed

Our three vans
enjoyed its flames
they make number four

Strangers

The rest area extends more than
a hundred metres
but they park so close
their headlights make our van
as bright as day

We can hear them pee
and they can hear us

French, we think
and in a combi

Perhaps they are nervous
of the empty spaces
perhaps they are used to
France's crowds

They pull away in the early morning
and we breathe again

GODS FEEL

The shorter drives and change from desert to seascapes means the journey takes on more of the atmosphere of a beach-holiday. The intense blues of the sky and sea compete as we head north up the Exmouth Peninsula to the resort town of Exmouth.

We visited Exmouth years ago when it was redder and rougher but there is green lawn now and tourist attractions housed in fashionable confections of concrete and glass.

We stay at a park that accommodates those in search of comfortable cabins; backpackers; and everyone (like us) in between. The park is conveniently near the Visitor Information Centre where we book our glass-bottom boat tour. This is a first for us. Usually we snorkel off the beach or from small cruisers.

Shining Silver

I stare down through the glass-bottomed boat
and wonder if this is how the gods feel

There is another world down there
going about its business

Shadows flash and bubbles rise
to be trapped against the glass

shining silver

like souls that seek
transcendence

Later we wander about Exmouth, as neat and pretty as coastal tourist towns usually are, and I buy a fantasy novel at the local Op Shop (Charity Shop) and drop off books at a book exchange in the main street. Book exchanges are found in roadhouses and caravan park laundries too and act like Australia-wide libraries but without the date-stamp. Take a book; read it; and deposit it at the next stop's book exchange for another traveller to enjoy.

The next day we head out to the Vlamingh Head Lighthouse, which turns out to be an austere grey rather than the more common bright white and red, and then continue to a cemetery of the same dull grey and with the usual black crows replaced by the silver and white of gulls.

Their sombre colours are out of step with the rest of the area; the sky an intense blue and the ocean bluer again and brilliant with white-caps. The Exmouth Peninsula has beaches as perfect in shape as crescent moons and shining with glass-clear waters and we snorkel at the aptly named Turquois Bay.

In Place

The current is strong and I freestyle hard
to stay where I am

There is a giant clam below who has
seen it all before

Its mouth opens and closes as if to
mime messages
commiseration perhaps or laughter more
likely

It knows that I will soon be gone
while it remains firmly
in place

Later at the park, the sky a blush with pink, a musician appears and sets up in an open, grassy area. We troop over carrying our chairs, drinks and nibbles (and money to show our appreciation) and make ourselves comfortable with the rest of the audience.

Player

He plays a guitar complete with amplifier
back-up music and CD's to sell

Dusk settles

We might be gathered around a fire
with flutes and drums
or in a tavern with a bard
and harp

We might be simple folk in a forest
where music is magick
or people who conjure orchestras from
phones

It is all the same

Music needs listeners to make
the melody complete

Want to explore further?
Onslow: https://onslowbeachresort.com.au/around-onslow/
Exmouth: https://www.tripadvisor.com.au/Attractions-g488342-Activities-Exmouth_Western_Australia.html
Useful reading
Karen Simpson Nikakis: *The Use of Narrative in Order to Break the Masculine Domination of the Hero Quest*. Ph.D. thesis, Victoria University of Technology, Melbourne, Australia 1997

LESS BEAUTIFUL

Carnarvon is perched on the edge of the Indian Ocean where the Gascoyne River empties into the sea and we will be camping there alone for a little while. We need to get the 4x4 serviced while our friends peel off north to their camp at Quobba Station.

Many Outback settlements owe their existence to gold but Carnarvon started life as a port where its famous One Mile Jetty was used to export wool, pearl shell, sandalwood, sheep and cattle, and import much needed supplies.

Carnarvon's other claim to fame is a space tracking station that helped the US land its first man on the moon. The tracking station is defunct but volunteers keep it running as a fascinating little museum. The One Mile Jetty has been less fortunate. It was closed due to damage and the hefty repair bill means it is likely stay that way.

It is still a brave sight as it reaches out into the ocean even as the tracking station's radio waves once reached out into space. As we wander the historic buildings near the jetty, it seems to me that Carnarvon is a town of opposites.

Being coastal means being the meeting point between earth and sea and being on a river means fresh water meeting salt. Nothing remarkable about that given every coastal settlement needs fresh water but Carnarvon's fame stems from structures that could not be more different: a timber jetty and a space tracking station.

And then, as I consider them, I realise they might both be aspects of a single thing: our need to reach *out* to connect with the outer world and our need to reach *in* to connect with our inner world.

We drive up the steep sandy road to Quobba Lighthouse which, unlike the Vlamingh Head Lighthouse, *is* bright white and red; the traditional colours that make lighthouses visible from the sea. The lighthouse's stairs and lantern are recycled so opposites meet again here, in the old and the new.

Light also has a strong symbolic relationship with *good* and, as a fantasy writer, I cannot look at a lighthouse without suspecting its *evil* opposite, the darkhouse, lurks beneath.

Western culture divides the world into love-hate; life-death; hot-cold; so why not lighthouse-darkhouse? Lighthouses are designed to keep sailors safe but in 17th and 18th century Britain, light was used to lure ships onto rocks to plunder their cargo and so I light-heartedly conclude (no pun intended) light can be used for evil too. The lethal deeds of smugglers seem far away though on this blue-sky day.

The wind whips off the ocean and crests its waves with white and a couple and their little girl perch on the slope on the leeward side. The father's binoculars are trained on the honeyeaters and silvereyes busy feeding on the banksia; their nectar-laden, orange-gold flowers as bright as fire amid the duller coastal scrub. We watch the birds too as we pause to chat.

Darkhouse

The lighthouse is impressive but the family
do not watch the sea for trouble
but the land behind

Birds break from flowering banksia
double back and break again

The father is happy to chat
about climate change
as if we banter about the merits
of our football teams

Tell me what you think, he invites
with a smile or is it a smirk?

It could be happening or not, he continues
it makes no difference

We look at his child and think of
the lighthouse's warning to ships
and of the wariness of birds

His smile or smirk remains firmly in place
but we are terrified

Our next spot on our touristy tour is to the nearby blowholes but
having visited the blowhole at Loch Ard Gorge on Victoria's south-
west coast, I am not expecting anything special. There is a long wait
at Loch Ard Gorge (named after a shipwreck) before each brief burst
of fume but the blowholes here turn out to be astonishingly different.

The coast consists of a rocky shelf that, when viewed from the land,
appears to be at sea level but is actually a couple of metres higher.
It gives a strange visual effect as waves crash into its underside and
send spectacular bursts of foam high into the air. In the multiple
places where tunnels have eroded in under the stone, spume shoots
10 to 15 metres skywards.

The sight is so wonderful I have to resist the urge to whoop. (I am
not a whooper). The show is so exciting I find it hard to drag myself
away but we eventually clamber back into the 4x4 and head north to
Quobba Station to catch up with our friends. And it turns out there
are more wonders to come.

Whales

At first I think it is a smudge
on the 4x4 window
marked with the death-flights
of countless insects
and then I see a second
far out to sea

a fume

Whales are there and later that night
as we watch the sun slide off
and away across the
endless blue
we see the fumes again
and then the whales
breach

dark silhouettes

We stand transfixed with pleasure
and wonder at their strangeness
dreading those who hunt them
and reminded that

while we enjoy our campfire
and the friendships
of many years
others die in our detention camps
for the sin of being
less beautiful

than whales

Quobba Station extends 80 kms (47 miles) along Western Australia's
red coastline and provides camping sites that overlook the ocean or
ones set back among sandy hummocks. Our friends have claimed the
former and I pick my way down from their vans onto the beach and
stop. I have never seen anything like it. It looks like a vast graveyard
of dinosaur bones. The coarse sand is littered with great chunks of
bleached and battered coral and giant clam shells.

I wander amid the wreckage in an effort to make sense of it. There
is nothing small or delicate; just coral and clams and I wonder why
these things have ended up *here* and then I wonder why *I* have ended
up here, and whether these questions really need answers. Perhaps,

in some odd way, our endless pursuit of *why* robs us of the simple but profound pleasures of *now*. The evening is filled with the thrill of breaching whales as we share a meal and then head back to Carnarvon for the night.

At 2.646 million sq kms (1.021 million sq miles), Western Australia is Australia's biggest state and largely arid unlike Victoria's gentler greenness. Everything seems big: horizons; skies; deserts; mountains; and the endless days of travel it takes to reach anywhere at all.

There is enormous beauty here as well and beauty does more than excite; it refreshes, by reminding us to look away for a time from the things that anger, sadden, frustrate or distress us; to rest our minds and to restore our souls. And beauty, with its restorative power, exists in all sorts of *small* places too that require no long treks into the Outback.

Our suburban unit is one of two built on what was formerly a single house block. We are at the back with a bare two metres between my study window and a high paling fence. I face this fence for most of the day as I sit at my desk to write. It is the usual greyed-wood that dominates the suburbs of Australia's cities and towns and was bare when we shifted in.

It is now covered with star jasmine; pink, white and purple climbing geraniums; honeysuckle; banksia roses; and a passionfruit with dreams of world domination. The flowers come and go and there is always something budding, blooming and browning. I have fixed the leafy face of a Green Man in the understorey and set two bird baths against the fence where blackbirds and pigeons dunk and flap, and where bees drink.

The neighbour's lemon tree towers above the fence top, sending me the sweet scent of lemon blossom, before it sets small green fruit, that I watch swell and yellow. The (badly laid) concrete path between me and the fence is softened by an overflow of ferns and violets and, with each new day, a fresh criss-cross of shining snail trails.

Even without my verdant outlook, there is plenty to heal the heart on my morning walk around an unremarkable suburban block. Despite the older, cream brick veneer houses of the 1970's increasingly giving way to townhouses of hard-edged grey bricks, there are gardens with shrubs and flowers; street trees full of parrots squabbling over eucalypt blossoms and, at this time of year, nature-strips circled with mushrooms and wreathes of other nameless fungal flowers. There is birdsong and the rattle of leaves blown along gutters, and some mornings, the drift of mist or the spritz of rain on my face.

The decluttering I have noted more than once allows us a quieter mind to look, not only at the spectacular things that seize and hold our attention, but at the small, unremarkable things that have the potential to be just as restorative and yet often go unnoticed.

If we must fight peak hour traffic each day to get to work on time, to deal with the growing mound of work on our desks that must be dealt with in accordance with certain timelines and standards, we are unlikely to dwell on the blue-black feathers of the crow that eyes us from a light pole, or consider how it views its surroundings, or the magical way our ancestors viewed *it* or consider that, like us, the crow has a heart that beats; a throat that sings; and eyes that make sense of the world.

There are times when we *must* prioritise one thing over another, for all sorts of reasons including safety, but we must also set aside time to attend to the things that make our lives more richly realised. Bringing back together the things we judge to be important *and* unimportant, is a form of transcendence that, despite the religious connotations of the word, is about creating or *re-creating* wholeness.

We speak of *rising above* certain things (usually conflict situations) and, although the term is used metaphorically, its literal sense implies we need to view things as a whole (like a bird might) rather than being *bogged down* in the more limited, *segmented* vista of the ground.

This is easier said than done in a world where we are male or female; hetero, homo, trans, fluid or some other categorisation; old or young; urban or rural; left or right on the political spectrum; fat or thin; fit or unfit; white-collar or blue-collar; and so on.

The way we are divided and defined, to the detriment of the unifying power of our shared humanity, comes home to me the next day, in the most mundane of places: the caravan park laundry.

Hard to Be a Man

The young male cleaner in the laundry
wears an Akubra hat and thanks me
when I make way for his broom

An older lady teases him
that washing clothes must be new to him
but he tells us, with quiet dignity
he has done his own washing
for eight years

He seems proud not to be *one of them*
a chauvinist, I think, but as a country lad
he does not use the term

His cleaning done, he departs
and the older lady quips
he must be gay

I tell her firmly that he is not
Oh, you can tell, can you? she challenges, still light-hearted
Indeed, I can, I reply

In truth, I am far from infallible
and not given to empty boasts
but the young man carries
enough on his shoulders

and, as I peg up my washing
I consider how hard it is
to be a man

There are no elders to guide them
no initiation rites of transformation
the rapers, beaters, deserters
all well-known
while the other path
the one of decent masculinity
is ill-defined, uncertain
and always filled with
doubt

Our friends come in from Quobba Station and take a day to do as we did: visit the sights; do their washing; and restock their food and then the next day we hitch on the vans and take the short drive south to Hamelin Pool.

Want to explore further?
Carnarvon Space Tracking Station: https://www.abc.net.au/news/2019-07-14/the-vital-role-played-by-carnarvon-in-the-apollo-11-moon-landing/11261800
On Mile Jetty: https://www.abc.net.au/news/2019-01-07/carnarvons-historic-one-mile-jetty-faces-$42-million-repair-bill/10687832
Carnarvon: http://www.aussietowns.com.au/town/carnarvon-wa
Quobba: https://www.australiascoralcoast.com/destination/quobba-and-red-bluff
Loch Ard Gorge blowhole: https://exploregreatoceanroad.com/the-blowhole/#.Xqv0nOgzaUk
Quobba Station: https://www.quobba.com.au/

DRAGONS

Egyptian pyramids? Mayan temples? We tend to think of such things when we consider the most ancient structures on earth and when we think of similarly ancient *creatures* we might think of dinosaurs but Hamelin Pool takes the prize for both or rather its special residents do.

Stromatolites look like small chunky pillars of coral or rock but are, in fact, one of the oldest *living* creatures on earth. Their existence is remarkable but their resemblance to the defunct stumps of an erratically built pier make them *un*remarkable to look at, in contrast to the surrounding area.

The park manager is welcoming, charming and helpful as she guides us into, what is a tight spot, thanks to low roofs and odd angles, and then it is a short stroll through a palely translucent shell quarry to the board walk and viewing platform for the stromatolites.

The quarry consists of metres-deep, hard-packed shells and is step-sided where blocks have been cut for buildings. The surrounding sand is pale too as is the silvery bark of the occasional salt-bleached tree, more wood than leaf that, as the sun westers, spiders the ground with charcoal shadows. I enjoy this walk multiple times during our stay as well as what turns out to be the most vivid sunset of our journey.

One of our friends is a professional photographer and I join him on the viewing platform early, keen like him, to watch the whole show unfold. It begins when the still water near shore pales to a silvered aqua that sharpens the stromatolites' reflections to the clarity of a mirror.

The water reflects the clouds too: soft smudges of white as brilliant as new-fallen snow. And then, as the sun sinks, the clouds turn gold, then tangerine, with stripes of turquoise sky between. There are slabs of mauve too, where cloud is thicker, and crimson where it thins.

The show is brightest over the ocean which becomes a great sweep of molten orange in contrast to the cooler pinks and blues that linger near the shore; a motley patchwork matrixed by the dark thrusts of stromatolites. The orange sky turns crimson, then pink, then purple as the ocean does, until sky and sea are doused in twilight's soft grey.

I am on the viewing platform on another evening, with a less spectacular sunset, when I see a jellyfish in the pools below.

Jellyfish

As the tide ebbs and the sunset fires
the ocean pink and gold
I watch a jellyfish
confined
in a shrinking pool
headbutt the stone

It swims forward
away from the open water
and I watch, powerless to help
knowing that
the only way out
is back

It is another sunny day when we head off in the 4x4's, pass the turn off to the Peron Peninsula and take the next one north, up the Carrarang Peninsula to Steep Point, the most westerly point on the Australian mainland. It will be a different type of driving today with narrow tracks and thick sand.

Paused

We deflate our tyres at the Ranger Station
obedient to the long list of requirements
designed to let us exit
the sand ahead
with a minimum of fuss
(and nuisance to others)

We crest the first giant dune and
as the land disappears
we pause, neither ascending
nor descending

All certainties are stripped away and I think of Tolkien
who wished for the excitement and danger of dragons
(but not in his own backyard)
and I think of his elves, of their long enduring
woven about with poetry and song

dream-like

neither asleep nor fully woken but
forever paused

I am not a fan of *man against nature*-type trips that test how far a
vehicle tilts before it rolls or whether winches really do pull vehicles out of knee-deep sand, and nor am I a fan of damaging fragile
ecosystems by thundering over them in tonnes of machinery, and I
am glad to report we do none of these things.

Lumbering up and down dunes on well-marked tracks turns out
to be a lot of fun and takes us to some truly wondrous places. We
stand with our faces to a stiff breeze where Australia's red rocks jut
farthest west into the Indian Ocean and admire the ocean's clash
with the soaring Zuytdorp Cliffs (named after a Dutch sailing ship
wrecked nearby), before we head off again along more sandy tracks
to a gentler meeting of land and sea.

Every beach is subtly different and this one is strewn with slender
white, five-legged starfish. Some are bigger than my hand, others in
miniature and all as perfect as the silver and gold stars that adorn our
Christmas tree each year.

We drive on, dipping and rolling like a ship through rough seas, over
sandhills clad in the grey-green of salt bush and cushion bush until
we pull up at a collection of blowholes. They resemble volcanic

vents with tunnels that extend 10 to 15 metres beneath the stone and, as the ocean roars in under our feet like an express train, multiple openings shoot fume high into the air.

It is easy to think of dragons as I thrill to the thunderous boom and watch plumes of spray erupt like smoke from a dragon's mighty snout. I have the same sensation in underground railway stations, especially in the London Underground. The train's roar comes first followed by its headlight deep in the tunnel's darkness, then a gust of air as the train thunders out.

I have noted that dragons symbolise transcendence in the same way as angels do and that they also symbolise the constructive/healing energies of the earth (explored in *The Emerald Serpent*). And, as I hear, feel and see the power of stone and water, it is good to be reminded of how small I am and how fleeting my life and, rather than feeling diminished, I feel glad to be part of something older and far greater.

Want to explore further?
Stromatolites: https://www.australiascoralcoast.com/destination/stromatolites-hamelin-pool
Steep Point: https://www.sharkbay.org/place/edel-land-steep-point/places-to-see/

THEFT

We leave Hamelin Pool's ancient stromatolites behind for Denham's more recent sculptural installations. The small coastal town's other attractions include the nearby Monkey Mia, where wild dolphins come ashore to be hand-fed, and the Francois Peron National Park. The national park is our first excursion and provides a new set of sandy tracks to more wild and beautiful places.

Sand

The red sand grows deeper
and as the 4x4 labours
I lean forward
as if to encourage it

We slide sideways to be seized
by more sand
so soft and pretty
and so unforgiving

Our second excursion is to Monkey Mia where we see dolphins slice the aqua shallows but opt for a whale-watching cruise instead. The cruise is enjoyable despite our only sighting being a lone turtle.

Our batteries continue to be troublesome and later that day, as we search our digital records for their purchase date, we discover our credit cards have been scammed. Fellow campers tell us Monkey Mia is a hotspot for scammers due to its high employment of back-packers. I have no idea of the truth of these claims but it reinforces my earlier point about the outsider/stranger being the first to generate suspicion.

Thieves are nothing new; they have been the bane of travellers since travelling began and digital thieves ply their trade from anywhere in the world. I try not to take the thefts personally but, as in the 2016 robbery, I feel under attack by people I have never met, let alone harmed.

Thieves are common characters in fantasy narratives where they are often presented as needing to steal to live (as Viv does in my *Angel Caste* series), or cheeky rascals thumbing their noses at their oppressors. We cancel the cards and later, after a very time-consuming process, have the money refunded but the theft means we must detour to Geraldton to organise new cards. In the meantime, we depend on a second set of cards that we rarely use, but fortunately, happen to have with us.

The park we stay at in Denham is neat with good facilities but it has a little surprise in store for me.

Time

The light goes out as I step from the shower
and plunges me into darkness

I trawl my memory
for the route back to the door
find the switch and
blink in the illumination

I am relieved it is not a power outage
and that, clad in towel and shower-hat
I am alone

The light is on a timer
the cleaning lady confirms the next morning
You get half an hour, she adds

I must have used other peoples' time on previous nights
like those who live on, diapered and dribbling
while the young die
in wars' stinking rubble

or in our
detention centres where *we* decide
they will live out
their time

Want to explore further?

Francois Peron: https://www.australiascoralcoast.com/destination/francois-peron-national-park

Denham: https://www.australiascoralcoast.com/destination/denham

BETWEEN

Our convoy heads off the next morning to enjoy a final coffee over-looking Denham Sound before another easy 373 km (231 mile) drive to the Galena Bridge Rest Area on the Murchison River. Our route takes us inland between the Zuytdorp and Toolonga Nature Reserves where their scatter of gums, paperbarks, mallees and wattles provide an oasis of difference amid the red sands.

The turn off to the rest area consists of rich-red compacted roads and uncertain signage but we eventually reach our destination, set up and head off for a walk through a surprisingly lush landscape. Slender white-barked eucalypts throw shadows over hummocks of verdant moss and the Murchison River's banks are thick with lime-green reeds.

The river's other side has even more impressive facilities than the shiny toilet block and picnic gazebo on our side. There are plenty of vans there and we say hello to their occupants who relax beside the river or stroll like we do with their dogs. We complete our circuit and are close to camp when we come across an abandoned caravan among the trees.

Against Their Will

The van is an empty shell
ribs exposed
roof long gone

It rests in a rocky hollow

wheel-less

like a ship thrown inland
by an angry sea

It is sad and somehow sinister
as if its owners met their end

here

not abandoning ship but wrenched from it
against their will

I find the caravan disturbing despite it being far from the first ruin we
have seen and I wonder if the van troubles me because we tow a van
and the notion that all things end is suddenly a lot less abstract and
a lot more personal. Chant (in *Heart Hunter*) finds the sight of the
Old Stead, the ruins of a once mighty settlement, similarly troubling
because her home of Berian-tur is under threat.

Heart Hunter: Excerpt 8

*The rain drifted away overnight to leave the Old Stead bright with
sunlit pools and the musical drip of foliage. It was beautiful but
Chant couldn't wait to leave. The stones whispered of the Sceadu's
fate if she failed her quest and the understanding made her skin
crawl.*

Chant completes her quest but yearns for things to be as they were
before. It is a very human desire to want to be surrounded by the
reassuringly familiar but there is no going back. Life is about change
even if, in some cases, the change is so slow as to be barely notice-
able. Those Chant loves in Berian-tur have altered in her absence
and, of course, the quest changes Chant irrevocably.

As noted, quests belong to the *Trials of Initiation*, the middle stage
of Campbell's hero quest structure where the heroes' previous state
has been left behind and their new state has yet to be achieved. In
fantasy, it is a space where heroes face new and alien challenges, often completely at odds with their previous experiences and, as I write
this (June 2020), a global virus has tossed much of the world into the
Trials of Initiation too.

Like many national leaders, Australia's Prime Minister speaks of us
*snapping back/returning to business as usual/coming out the other
side,* and while there is much debate about what the world will be

like on *the other side*, one thing is certain; it won't be the world we left behind.

As of now (June 2020), Australia has suffered less than many other countries but even if Australians get their jobs back; their businesses back; their savings and superannuation back; and take their postponed holidays; their outer and inner worlds have been fundamentally and permanently changed.

Gone are the sureties that the career built over many years will keep them secure; the multiple hustles in the gig economy will pay their bills; the things they need will be on the supermarket shelves; the ills they suffer will be cured by vaccines or pills; the life-saving equipment in hospitals will be available to all, regardless of income or age; that they will see their friends when they want to; visit restaurants and local markets on sunny weekends; keep fit in pools and gyms without the fear of being fatally infected or fatally infecting others.

The Australia where, in May 2019, we hitched on the van and went wherever we wanted, is gone, and we do not know when or in what form it is coming back. The parts of the world we had planned to fly to, train-ride through and cruise around in 2020 are gone too in their former state, and we do not know when or in what form they will return either.

Like the hero who *Refuses the Call*, I and millions like me, have been thrown out of our comfortable *known* worlds and are yet to land in new ones. We remain in the liminal, dealing with the *Trials of Initiation*, as best we can.

Waiting is frustrating and doubly so when there is no end date to our confinement but we only have to wait in the *outer* world; our inner worlds are still free to thrive and, as discussed, they thrive more freely when clutter is removed.

With the contraction of the outer world (and all its distractions) the inner world has the space to blossom and to offer compensatory solace. It is not a matter of the inner world *displacing* the outer world but of our mind, in its totality (consciousness and unconsciousness), expanding to keep us whole.

It is no surprise my creative friends are super busy with their writing, quilting, weaving, drawing and painting but we do not have to see ourselves as creatives to be aided by our inner world's creativity in this new, decluttered world. My avowedly *non-creative* husband has been busy sorting hundreds of his photos and watching countless YouTube videos on how to digitally enhance them, and I am urging him on, keen to collaborate on a *visual*-journey project that parallels *this* textual journey.

My husband has also raked out the bread-maker and filled the house with delicious waftings of new-baked bread. Nor is he alone. Flour is scarce on the supermarket shelves as Australian's take to baking, particularly of bread. I find the sudden passion for bread-making interesting. Bread is a form of sustenance with roots deep in human history and I wonder if people have turned to the familiar tradition of bread-making because the outer world is suddenly so unfamiliar and whether the *creative* act of making bread satisfies the inner world too.

But it is still July 2019 when I stand in the mossy undergrowth beside the Murchison River and contemplate the ruined caravan and the virus that is to change the world is yet to be named and its consequences yet to be felt.

Want to explore further?
Galena Bridge Rest Area: http://www.freecampingaustralia.com.au/free-camps/western-australia/galena-bridge-rest-area.html

DISRUPTION

The next day we head to Geraldton to sort out our scammed credit cards and our friends to the resort town of Kalbarri where we will join them later. The highway turns inland through a landscape surprisingly like Victoria's with rolling green hills and scattered gums.

The second surprise is the town of Northampton which turns out to be one of Western Australia's oldest settlements. It certainly looks like it with timber buildings topped by wooden facades and broad bull-nosed verandas that we decide to investigate on our way back.

Geraldton is a neat regional city with plenty to see and do but our priority is to replace our credit cards. Going through the process takes time, despite the bank's helpful staff, and we leave with assurances our new cards will be sent to our home address. I sincerely hope so because we are to fly out of Australia less than a week after our return.

We trek back to our parking spot and pause to admire the Sancta Maria in Ara Coeli church. It has an eye-catching, chunky red brick turret topped by a conical slate roof and is very different to the humbler churches we passed earlier on the journey.

Northampton turns out to be just as interesting up close, especially its cavernous shop of clothing, sewing supplies, and historical sewing-machines. One of our friends is a textile artist and quilter and I mention the shop to her that evening as we share coffee at the camping ground.

No one welcomes theft but had it not been for the credit card scammers, we would not have seen Geraldton's lovely church or discovered Northampton, and our textile artist-quilter friend would have remained ignorant of its sewing shop which she later detoured to visit too.

The incident reminds me that while not every cloud has a silver lining, some black clouds have very bright linings indeed. There was a time when my husband's work stress was so high, he feared he was having a heart attack and detoured to our local medical clinic on the way home.

They thought he was having a heart attack too and he finished his journey in an ambulance. His heart was fine but our caring family doctor ordered some broader tests and the caring specialist was super vigilant and my husband was treated for a condition that, had it not been discovered, would have soon proved fatal.

The next day we go exploring and end up at the Z Bend: a sharp bend in the Murchison River Gorge. We have been spoiled on this trip by enjoying magical places with only the birds for company but the Z Bend is popular.

Bound

We tramp with countless others
along a path
that winds down to
the river

The air is as close-packed as the crowd
and grows hotter as we descend
as if the heat sinks
rather than rises

People jostle and a child wails with the
tearless howling of the
thwarted

The water offers no release
bound tight with selfies
that souvenir
its scent and subtle voice
and carry it away

in backpacks crammed
with chatter

The Z Bend reminds me of other *attractions* I have visited with similarly numbing results. The increased accessibility of world travel means the crowds at some sites resemble those of major sporting events, often with similar behaviour. A few years ago I was caught up in a pushing, shoving scrum in front of the Mona Lisa in the Louvre and later in 2019, when we head off overseas, I encounter similarly crushing masses in the Sistine Chapel in the Vatican and in the tombs at Giza's pyramids.

I have described my dislike of crowds but I pause to consider whether the people around me are pursuing their own soul-journeys too. Their chatter does not suggest it. Noise is a form of clutter that distracts from the nourishment beauty offers *when* time and space are devoted to its contemplation.

Kalbarri marks our groups' last night together and we scout out a restaurant to commemorate the trip but the meal turns out to be memorable for other reasons. One of our friends is vegetarian and to keep it simple, usually orders salad or vegetable dishes without the meat. This variation seems too much for the restaurant staff who have trouble communicating with each other, the chef, and with us.

The evening turns into a comedy of errors, with all of us growing increasingly annoyed, except for the vegetarian, who dissolves into infectious laughter that leaves us all struggling to keep straight-faced.

Want to explore further?
Northampton: https://www.australiascoralcoast.com/destination/northampton
Geraldton: https://www.australiascoralcoast.com/region/geraldton
Kalbarri: https://www.google.com/maps/place/Kalbarri+WA

WAYS

The route we chose for our outer *westward* journey deep into
Australia's red wilderness was not the only one available. We might
have gone straight north through New South Wales to Queensland,
west through Mt Isa, north again at the Three Ways Roadhouse near
Tennant Creek to Katherine and west again through Kununurra and
Fitzroy Crossing to arrive at Broome, far north on Western Australia's coastline.

And now that we head east, we can drive south to Perth, south-west
to Esperance and north to Norseman to pick up the Eyre Highway
for the long trek east across the Nullarbor Plain to Port Augusta. Or
we can, as we do this time, pick up the Eyre Highway at Norseman
via Mount Magnet, Leinster, Leonora and Kalgoorlie.

Once in Port Augusta we can choose to head south-east to Peterborough and Ucolta to join the Barrier Highway and follow it north-east
to Broken Hill, Wilcannia and Cobar, south-east through Bathurst to
Sydney and then south for 878 kms (545 miles) to Melbourne. We
can also choose to repeat out outward journey although, as I have
noted, the view is different going in the opposite direction and we are
not the same person who set out in our outer *or* inner journeys.

A cursory glance at a map of Australia shows that the red lines of
highways hug the coast, with only the single red line of the Stuart
Highway dissecting the continent north-south. There is no red line
that dissects the continent east-west. What *does* exist is the Great
Central Road that runs from the west to terminate in the centre of
Australia at Yulara (the site of Uluru and Kata Tjuta).

Known euphemistically as *Australia's longest short cut*, the Great
Central Road is 1147 kms (712 miles) of unsealed road with a reputation for roughness. Only one of our travelling companions was
keen to use it when we planned the trip and, given the risk of major
damage leaving us marooned in the middle of nowhere, we all end
up taking the Eyre Highway back across the Nullarbor.

We wish our companions safe travels and set off to our first stop of Mount Magnet. We fuel up and pause to chat to a couple in charge of a pigeon-racing truck. The truck's tray is piled high with empty cages which tells us the pigeons have already been released to race each other home.

We discover the couple *have* travelled the Great Central Road and, wondering if we have missed an opportunity to experience even more wonderful Outback sights, I ask about the road's condition. It is the woman who answers: *The first 900 kilometres are hell,* she says, *and then it gets worse.*

We drive on, glad of our choice of route and as we near Sandstone, discover that rains have filled the dips to either side of the road. The water creates small green lakes and wakes early wildflowers so that drifts of colour add to the water's shine. Western Australia has over 12,000 varieties of wildflowers (one of the largest collections in the world) and on an earlier trip we seemed to spend more time admiring and photographing them than driving. We are too early for the main show but the flowers are still a delight.

Blur

The road is
rimmed with water-sheets
that invite wildflowers

Some accept and wend their way
up through sand and stone
to bloom in
drifts of white and blue
that blur as
we pass

We leave Sandstone behind and, as the sun sinks, search for the Peter Denny Lookout free camp. We have enjoyed some great free camps but they are not always easy to find.

They might be nothing more than tarmacked sidings with a rubbish bin and designated for road train use only; or be listed as suitable for *small* rigs and have no facilities; or have everything: water, toilets, dump points, rubbish skips, phone coverage, picnic tables, fire pits and big rig spaces.

Some have no signage at all and are only spied as we whizz past while others do not seem to exist, despite being listed on wiki's and in our free camp book; hence the keenness of our hunt. Long hours of driving make it sensible to be off the road before dark, as do the risks of hitting kangaroos or emus (or wombats and koalas in some regions).

The Peter Denny Lookout turns out to be well-signed and we pull in. There are half a dozen vans spaced out amongst the eucalypts and we select a spot a polite distance from our neighbours. The general rule of free camping is to do it in company and as we now travel solo, that means the company of strangers.

It is common for lone campers to pull into a free camp and wait, and if no one joins them, to move on. Australia is a reasonably safe country but even so, we have had some truly awful crimes committed by rapist-murderers who stalked their victims along deserted Outback roads.

Camping with others provides a sense of camaraderie too and a chance to exchange information useful to the journey ahead: the good fuel and food stops; the good camping sites; the towns that welcome travellers with thoughtful facilities and signage and the towns that do not. People share more personal tales too and as I navigate my own soul-journey, I am keen to hear theirs.

The Peter Denny Lookout is named after a former local councillor but the *lookout* part remains a mystery until I wander over to the edge of the trees and discover the land falls away in a dramatic and totally unexpected way.

It is another one of those beautiful surprises that reward us when we step away from the familiar and open ourselves to what the *unfamiliar* might hold.

Want to explore further?
Great Central Road: https://www.chartandmapshop.com.au/blog/the-great-central-road-drive-from-laverton-to-uluru-with-a-caravan/
WA Wildflowers: https://www.westernaustralia.com/au/things_to_do/forest_and_flowers
Peter Denny Lookout Free Camp: https://planner.hemax.com/Place/Details?id=430dbd29-5569-433a-9c13-d50f8f7b50b1

IMMORTALITY

I stare in mystification at the objects that litter the verges. Too perfect for stones so emu eggs perhaps? But too many and emu eggs are teal green not pale yellow and then, as I dredge my memory, I recall having seen these odd things before on another trip: *paddy melons*.

At the time I thought a road train had spilled its load of fruit for they were scattered along the road side as they are now: creamy yellow with smudged green stripes and the size of rockmelons.

They seemed completely out of place, as indeed, they are. Paddy melons are native to Sub-Saharan Africa, not Australia, and were introduced by Afghan traders in the mid 1800's, either for camel fodder or accidentally, along with the (now feral) camels that roam the Outback.

They conjure visions of juicy watermelons, a distant relative, but in addition to being a pest plant, paddy melons are considered inedible, although I have seen them used in light-hearted bowling competitions in Outback parks.

Paddy Melons

They strew the highway edges like clutches of
carelessly laid dragon eggs
but there are no dragons
here

Perhaps the spawn of road trains then
that roar like dragons but fail to fly

earth-bound metal worms
unbreathing but
unstoppable

We continue east to the Goldfields Highway at Leinster, and then south through Leonora to Menzies and I realise that, despite having stared out the 4x4's window for nearly two months, I am still astonished by what the Outback reveals. Menzies owes its existence to a goldrush in the late 1800's but its other claim to fame relates to Lake Ballard, 51 kms to the north-west. Like Kati Thanda – Lake Eyre, Lake Ballard is a saltpan although far smaller and lesser known, at least for its grandeur and glitter. What it *is* known for are the 51 metal figures spread over its 10 square kilometre, usually dry, lake bed.

The *Inside Australia* installation was created by the English sculptor Sir Antony Gormley who took three dimensional body scans of 51 volunteers from Menzies (men, women and children) and, using local materials to create an alloy, transformed the 51 body scans into the sculptural figures he set in the salty lake bed.

We take the smooth dirt road to the free camping area and although the prime positions on the lake's perimeter are occupied, the whole area is so picturesque there are no bad places to set up. We back into a hollow between two deep red dunes and head off to explore.

I had expected the saltpan to be the same silver-bright as Kati Thanda – Lake Eyre but it is covered in a thin layer of reddish silt deposited during the last (rare) inundation. The 51 figures are more of a *rust*-red in colour, gaunt and skeletal, and with barely articulated faces. The women have breasts like garden trowels, the men similarly stylised penises, and only height separates adults from children.

Because the figures are scattered over 10 square kilometres, few are visible from any given point and it is only as we reach each distant figure that we can decide the next one to visit. The lake bed is wetter in some places which makes some routes slippery and boggy, and the mud and risk of falling increasingly determines our direction.

The strange solitary figures create an otherworldly sense but my attention is increasingly drawn to a small conical island that rises steeply from the lake bed.

It resonates in the same way as other sacred places do and, as I stare from the island to the figures, my fantasy-writer's brain wonders whether it is the island that is really important here and whether the figures are simply diversions to keep the island safe.

Immortality

He promised us immortality and I suppose
he delivered, after a fashion

There are 51 of us, the entire clan he claimed
our flesh reduced to hardy metal as red
as the shifting sands

We are too scattered to embrace, too far flung to share
song or story, but still we guard by drawing
the gaze of others away from him

He crouches in mountain form and gathers us around his knees
like children neither living nor truly dead
but simply enduring

The First Nation name for Lake Ballard is lost but it is a special place, whatever its naming and shares the same stillness as Uluru's quieter corners and Kata Tjuta's sweeping shadows in its wondrous Valley of the Winds. The sculptor Gormley chose this site for his own reasons but I suspect he felt the sacred here too and used the sculptures to express his understanding of it, even as I use prose and poetry.

Thousands of years before, the First Nation Wongi/Wangkatha people knew this place was special and told of it in their Dreaming stories. There are six other islands, apart from the one I notice near the camping area, and the Wongi/Wangkatha people's Dreaming links them to the Seven Sisters of the Pleiades constellation. In the Wongi/Wangkatha Dreaming story, the seven sisters were tempted down from the sky by the lake bed's glittering surface then forced to transform into islands to escape attack.

Sculpture, poetry and the divine descending to assume earthly shapes are all ways we might attempt to express the sacred. There are other expressions of the sacred too, that lack any artifice, and that we enjoy as we perch outside the van to watch the sun set. Shadows stretch across the saltpan and, as the sky becomes a vast star-stencilled dome and bathes us in its silvery light, the sacred seems as tangible as the silken sand beneath my feet.

Want to explore further?
Paddy melons: https://www.bushheritage.org.au/blog/learning-more-about-camel-melons
Lake Ballard: https://traveloutbackaustralia.com/lake-ballard-gold-fields-western-australia.html/
Lake Ballard: http://www.youtube.com/watch?v=VeIDvX23HYs

RICHES

We linger to enjoy the lake bed bathed in the sunrise's gentler gold
before we head south to Kalgoorlie, a town of around 30,000 that,
likes Menzies, was founded on the prosperity of gold. It is less than
a two hour drive which gives us plenty of time to book into a park,
unhitch, and head into town.

The local market is in full swing and we wander between the stalls of
cheap clothes, cheap sunglasses, and fast food vans, then search out
a pub (public house/bar/hotel) on the main street for a counter lunch.

Country hotels are similar all over Australia: dim, smelling of beer,
and furnished with polished-wood bars, Laminex tables, and floral
carpets. The regular drinkers perch on stools at the bar and families
claim the tables to drink and eat. Pokies (gambling machines) ping in
the background and a pool table in a far flung corner will have been
commandeered by younger men.

Counter meals commonly include beer-battered fish and chips; steak
with mushroom or pepper sauce; beef or chicken pot pie; roast of the
day; bangers (sausages) and mash; parmigiana; and soup of the day.
Meals are enormous and everything comes with chips. On the faint
chance patrons have room for dessert, the usual offerings are chocolate, strawberry or vanilla icecream, sometimes with banana and nuts
to make a banana split, or sticky-date pudding.

We enjoy the meal and, rather over-fed, roll on down the street,
admiring the grand buildings characteristic of gold rush towns. Kalgoorlie is the twin town of Boulder, and Boulder the less affluent of
the two. At the time of the gold rush, Kalgoorlie housed more of the
mine owners and merchants, and Boulder more of the miners and,
while the class divisions have largely gone, the historical difference
in wealth is clear in the architecture.

Kalgoorlie's gracious buildings and Boulder's more utilitarian
ones remind me that cultures define *and* mark wealth in different
ways and that, even in materialistic Western cultures, wealth can be

defined by family love and support; friendship; believing oneself in God's/the gods' care and, in each instance, be marked by commitment; loyalty; and living a life in keeping with God's/the gods' teachings.

In *The Kira Chronicles*, Kira's home of Allogrenia distributes its wealth (food, clothing and shelter) equitably and healing, which is central, is *always* given, selflessly and without expectation of reward. But when Kira leaves Allogrenia, she is shocked to discover that food, clothing, shelter and healing are traded and that those with nothing to trade, go without.

The Kira Chronicles: Excerpt 11

Three days after Caledon had gone, Jesa was shifted to the Small Room, and a few days later, Aranz came to Kira's alcove with a beautifully carved wooden box. 'The Spursman child has been collected by her uncle. This is for you,' he said, and handed Kira the box.

Kira grimaced. 'Healing is given. Besides, her brother died.'

'I've explained to you why the trade is necessary,' said Aranz curtly.

'Then give it to Dumer. I eat the Sanctum's food and sleep on the Sanctum's pallet.'

'The Sanctum's needs are gifted by King's Hall, for Tain Kings have always loved and cared for their people. I suggest you trade it for clothing or a comb. Speri will be back on the morrow and I'll ask Physick General Dumer to release her to help you.'

He gave a brief nod and stalked off but Kira's face burned at his thinly veiled insult.

These forms of wealth reside in the outer world which raises the question as to how wealth is defined and marked in the *inner* world or whether indeed, *outer* world notions of wealth are relevant. I have described the necessity of decluttering, both in the outer and inner worlds, and that the process reveals what is *truly* important and in doing so, carves out the space and stillness to recognise and appreciate it.

And oddly, as I struggle to define what constitutes wealth in the inner, *soul*-journey, I wonder if wealth is actually defined by *absence*. This is not the type of absence that casts us adrift, like a ship with a broken anchor, but the absence of things that distract, exhaust and distress us, to leave us to rest in a place of sacred peace.

Want to explore further?
Kalgoorlie: https://www.abc.net.au/local/photos/2013/04/18/3740254.htm

VENOM

Jimberlana, as it is in the local First Nation tongue, is our first fuel stop as we head south. Towns can be named after geographical features (Mt Isa, William Creek); man-made structures (Wisemans Ferry; Murray Bridge); or retain their First Nation names (Canberra; Ballarat). They can even be named after a horse. The town of Norseman might owe its existence to another of Australia's gold rushes but it owes its name to a prospector's horse that, according to the tale, pawed the ground to reveal gold.

Norseman promotes itself as the gateway to the *Nullarbor* Plain (Latin for *no trees*) but as we turn east onto the Eyre Highway we pass through the largest semi-arid woodland in the world. The open forest is a beautiful sweep of glossy-trunked, spindly-branched trees with leaves a shine in the sunlight and, given its status, I am mystified the woodland is not better known.

Our second refuel is at the Balladonia Roadhouse and we pull off shortly afterwards for a quick lunch before we push on. There are several free camps along the Nullarbor but we aim to reach the Baxter Rest Area, 490 kms (304 miles) from our start at Kalgoorlie. The rest area has the attraction of mobile (cell) phone coverage which means we can catch up with our former camping companions, make park bookings, and touch base with friends and family.

The Eyre Highway between Balladonia and Caiguna claims to be the longest section of straight road in Australia and at 146 kms (91 miles), one of the longest *straight* stretches in the world. Baxter Rest Area is only 66 kms shy of Caiguna and, guessing we are in for a long and uneventful drive, we do something unusual for this trip, and turn on the radio. The reception is good and an interesting interview is in progress.

The Man on the Radio #1

The man on the radio is talking about taking
psychedelic drugs to reset the mind

My interest wakens

For depression perhaps, I do not know;
I missed the first part

He tells of inhaling toad venom
squeezed from its glands and dried
to brown sugar

The inhalation (as it turns out)
is catastrophic

His ego is annihilated and he loses all connection
suffers dissolution and then thankfully is
tethered to the *real* again

whatever *real* is

What we call *mind-altering substances* have a long history in human
societies, sometimes legally, sometimes illegally, and sometimes
moving between the two states. The poet Samuel Taylor Coleridge
famously wrote his poem Kubla Khan in 1797 under the influence of
opium and the visionary work of shamans is often aided by *mind-altering* substances.

Such substances are also used in modern Western medicine to treat
various psychiatric illnesses. I had ample opportunity to sample
(illegal) mind-altering substances in my teens and early twenties but
declined. Even then I had a barely articulated belief that if I were
going to make stupid mistakes in my life, it was *me* who was going
to make them, not some drug or addiction sitting like a monkey on
my shoulder.

I feel even more strongly about it today, many years later, and am also wary of *legal* substances that have similar effects. In the outer world, we must obey the law; fulfil the requirements of our employment; meet the obligations of family, friends and society; but our inner worlds are ours alone; precious; vital to our well-being; and not to be risked.

We reach the Baxter Rest Area as dusk purples the land. The rest area is well sign-posted and well laid out, with a tarmacked strip nearest the highway for road trains and sites spread among the trees for bigger rigs like ours. There are half a dozen caravans and RV's already set up but there is plenty of space and we make our calls to our friends and catch up on what is happening in the world.

The rest area is close to the highway but quiet, apart from the usual squabble of cockatoos, corellas and crows. After a long drive, we make an early night of it and drift to sleep watching the Outback's stars a fire through the hatch above the bed.

Want to explore further?
Balladonia: https://www.aussietowns.com.au/town/balladonia-wa
Norseman: https://www.touristradio.com.au/norseman/

FELLOW TRAVELLERS

It is fortunate we make an early start the next morning because our destination turns out to be more than 600 kms (372 miles) away. We pass through Caiguna and stop at Cocklebiddy for fuel. The last time we visited there were roadworks and the road plumed in red dust. We towed a modified plumber's trailer with a metal hutch on the back that, when we pulled up for fuel, we discovered had sprung open. Camp chairs and lamps were gone, never to be seen again.

The road is sealed this time and we suffer no mishaps. The name *Cocklebiddy* has a quaint, English-village feel about it, but nobody seems to know its origins. It might be a corruption of the First Nation name for the area, but that too is unknown.

An amusing sign at the front of the roadhouse tells us that Cocklebiddy's population is eight people and over a million kangaroos, but its humour belies the fact that Cocklebiddy's harsh landscape and isolation make it a difficult place to live. We go on to another similarly isolated roadhouse.

Better Days

The motel next door is boarded up
with rough-edged roofing metal
and the roadhouse has seen
better days

We fuel up and I go in to pay

She is a migrant
with a face drained of joy
and I wonder when she last smiled
or even laughed
and sense her misery has nothing to do
with me

A child cries in a back room
and a toddler rushes out
to clutch her legs

She makes coffee for the sudden influx
of travellers and speaks to the toddler
in her own tongue but does not
look down

She is in a place less forgiving than
others she might have chosen
or more likely
had chosen *for* her

Good money
if you can last ten years but as I watch her face
I wonder if the cost will be
too much

Our surroundings start to resemble their name of *nullarbor* as we
move steadily eastwards. The pinkish-yellow soil is strewn with
stones and covered in clumps of bluebush, saltbush, spinifex and the
occasional spindly mulga, and crows crowd the verges, busy with the
usual carnage delivered by passing vehicles. Hawks and the bigger
wedge-tailed eagles ride the thermals but my attention stays on the
crows.

Shining

The horizon peels back
like a carton of long-life milk
and crows breakfast
on roadkill

A murder of crows becomes
a feast of crows
dressed for dining
their feathers black and shining
in the early morning light

The last time we drove across the Nullarbor we headed west. It was
our first big foray and we drove from Melbourne (Victoria) to Perth
(Western Australia) exploring places like Wave Rock and New Norcia (Australia's only monastic town) along the way.

Once in Perth, we made a sudden decision to put the vehicle and
camping trailer on the Indian Pacific train for the return journey. At
4,352 kms (2,704 miles) from Perth to Sydney (New South Wales),
the Indian Pacific is one of the longest train journeys in the world
and my husband was keen to experience it. The train by-passes Melbourne so we disembarked at Adelaide and drove the final 726 kms
(451 miles).

Taking the train turned out to be a fortunate decision. We had some
over-heating issues with our 4x4 on the journey over the Nullarbor
and, while the train was airconditioned, it was more than 40C (104
F) outside, something we discovered when we briefly disembarked at
the aptly named settlement of Cook.

A mechanic later told us the vehicle would not have brought us home
and being stranded in those sorts of temperatures can prove fatal.

And, as white crosses appear along the roadside, I am reminded that
the Outback holds other dangers too.

Endless

White crosses mark
the spot where
life ended

So many crosses on
one of the straightest stretches
of highway in the world

There are no trees or murderous rocks
so maybe weariness claimed these victims
or the wish to cut their time in this world
short

unlike those they left behind
whose grief is
endless

Falling asleep at the wheel is a major cause of fatalities in Australia,
where driving long distances is common once urban areas are left
behind. There are numerous signs along Australian highways warning that *Drowsy Drivers Die* and to *Stop Revive Survive* and we pass
many rest stops designed to keep drivers safe. We pull into them to
stretch our legs and top up with coffee.

The Nullarbor's openness makes for stunning driving and stony
tracks lead off to the very edge of the Great Australian Bight where
travellers can gaze out over the plunging cliffs to where (they imagine) Antarctica's pristine wilderness gleams. We did so many times
on our first crossing and I remember the shock of seeing the familiar
red desert terminate in knife-cut-sharp cliffs.

The abrupt ending of the familiar is something that Kira (*The Kira
Chronicles*) and Warrain (*The Third Moon*) also grapple with. In
Kira's case, it is most jarring when she first sees the lands beyond
her forest home.

The Kira Chronicles: Excerpt 12

*The alwaysgreen's scent reminded her of everything she was about to
lose, and she had to force her feet away from its Shelter to the very
last of the fallowoods and when she reached it, she had to grip its
trunk to stay upright. The world had been devoured by an immense*

sweep of sky. It curved up to unimaginable heights and down again to the skin of the earth itself.

Warrain too struggles with a shocking change to his known world.

The Third Moon: Excerpt 3

I crawled laboriously to the top of the ridge and peered over, and what I saw remains branded in my brain to this day. A great surge of ocean rolled up the valleys, turning spurs into promontories and drowning all else. Even the mighty spurs that divided Sapphire, Turquoise, and Amethyst Bays had been reduced to the splayed fingers of a giant hand, grey against the ocean's blue. Station One was gone and I was terrified Haven would follow...

The jolts Kira and Warrain experience in the outer world, as the familiar is stripped away, allows the changes necessary to their inner worlds. Kira learns her despised warrior kin are not the antithesis of healing after all and that, among the people who murdered her family, there are those who suffer as she does. And in coming to understand how his new planet functions, Warrain comes to understand himself.

The Eyre Highway draws closer to the coast as we near the Western Australia – South Australia border and we stop at Eucla for fuel. Eucla is known for its abandoned Telegraph Station that, depending on the wind, appears and disappears from under shifting sands. Parts of it were visible on an earlier trip but we are more intent on covering the kilometres than searching for it now.

I peruse our camp book and wiki for somewhere to spend the night as we cross into South Australia. Our road atlas shows rest areas but many are lay-bys where overnight stays are prohibited.

We have the usual problem of missing the badly signed or unsigned *legal* stops and driving a big 4x4, towing a big van, means we cannot slam on the brakes or whip into a U-turn. It is the first time we have trouble finding *any* free camp and, as dusk thickens and we grow wearier, we decide that if we miss the last on our list, we will spend the night beside the road.

We count down the kilometres and the turning looms out of the gloom on our right. It appears to be some sort of whale watching company, which does not sound promising, but we head down the road towards the ocean and just before the gate for paid entry, see a fenced, tarmacked area signed as a Free Camp.

It is popular, with vans nose to tail around the perimeter fence and lined up side by side in the middle. The only option is to join those in the middle, close enough to the neighbouring van to allow room for later arrivals, and hopefully not so close as to invade the incumbents' privacy.

I need not have worried. They greet us cheerily and invite us to join them. I cook up a quick meal and, armed with our chairs and a bottle of wine, we settle in their circle. As my eyes adjust to the dark, I see the circle includes dog beds, with various dogs in residence. As a *dog-person* (cats are fine too!) the doggy campers are a welcome sight.

The dogs approach with hopeful eyes on our food but only get a pat. We share wine and later chocolate with their owners who we would not have met had we found the earlier camps or indeed, had we not set out on a journey in the first place.

The circle breaks for the night but as I cart my chair back to the van, my husband gets into conversation with one of the women; a conversation he later relates to me. I had assumed the group were all couples, and they are, except the woman is driving her own rig (with her dog), and her partner is driving his rig (with his dog).

The woman tells my husband she was widowed and, grief-stricken and lonely, consults a clairvoyant, who tells her something along the lines of *love is closer than you think*. She continues to travel with the friendship group but, one day, trips coming out of her van and the man catches her. And as his arms come around her, she finally understands the clairvoyant's message.

It could be argued if members of a friendship group end up single, they are likely to re-partner within the group (given the existing friendships) but it could also be argued that, in her grief, the woman could have chosen to withdraw from the world and, in *choosing* to continue her journey, remained open to the possibility of future happiness.

Many of those at the free camp are waiting for the whale watching facility's gates to open the next morning, but we are on a tight schedule and push on, something I later regret. Some of our camping companion friends *do* visit a few days later and report the whale watching was wonderful. As someone who rarely sees whales (the ocean is thick with them the day *before* I visit a viewing site and the day *after*), I am sorry to miss them yet again.

Want to explore further?
Cocklebiddy: https://www.aussietowns.com.au/town/cocklebiddy-wa
New Norcia: https://www.newnorcia.wa.edu.au/
Great Australian Bight: https://parksaustralia.gov.au/marine/parks/south-west/great-australian-bight/
Eucla: https://www.aussietowns.com.au/town/eucla-wa

ECHOES

Our journey continues in a series of large hops across the continent; out next destination being The Gums Rest Area in Kimba, 596 kms (370 miles) away. We are always less keen to explore once we turn for home but that is not the main reason we cover big distances. I am keen to revisit Uluru and Kata Tjuta (known for a time by their European names of Ayres Rock and The Olgas) and have persuaded my husband to detour north again despite it pushing our return date to just six days before we fly out.

We passed the turn-off to Uluru and Kata Tjuta earlier on the trip and it would have made sense to detour then, rather than backtrack now, but certain events made it impossible. The Uluru-Kata Tjuta National Park was returned to the Anangu, its First Nation owners, in 1985. For many years they had been disturbed and distressed by visitors climbing Uluru and had requested that, out of respect, visitors *not* climb it.

Uluru is sacred and climbing it has been compared to clambering about on the tops of cathedrals. Some climbers graffiti it and, in need of a restroom, urinate and defecate on the top. A number of climbers have also died from the heat and exertions of the climb.

The climbing of Uluru continued unabated and so, in November 2017, the Anangu announced the climb would be closed as of October 26, 2019. It was a long period of warning but the reality of the closure only really attracted media coverage in the months prior and then, colloquially speaking, all hell broke loose.

Apart from the uproar from non-First Nation people who insisted they owned *the Rock* (as it is called), there was a rush to climb it before the climb closed. Visitors to the Uluru-Kata Tjuta National Park must stay at the Ayres Rock Resort at Yulara which provides back-packer facilities through to luxury accommodation and the resort was quickly booked out.

It meant campers took over nearby free camps, road sides and private property, often with no regard to the proper disposal of rubbish or human waste. Chaos ensued and Rangers and the police moved in. It also meant we had to wait to several weeks to get a booking at the resort.

Apart from wanting to enjoy the magic of Uluru and Kata Tjuta again, we want to see Bruce Munro's *Field of Light* installation at Uluru's base. Other friends have planned to visit it too and we manage to overlap our bookings to enjoy it together.

We refuel at Ceduna and pull into the next rest stop afterwards for lunch. It is well past midday but only hunger prevents me suggesting we drive on. Most rest stops are pleasant, even those that are simply tarmacked lay-bys next to highways, but this one is different.

It has a bleak hostility that comes from somewhere other than the broken glass, graffitied rubbish bins and shelter's artwork of a hand that looks to belong to a drowning man. I do not believe natural landscapes (or human-made ones) are inherently evil, although we might perceive places of execution or torture as such by association.

But I am not the first person to wonder whether the more violent of human emotions such as hatred, anger, pain and fear leave a residue behind. I wonder too whether the visual forms of this residue might be ghosts, wraiths and apparitions; their aural forms voices, rattling chains or marching feet; and their tactile forms sudden drops in temperature or the sense of being touched.

Hampton Court in the UK is well known for the sound of screams, supposed to be of Henry VIII's fifth wife, Catherine Howard, as she fled in terror to beg the king for her life and a few years ago, closer to home, a friend related a strange incident her husband experienced at Port Arthur in Tasmania.

Port Arthur was a penal colony in the 1800's, with all the cruelty associated with that era, and its historic ruins are now a tourist attraction. Her husband was standing next to a wall when he heard male voices speaking behind him in an older English dialect. Imagining some sort of re-enactment was going on and expecting to see actors in period costume, he took several paces to where he had a clear view of the wall's other side. There was no one there.

Taken aback, he mentioned it to a nearby guard who confirmed other visitors had reported the same thing. (Port Arthur's historical reputation for violence was later overlaid with another atrocity when, in 1996, a lone gunman shot 35 people to death and wounded a further 23.)

My friend's husband is firmly rational but could provide no rational explanation for what he experienced. Nor can I explain the rest area's bleak oppressiveness. Rational explanations are part of the outer world and perhaps my feelings stem from the inner world. All I know is I am happy to leave.

Hard Men

There are unmarked places and others
too barren to stop at

battered, graffitied
the haunt of boozers
and addicts

of hard men who travel alone
and of boys who would
be men

who claim fame with a spray can
and the tenuous mateship
of others like themselves
or who pretend to be

places where beer makes bonds
that sobriety breaks

We mainly travel in silence but today we turn on the radio for the
second time on this trip and what I hear seems curiously relevant to
the inner journey I explore.

The Man on the Radio #2

I listen to the man on the radio:
Julian McMahon
a storyteller by any measure
despite his title of lawyer

He defends those on
death row:
Van Tuong Nguyen
Andrew Chan
Myuran Sukumaran

and watches them go from
small-time crims
to mature young men

in prison

making a life for themselves
making a *better* life
for others

then hanged or shot
a waste on every level
but worth the fight
the storyteller says

to lessen the number who face
the hangman's noose
or firing squad
to appease everyone and everything
except what is right

The storyteller/lawyer journeys with these young men and their families, sometimes for years and almost to the gallows, so his outer journey is traumatic, but he hints at his inner journey, and how it nourishes him, and when he speaks of the broader aspect of his fight, to lessen the number of young men who suffer the same fate, his voice lightens.

We are about 70 kms (43 miles) from The Gums Free Camp in Kimba, when a dash light flicks on. This is never good news. The manual tells me something about water ratios in fuel and gives me strict instructions to cease driving and immediately seek advice from a qualified Toyota technician.

Qualified Toyota technicians are not readily available on Outback roads (!) and we ring through to Roadside Assist at Port Augusta (158 kms/98 miles from Kimba) and are told they will send a serviceman to The Gums. We drive on, my eyes glued to the light; my ears straining for a choke or rattle that heralds the 4x4's demise, but we arrive at The Gums without incident.

It is a great little free camp in the middle of Kimba, with toilets and water, and a grocery store on the corner, that opens like a TARDIS to reveal goodies I have not seen in weeks: crusty bread, fresh fruit and vegetables, and custardy things.

The young serviceman turns up right on time and cheerfully confirms there is nothing wrong. He shows us how to reset the warning light which we do a number of times for the remainder of the trip. (We discover on our return home that the fuel filter is full of dirt, probably from dirty fuel, but at the time are simply relieved it is *apparently* easily fixed).

Apart from the generosity of its lovely free camp, Kimba is home to the Big Galah. I have described the popularity of *big things* in Australia and our (small) children enjoyed seeing the Big Galah on our last visit, as did we, but for different reasons.

It is hard to capture the essence of any animal in sculpture and we found the chunky, beady-eyed and sturdily anchored galah hilarious. I find more charm in it this time because I see it matches the galah's reputation for cheekiness (*galah* is Australian slang for a harmless idiot). This is just human fancy for, as I have noted, animals have their own *true* natures.

Tourist signage tells us Kimba is exactly halfway across Australia; a claim I find puzzling until I realise it refers to the midpoint between Perth and Sydney. A host of places could lay claim to the honour depending on their latitude and yet I cannot blame Kimba. Many a small town can add to its economy by giving tourists a reason to pause, buy fuel, a coffee and a souvenir, and Kimba has already gifted us a terrific rest stop and goody-laden grocery store.

Want to explore further?
Uluru and Kata Tjuta: https://parksaustralia.gov.au/uluru/discover/history/
Port Arthur: https://portarthur.org.au/
Big Galah: https://www.inspirock.com/australia/kimba/the-big-galah-a6267979003

ENDINGS

We are not long on the road before a mist closes in or, more accurately, we enter a mist. The trees become wraith-like and those nearest the road gleam and drip with moisture.

Mist

I have seen no mist for months
just red dryness
and it does strange things
to my mind

as if time folds back
upon itself
and I am home again where mist
is no stranger

The mist clears but the feeling
of displacement remains
and I wonder where
I really am

Perhaps we are not
as anchored in time and place
as we believe

but flashes of sunlight
caught between tree shadows
fleeting, ephemeral
and unconfined

The mist reminds me of the liminal once more: the space the hero passes through between leaving their old life (Campbell's *Separation or Departure*) and entering their new life (Campbell's *Return*). Mist seems appropriate for this stage (where the hero is tested and changed in readiness to assume a new identity) because mist lacks the opacity of cloud and the clarity of air and so exists as a state in between.

The Marshlands (in *Heart Hunter*), where the saturated earth is neither liquid nor solid, serve the same purpose. It is here that Tel first acknowledges Chant's beauty and where she pledges not to abandon him. Likewise, it is in the snowstorm in *Messenger*, where the air is neither purely gaseous nor solid but a slurry composed of both, where Jeph commits to Severine not for her father's sake, but for her own.

The liminal as a place of transformation is far more explicit in *I Heard the Wolf Call My Name* where the heroes' initiation rites take place in the Cloud Crown, a ring of cloud that divides the unfamiliar peak of a soaring mountain from the familiar lands below. The liminal heralds changes, big and small, and I think of the former as I watch the ghostly landscape.

Extinction

The sky is a soft grey
like the time before dawn
but the sun is well up

Perhaps it is the twilight of the gods
when their powers wane
and are not renewed

Perhaps it is *our* twilight

Rats confined on an island
eat out their food
then turn on each other

I fear that we are no different

The weak die first
then those unwilling to murder
but even the most callous of brutes
dies in the end

Extinctions are nothing new
but we *know* the end
towards which we march
and I hope that, what comes next
will be content with its small tree
or deep burrow

and leaves the other things
that call this planet home
the space to breathe

Those familiar with J.R.R. Tolkien's *Lord of the Rings* trilogy, and Peter Jackson's film version of the works (2001-3), know the story unfolds towards the end of the Third Age, when the age of elves is giving way to the age of men. This is a time of upheaval as Campbell's *Trials of Initiation* always are. Even the name of the realm (Middle-earth) suggests the transition.

At the time I contemplated the mist-swathed trees in Outback Australia (July 2019), I had no sense of the upheavals to come (due to a global virus) but now, as I write this (in June 2020) I know on a very personal level (as do millions of others) what it means to have the familiar and *dependable* world torn away to be replaced by who knows what.

The mist clears and we pause in Port Augusta or Curdnatta (*sandy place* in the local First Nation language) for fuel and coffee. The town is bigger and busier than I remember and we have trouble finding somewhere to park long enough to gulp down our coffee. Port Augusta was always the first stop on our mad, three day dashes to Australia's red centre and where we stocked up with fresh food and long life milk on other expeditions.

The town is perched right at the top of Spencer Gulf which cuts, like a narrow V, deep into the continent and so becomes a crossroad for travellers who head west across the Nullarbor; east to Sydney; south to Adelaide; and north to Darwin. We head north this time though our destination is Uluru and Kata Tjuta, not Darwin.

We have travelled this section of the Stuart Highway many times before but the climb up to the Arcoona Plateau north of Port Augusta never fails to thrill. As we leave the Spencer Gulf's blue behind and the Outback opens up in all its breath-taking vastness, I remember our regret on earlier trips as we headed south, *down* to Port Augusta.

The descent meant a return to our responsibilities as employees and to the mundane confinements of everyday life like keeping the grass short and putting the bins out on rubbish collection day.

Port Augusta claims the title of *Gateway to the Outback* (as does Broken Hill in New South Wales) and both deserve the accolade. For those of us more familiar with the green of the southern states' coastal rims, Port Augusta and Broken Hill are when the soil shifts hue and the horizon peels back to reveal things utterly, shockingly, gloriously new.

There is a wonderful scene in the iconic 1994 Australian movie: *The Adventures of Priscilla, Queen of the Desert*, where inner city travellers are so shocked by their first sight of the Outback, their vehicle stutters to a stop and they remain there frozen, mouths agape, too stunned to move.

It is 372 kms (230 miles) to the Bon Rest Area and we enjoy the sweeping vistas on either side as we reminisce about our first glimpse of the Outback's rich red soils; our first close-up of hefty wedge-tail eagles at feast on roadkill; our first sight of the Flinders Ranges' ancient bones; and our gladness on that first journey and every journey since, that we made the effort to set out.

The Stuart Highway swings north-west near Woomera where we divert for fuel. Woomera Village is a purpose-built town established to service the large military installation (a prohibited area) engaged in weapons testing, that historically included rockets, hence the name.

These are First Nation Kokatha lands, or were before the Australian Government acquired them, but the word *woomera* (a hunting device used to increase the range and force of a thrown spear, as noted) comes from the First Nation Dharug people whose lands lie west of Sydney.

We pull into Spud's Roadhouse with its warning sign: *No shirt; No shoes; No entry* where we have stopped before. It generously provides good clean toilets and a great sweep of white, silty gravel (necessitating sunglasses when the sun is out) that, on previous trips, allowed our children to kick a football and run about. This time it provides a space to stretch our legs and take in the crisp air.

As we continue through Pimba, slashes of sparkling white gleam beyond the olive-green of mallees: Lake Hart, Lake Johnstone, Lake Gairdner, Lake Ross; all salt pans like Kati Thanda-Lake Eyre, at least until the rains come. Away to the east, beyond the salty glitter of the lakes and running roughly parallel with us, is the Oodnadatta Track, our route north a few short weeks earlier. It seems like a lifetime ago.

The Stuart swings north again as we head towards the opal mining town of Coober Pedy but we stop 169 kms (105 miles) short at the Bon Rest Area. It is late afternoon, the time when travellers set camp after a long day driving and Bon Bon is popular. We pull in behind another van, leaving a two or three metre space, as Outback etiquette requires. There are toilets, sheltered picnic tables, and rubbish skips.

The sky begins its tussle between the turquoise-gold of sunset and the deep indigo velvet of night, and we briefly greet the travellers in front before eating and settling in for the night. We enjoy the usual star-storm and a good sleep before sunrise comes in all its cool-edged, sparkling glory.

To save our van's toilet cassette I visit the rest area's toilets which turns out to be a mistake. Pit or drop toilets are common all over Australia; provided for the convenience of travellers on the road, in bush/free camps, or in National Parks, and are very much appreciated by those old enough to remember when there were no toilets at all.

Pit toilets are efficient too, with bacteria doing the hard work of breaking down the waste but, unfortunately, these useful bacteria are destroyed by the chemicals of van toilets. Most van owners are knowledgeable and responsible enough to use dump points to empty their cassettes, but not all, which I suspect is what causes the problem at Bon Bon.

Graffiti

I have used drop toilets many times:
some with water
some with brushes and
great tubs of disinfectant
some with sawdust
some with nothing at all
but none that stink
like these
I read the graffiti on the walls
while trying not to breathe

This land is sacred
don't drop your butts

The injunction is heartfelt
but incongruous; as if all that risks
the destruction of *their* culture
is the fag end
of ours

Disposing of waste is a problem at anytime, given Australia generates so much of it, and we are very conscious of it as we travel. Some of what we produce is obvious: grey water (from washing clothes, dishes and ourselves); black water (from the toilet); cans, bottles, bags and wrappers (from food); and some of it less obvious: diesel fumes; tyre rubber on the roads; fire ash.

Of course, physical decluttering creates waste too, although hopefully mitigated by the things we shed being used by others rather than going to landfill, while the decluttering we undertake as part of our inner journey has the advantage of creating no waste at all.

Want to explore further?
Port Augusta: https://www.aussietowns.com.au/town/port-augusta-sa
Woomera: https://www.aussietowns.com.au/town/woomera-sa
The Adventures of Priscilla, Queen of the Desert:
https://en.wikipedia.org/wiki/The_Adventures_of_Priscilla,_Queen_of_the_Desert
Bon Bon Rest Area: https://www.youtube.com/watch?v=Lgtk1QZ_PSY
Bon Bon History: https://www.bushheritage.org.au/places-we-protect/south-australia/bon-bon

DESERT GEMS

A multitude of small and beautifully formed Egyptian pyramids herald the town of Coober Pedy. They glow palely, perfectly symmetrical but not the tombs of Pharaohs who strayed into strange lands but the heaped tailings of countless opal mines. We admire them from the 4x4 knowing it is unwise to give in to the temptation to explore. Apart from the legalities of trespassing on miners' claims, there is a real risk of suffering a fatal plunge down a mine shaft.

The town's name comes from a First Nation language (though which one, when *and* the name's meaning is debated). One source suggests Coober Pedy is an Anglicisation of *kupa-piti* (boys' waterhole) while another suggests it means '*white man's hole* (in the ground)'.

The latter, in turn, suggests no First Nation occupation of, or name for the area before the arrival of Europeans which seems unlikely given there were over 500 First Nation *nations* prior to European invasion; seasonal nomadism was common; and trading routes were diverse.

Whatever the truth of its pre-European history, Coober Pedy and other sites like Andamooka, White Cliffs and Lightning Ridge make Australia the world's chief source of opals. Coober Pedy is also known for its underground houses and hotels; the result of the land's harshness where summer temperatures regularly reach the high 40 C's.

We keep to the Stuart Highway's black strip but on other trips, camped at a park where the owner happened to be Greek. This is unsurprising given many Greeks came to Coober Pedy after WW II in the hope of wealth and to escape post-war poverty in Europe. The owner and my husband had friends in common which is also unsurprising as Australian Greeks seem to know each other or *of* each other and my husband disappeared for a couple of hours to chat with him over Greek coffee.

I have noted the historical suspicion of the stranger, but meeting *countrymen* far from home seems to have the opposite effect, probably because we welcome the comfort of the familiar. Greek Australians will immediately enquire about each other's home island to place each other in historical and geographical context and likewise, I find myself drawn to Australian accents overseas.

Being thousands of kilometres from home, albeit still in Australia, might be part of the reason I am so happy to meet up with friends at Kulgera, 459 kms (285 miles) further north. I have described the rush to climb Uluru and the difficulty of getting a site at the Ayres Rock Resort, so we won't be camping *together* for a couple more days.

We pull up behind the Kulgera Roadhouse where our friends are camped and clamber through a slack wire fence to exchange news of our travels over coffee and cake before we bid them farewell and continue north. We intend to overnight at one on the free camps between Kulgera and the Erldunda Roadhouse but while we see the occasional camper off in the distance, who seems to have gone cross-country through the mallee, we find none of the listed free camps.

It is fully dark when we call it quits and book into the campground behind the Erldunda Roadhouse. The roadhouse is right on the intersection of the Stuart Highway that takes us north and the Lasseter Highway that strikes west to Yulara (and Uluru and Kata Tjuta). Like many of the bigger roadhouses, it is very well equipped with a shop and restaurant, and we enjoy a country roast and a beer before having an early night.

Want to explore further?
Coober Pedy: https://www.gemsociety.org/article/opal-mining-coober-pedy/
Coober Pedy: https://southaustralia.com/travel-blog/best-experiences-in-coober-pedy
Erldunda Roadhouse: https://www.erldundaroadhouse.com/

INITIATION

Alice Springs is only a couple of hours north and we drive on through a morning as clear as glass. The land's colour palette is the same red sand, sage-coloured mallee and blue sky as usual, except in truth, there is no sameness about the Outback at all. Shadow runs; stone scatters; silvered and blackened wood; strews of discarded mallee leaves creamed, beiged and bronzed by the desiccating sun; blood-rust-red sand, dimpled with tracks or smoothed by wind; each view is different when we take the time to *really* look.

We have stayed at most of the caravan parks in *Alice* (as it is known) and we choose one, back the van onto the site, unhitch and go to drive forward and ... nothing. The 4x4 will neither start nor shift from park to drive. Another call to Roadside Assist follows and a mechanic appears in less than an hour, settles in the driver's seat, and the 4x4 performs. No problem is identified which I do not find reassuring given we have thousands of kilometres between us and home and much of it out of phone coverage.

I tell myself (more than once) there is no point fretting. For some reason, the 4x4 would not move and now it will. We have a quick lunch and head out to enjoy the things I missed on our earlier visit (thanks to the no-show sparky) and our first stop is the Olive Pink Botanic Garden.

Olive Pink (yes, it *is* her real name) started the garden in 1957 (or Reserve as it was called) along with (un-named) First Nation Walpiri gardeners. The climate was no kinder then, so carving out *any* garden at all was a massive feat, and the garden is still here for us to enjoy over 60 years later. I have noted my interest in gardens *and* cemeteries and I consider the link between the two as I admire the efforts of Olive and the Walpiri gardeners.

Even given legal and hygiene requirements, the rituals that surround human burial in orderly lines, in designated places, enclosed by boundaries such as fences, seem evidence of the human want to control natural phenomena such as death and similarly, gardens evidence of the human want to control Nature.

245

In natural settings, flora is positioned according to pollination and seed-fall (or seed-*carrying* by wind, water, birds or animals) and what grows or dies varies according to the vagaries of winds, rains, heat and cold; soil types; crowding; browsing animals and pest attacks. But in a garden, flora is planted in certain places, in particular configurations, where heat, moisture, competition, pests and so on can be manipulated.

Both struggles for control (over human death and Nature more broadly) take enormous amounts of time and effort. There is always a new virus or disease to be fought off and in land-hungry cities, the deceased have limited tenure. Grand gardens, centuries in the making, can be destroyed by super storms or exotic diseases, and humbler gardens face the continuous onslaught of weeds.

As I consider the warning-signs of snakes and goannas, I ponder that if cemeteries *do* seek to control death and gardens to control Nature, then both are doomed to failure. Controlling things is a very human desire and one more at home on the outer journey. In contrast, in setting out on our inner, *soul*-journeys, we *relinquish* control over the familiar and, in opening ourselves to the new and unknown, actively seek the death of the old self, without which, our soul-journey cannot progress.

My progress (in the outer world garden) is slow, partly because I contemplate the life work of a remarkable woman and remarkable First Nation Walpiri gardeners and partly because desert plants tend to be subtle in the beauty of their leaves and in their small and often hidden flowers, and I need time to appreciate them. The warm day fills the air with the peppery scent of desiccated eucalypt leaves as they dry-crack-crack under foot, and I glance down at them often, alert to the shine of scales.

As we sit outside the van that evening, my husband makes up for days of enforced solitude by chatting to everyone who passes. I am supposed to be writing but am distracted by the magpies at play in the branches above and by a fellow camper with a cockatoo perched on his shoulder.

Sulphur-crested cockatoos are intelligent and far from docile and I would not want its hooked, seed-cracking beak as close to my eyes. The man seems to have no such worries. The cockatoo is a long-time pet that has travelled all over Australia with him and his wife and as its wings are clipped, it is not going anywhere without them.

Staying in a caravan park means long, hot showers and catching up with the washing, and we are more presentable as we head off to Alice Springs' Todd Mall markets the next morning. It is another sunny day, and the mall crowded with tourists and locals. I am hoping for market tables of preloved art glass and ceramics, which I covet as little time capsules of their previous owners lives, but there are none; just home-baking, baby clothes, scented candles and a van that whips sugar into the lurid-coloured fairy floss (cotton candy) loved by children.

We find a table outside a café and have settled in for coffee when I see him.

Quietness of Truth

The market crowd is a microcosm of
every fair in history:

the locals at ease
the tourists padded by age and money
the dread-locked young
outsiders in any century

and the displaced *natives*
clothed in the garb
of the invader

but not in their ways
nor in the ways of
the time before

free, lost or caught between

Then he walks through the crowd
tall and lean
his steps measured
his hat part cowboy, part Akubra
his gaze all Elder

He carries his silence
about him like an echo
of other times
his soul scarified with initiation rites
if not his skin

He has no need of bluster
to know his place
just the quietness
of truth

The First Nation man carries himself with dignity and grace and reminds me that the breach between First Nation peoples and those others of us who call Australia home, has never been mended. This has troubled me since I first ventured into the Outback and saw the living conditions of some First Nation peoples.

First Nation people can expect to live significantly shorter lives than non-First Nation people for many reasons; some simple, some complex, and successive Australian governments have instigated policies and/or interventions to address these reasons and spent millions of dollars in the process.

Those who claimed Australia for Great Britain declared it *terra nullius* (land empty or unoccupied), which means no compensation was offered and no treaties entered into. In dispossessing Australia's First Nation people, the British claimants effectively denied in excess of 60,000 years of First Nation occupation and fractured over 60,000 years of rich cultural traditions.

Dispossession of land was fundamental to this fracturing but massacres, mass poisonings, European diseases, enslavement, removal of children, suppression of cultural practices, policies of assimilation and active discrimination (the right of First Nation people to vote was only granted in 1962 following a referendum) added to the wreckage.

In contemporary Australia, there is a sharp divide between (mainly European) Australians who disparagingly refer to past wrongs as a *black armband* view of history; who shrug and say we should all move on; or who deny any injustices/atrocities took place at all; and those Australians who want past wrongs acknowledged; apologies offered; and a way forward negotiated with First Nation people as equal partners.

This divide simmers away to erupt now and then when historians/writers bring new bloodied events/injustices to light or contradict the historical view of First Nation people as primitive savages; or when a blue-eyed, fair-skinned person claims First Nation status (for perceived personal gain); or when First Nation people exercise their rights over their property, as in the upcoming closure of Uluru's climb.

My non-First Nation understanding is this: in First Nation culture, land is *country*, and when First Nation people speak of being *on country*, it means more than roaming across the physical features of their ancestral lands.

It means what *they* are as a people (physically, spiritually, mythically, culturally) and what the *lands* are (geographically, florally, faunally), and to be separated from/dispossessed of their *country*, is to be fractured in the most intimate and profound of ways. Thus land rights are central to First Nation struggles for recognition of their 60,000 years plus occupation of their homeland.

We wander on to the Araluen Arts Centre where I come across the words of Vincent Lingiari, a First Nation Gurindji man who pioneered the fight for land rights in Australia (and won). I stand in contemplation for a long time, profoundly moved. I have post-graduate qualifications in teaching English as a second language and I think of

249

how sometimes, in rough-hewn words, English spoken as a second language can express the most heart-felt of truths.

My name is Vincent Lingiari, came from Daguragu, Wattie Creek station. Yala-ngurlu nguna yanana, Wattie-Creekngurlung, nguna yani, murlangkurra; ngunanyjurra yani. Ngunayini yani jarrakap-ku jangkakarni kartiya-wu, murlangkurra, well nyawa na nguna marnana jarrakap [Then I'm travelling, I came from Wattie Creek, here; I came to all of you. I came to talk to the big (important) kartiya here, well this is what I'm saying] That means that I came down here to ask all these gentleman here about the land rights. What I got story from my old father or grandfather, that land belongs to me, belongs to Aboriginal men before the horses and the cattle come over on that land where I am sitting now. That is what I have been keeping on my mind and I still got it on my mind. That is all the words I can tell you.

Gurindji/Malngin leader Vincent Lingiari spoke these words as the introduction to the song, 'Gurindji Blues', written by Ted Egan in 1969 and recorded by Yolngu leader, Galarrwuy Yununpingu in 1971. (https://www.cdu.edu.au/sites/default/files/artcollection-gallery/docs/simm-teachers-notes.pdf accessed December 2019).

Want to explore further?
Olive Pink Botanic Garden: https://opbg.com.au/
Todd Mall Market: https://www.toddmallmarkets.com.au/
First Nation people and country: https://www.aboriginalart.com.au/culture/tourism2.html
Vincent Lingiari: http://ia.anu.edu.au/biography/lingiari-vincent-14178

SACRED STONE

From Alice Springs we back track south to Erldunda and this time we *do* take the turn west along the Lasseter Highway towards the Ayres Rock Resort at Yulara, a journey of 246 kms (152 miles).

The first thing travellers see, about an hour and a half from the turning, is Mt Connor (Atilla/Artilla in the First Nation tongue), a flat-topped mountain (mesa) that thrusts from the sparse forests of desert oak and golden spinifex. Its vaguely similar shape and size to Uluru means many first-time visitors mistake it for its more famous relation.

The Lasseter Highway takes us on past *Atilla* until we glimpse the real thing, clad in the soft purple garb Uluru dons for those who view it from a distance. I have seen Uluru many times although not for some years but, such is its presence, I have to remind myself to breathe.

Uluru

As the Rock looms on the horizon
I think of how the first humans

might have stopped
shaded their eyes
and considered
what god it was

How songs might have been sung
and tales told

hesitant
stumbling

too small to enclose
what only sky and earth can hold

yet still mighty leaps
in speaking the
unspeakable

The Rock grows redder as we draw nearer but then we turn off into the resort and join the queue to book in. I fear the camping ground will be crowded but the rush to climb the Rock has eased with the school holidays' ending and it is quiet inside. The sites are large and we pull in a couple of vans from our friends and set up. The Rock can be seen from viewing platforms atop sandy hillocks scattered around the park and though I cannot see it from the lower land near the van, I can sense it.

Kata Tjuta, 57 kms (35 miles) further on, has a mighty presence too, but not the same as Uluru. While both are sandstone formed from sediment laid down in ancient oceans millions of years ago, Uluru is a single stone (monolith), 348 metres (1142 ft) at its highest point and with a further astonishing 2.5 kms of stone underground (hence its description as a *land iceberg*). In contrast, Kata Tjuta is made up of 36 domes (Kata Tjuta means *many headed*) with the highest being 564 metres (1850 ft).

But all the statistics in the world are useless in expressing the mysterious power of these formations. I faced the same struggle on earlier visits and then, as now, resorted to the language of poetry. It did not take me long in their presence to decide Uluru's resolute solitariness made it male, and Kata Tjuta's sensuous dips and curves made it female.

Desert Lovers

Uluru and Kata Tjuta face each other
across the desert sand
steeped in the silence of long-time lovers
who have had words

Uluru stands erect, stoic
like a man
braced against accusations
of unfeelingness

Pools have formed along his flanks
sacred places where
king-fishers dive and dart
blue as the sky

Kata Tjuta opens herself slowly
lets her wind-filled valleys
share their silences
with the stars

Her ghost gum limbs
beckon the moon
to her embrace

and when the sun rises
she warms and sends out tender flowers
of palest pink
across the desert sand
to Uluru

and he accepts
them

Impatient to reacquaint myself with the Rock, I jog to the nearest
viewing platform but cannot linger. We have a bus to catch to the
Field of Light Uluru. According to the brochure, Bruce Munro's
installation consists of *50,000 spindles of light, the stems breathing
and swaying through a sympathetic desert spectrum of ochre, deep
violet, blue and gentle white*. A less poetic description would say the
installation is made up of 50,000 lights on flexible stems that created
a multicoloured carpet after dark.

The bus delivers us and our friends (and fellow ticket-holders) to a viewing site where wine and nibbles are served as we watch the sun set over Uluru and the swathe of lights at its feet twinkle to life. And then, as the darkness deepens, we descend to wander the pathways between them. They are pretty, in the same way fairy lights are, but not powerful in the way *faerie* lights might be. There is no mystery and no sense of other-worldliness and I find myself gazing up at the brilliant silver of the stars instead.

Pretty Blooms

A sweep of colours
winks across the spinifex

crimson, gold, indigo, silver

metal blooms of
pretty glass

while above

mono-coloured stars
achieve a splendour
all their own

The next day we wish our friends safe travels as they depart and then we head out into the Uluru-Kata Tjuta National Park. From the park entrance, it is a half hour drive to Uluru and my husband drops me off where people queue to climb the Rock.

The First Nation Anangu owners call the climbers *minga* (ants) and as I watch the thick trail of people labouring up Uluru's face, I see why. My husband intends to drive around the perimeter road on a photographic journey while I walk the 10 kms (6 mile) track around the base.

I set off clockwise, excited but also deeply calm and thankful to be back. My memories are of a soft red sandy track; golden grass higher than my head; dull green desert oaks: some like closed umbrellas, others like open ones; the songs of pied butcher birds; and always the mighty crouch of the Rock: smooth, cragged, bright, shadowed and impossibly red. I am not disappointed. It is the same as my memories and I feel the same too.

Others walk, but quietly and strung out; the walk less popular than the climb. I mostly walk alone, although I am never truly alone, with the red sweep of stone at my right hand, stark sometimes, and sometimes softened by gold and green.

The walk is meditative and other-worldly, as if I have slipped the constraints of the outer world and wander somewhere in an inner one. Part of me is aware of the blue sky, the red rock, the warm and cool air as I move between sunlight and shadow, but the sensations are like surface ripples on a lake while I dwell in the still greenness of its depths.

I surface abruptly as I complete the circuit and clear Uluru's shoulder into the harsher sunlight that rims the tarmacked road and its sweep of traffic. Foot traffic increases and *minga* who have climbed or who wait to climb, wander in search of selfies. I perch on a seat and watch the climbers and, as I swig from my water bottle, I wonder at their need to conquer.

My husband climbed the Rock with a friend many years ago when, due to work commitments, I flew home with the children, and he and the friend drove. I was annoyed with him then and even more so now when my sense of the sacred is stronger. He and the friend's motivations were wanting to do something unusual and to take in the view from the top.

They had no thoughts of trespass, disrespect, or insult to Uluru's owners and I have to remind myself the present climbers' motivations might be similar *or* something else entirely. All I really know are my own motivations in *not* climbing.

Uluru's Anangu owners are to close the climb for the reasons noted and the walk around Uluru's base has altered too. The sacred men's sites that I respectfully turned my face from on previous walks and the sacred women's sites that I did not, are now fenced off. The small cave on a neighbouring hump of stone where we shared oranges with our small children, is no longer accessible. I cannot complain. Uluru does not belong to me and its owners remain generous in their willingness to share.

Owned

I walk around the Rock
as I have so many times before
and watch the folk who climb it
as I have before

They are different now
there is an urgency about them
and an anger

They are to close the climb
deny *us* our rights
for *money,* of course
or sheer *bloody mindedness*

Who do they think they are?

This is *our* rock and
our right to climb

My walk has changed too
there are more prohibitions
and more fences

The first time I visited Stone Henge
I walked amongst the stones
laid my palms flat
against their pitted faces
as Roman, Celt, Angle and Saxon
had once laid theirs

Those stones are fenced off too
my last visit a more mechanical homage
than my walk around the Rock

But the redness is the same and the bulokes
the silver and gold of grasses unchanged
like the Rock's vast ineffable beauty
that we never owned

That evening we join the crowd on the viewing platform to watch the
sun set over Uluru. There are viewing sites people can drive to for
the *sunset experience*, and others where tours provide gourmet meals
with waiter service, crisp white table cloths, and sparkling wine, but
I am content to eat more simply in the van before I watch the Rock
shift from blood-red to rose-red; purple to mauve; cool grey to black;
and as darkness infills its outline, to lift my eyes to the sky's mono-
chromatic star-pulse.

The next morning we drive out to Kata Tjuta and the Valley of the
Winds walk. Those who visit the Uluru-Kata Tjuta National Park
will know the Valley of the Winds walk and if they walk it, will have
added it to their never to be forgotten, often life-altering experiences.

The Valley of the Winds walk tops my own list of the life-altering,
followed by Uluru's base walk; the pristine, glittering salt pan of
Kati Thanda – Lake Eyre and beyond Australia, the deserted, wintry
sites of Stone Henge, Glastonbury and Tintagel; the sweeping,
silver-streamed Scottish Highlands; the blue-ice-volcanic-black of
Iceland; the crater-rim vistas and animals of Ngorangora Conservation Area (Tanzania); the lavender sands and hulking tors of Wadi

Rum (Jordan) (the backdrop to films like *Lawrence of Arabia*, *The Martian*, and various *StarWars* spin-offs); the glimmering pearl-like Taj Mahal (India) and the astonishing and humbling La Sagrada Familia (Gaudi's Cathedral) (Spain).

There are only two built environments on my list but the Taj Mahal is actually a tomb and the organic, forest-like interior of La Sagrada Familia owes as much to Nature's beauty as to visions of the hereafter. The list says something about the power of the natural world to ground us, both literally and metaphorically, and when I recall these places, the sacred seeps back along with the memories.

The Valley of the Winds walk is only 7.4 kms (4.5 miles) but a lot more demanding than Uluru's flat sandy track. My husband decides to join me but we end up mainly walking apart. Thanks to his fairly recent knee-joint replacement; differences in our fitness levels and walking speeds; and his want to take *good* photographs, I spend a lot of time ahead, or contemplating my surroundings while I wait for him.

Kata Tjuta is a series of sensuous soaring domes and scooped valleys of the same wondrous red as Uluru but slashed here and there with white-limbed gums; the gold of spinifex; and the darker greens of mulga, acacia and desert oaks. Shadows bathe parts of the walk and sunshine fires others, and there are deep quiet places, and places where the curved stone opens like a window to reveal sweeping, light-drenched vistas.

Kata Tjuta

There are reds here
not of crayon or palette
but of chalice and cross

Reds of new blood and old
imprisoned in every grain of sand
in every sweep of stone
that settles to rest
like a beggar's cupped hands
or the open palms of prayer

This is no ocean of breaking waves
that clash in jagged peaks
to claw the sky
but a blunted surge and swell
that rolls on
towards a horizon made red
by a setting sun

In the quieter places
between the rise and fall of stone

lie pools of darkness
where ghost gums shine like candles
set in story altars

to lattice the ruby light
of stained-glass skies

Here the butcherbird and currawong sing
bright hymns of praise
and ride the wind like Noah rode the waves

straining forward over the prow
as he searched ahead for the holy places

the sacred places
of deliverance

Want to explore further?
Uluru Field of Light: https://www.ayersrockresort.com.au/events/
detail/field-of-light-uluru
Uluru Climb Closure: https://parksaustralia.gov.au/uluru/news/uluru-
climb-to-close
Uluru – Kata Tjuta National Park: https://parksaustralia.gov.au/uluru/

SYMMETRY

We set off early the next day for the final part of our journey. I twist my head around to imprint Uluru's soft purple on my memory and ponder whether the hidden part under the sand that tethers it, mirrors the unconscious that tethers us. All too soon, Uluru is eaten by the horizon and I stop putting kinks in my neck.

We reach Erldunda and swing south onto the Stuart Highway. We are truly going home now; no more detours; no more diversions. But there is still plenty to consider as we drive and plenty of time to do so. We pass Kulgera where we caught up with the friends with whom we shared *Uluru's Field of Lights* and then our tyres hum over the line on the map to leave the Northern Territory behind and South Australia stretched out in front.

I take pictures of the highway as it stretches in an every-narrowing strip to the horizon; of the sweeps of stony soil, mallee and spinifex to either side; of the bluish-purple hummocky mountains in the distance; and of the red slashes of those closer. These flat images belong to the outer world but I hope they will nourish my inner world too when I am back in Melbourne's smaller skies. There are more mundane sights out the window too that remind me we must function in the outer world to stay safe.

Cows

Watch for cows, the sign says
the highway here
one long and unfenced paddock

I watch for cows

I know what a cow will do
to a 4x4, a van, to *us*

and I know
what we will do
to a cow

They lay on the verges
legs erect
bellies full of gas

Rubber stripes the road
burned from car tyres in desperate detours
or laid in straight lines by road trains
chased by trailers in
no mood for swerving

The kilometres click over and we stop for fuel and coffee and food
when we must. We pass through Marla, a few kilometres north of
where, earlier in the journey, we emerged from the Oodnadatta
Track: red-dusted, glad of tarmac, and abuzz with Outback visions.
Those early days of journeying seem a life time ago now and perhaps they are. Perhaps, in turning for home, my *mind* has already
turned from *this* discrete life and journey, to a *new* discrete life and
journey.

I stare east, far from ready for *this* life's journey to slip away. Beyond the desert sweep, Kati Thanda-Lake Eyre lies, in all its silver
splendour; its salty water awash with pelicans on their own journeys.
As the sun slides to the horizon, Coober Pedy's mine-spoil pyramids
emerge: their western faces gilded by the setting sun; their eastern
faces shadowed. Their neat gold and black halves seem a perfect
metaphor for our outer and inner journeys; where we seek our own
symmetry by acknowledging the hidden part of ourselves.

This journey has not revealed whether symmetry is possible but it
has allowed time and space to nourish the parts of myself in need
of more than food and shelter and in the process, exposed a strange
paradox. When we journey from the familiar into the unfamiliar,
and explore these strange outer *and* inner landscapes, we make them

more familiar and in doing so, *we* change, so that what was once familiar, becomes less so.

Because I am not the same person who set out, in either my outer or inner worlds, I do not view what was once familiar in the same way. In simple concrete terms, we travelled north on the Stuart Highway and now we travel south, and not only is the view objectively different, but because *I* am different, the view is subjectively different too.

Journeying and *home* seem less like opposites now and I ponder the slippery definition of *home* and the assumption that *home* is static in place and time. For the last nine and half weeks, home has been a caravan; or a 4x4; or the places we stayed, sometimes briefly, sometimes for several days; that we *walked* away from to later return or *drove* away from to later return.

Perhaps the highway, *the long graveyard of the wild and unwary*, is a type of home too, where any stop is no more than a *pause* as I poetically suggested early in this story. And as I suggested later, as this story revealed itself: an inner journey can unfold, suddenly and dramatically (via a personal tragedy or an impersonal one like a global virus) without any of us setting foot outside the doors of what we call *home*.

As we leave Coober Pedy behind, I focus on the outer world, in search of a particular turn off. Roughly 745 kms (462 miles) from our starting point this morning at Yulara and 12 kms south of Coober Pedy, lies the William Hutchison Memorial Free Camp (or *Hutchinson* as it is sometimes spelled). I see no signage but we gamble on a turn-off roughly in the right place and see the small, brass-plaqued stone memorial only after we are well off the road.

There is no evidence of a free camp, or other campers, which is worrying given the sun is well down and travellers have usually stopped for the night. We drive on another thirty metres and then the land drops away to reveal a well set out and expansive free camp dotted with vans and converted buses.

Orange campfires glow, startling in the dusk and sending slim streams of smoke to join the purpling air, but we loop around and park on the higher ground, nearer the Stuart, something I later regret. For some reason, as I lay in bed that night, I imagine we are vulnerable to drunks who might think it a grand idea to drive out from Coober Pedy and deal out trouble, and I *do* hear a surprising number of suspicious noises that result in nothing more than a bad night's sleep.

After we stop, I use my phone to take a 360 degree video shot of the area that I have looked at many times since, as if to absorb its essence. It captures the vast arc of turquoise sky, fired along its landward edges with orange and gold; and the great sweep of red-gold-olive green mottled plain that rolls away to the horizon. It has been a common sight on this journey but I never tire of its understated beauty, or stop being surprised by its ability to calm and centre me.

As we breakfast the next morning, I have a chance to learn more about Will Hutchison who, as a 15 year old, is credited with discovering opal in the area. Unfortunately, five years later, Will went for a swim in a nearby river and drowned. Outback cemeteries tell me that many a young man was claimed by drowning but I wonder whether, in Will's case, the earth extracted compensation for Will's unwitting part in the *theft* of its fire-shot opaline gems. The notion has a certain tragic symmetry as a metaphor for gain and loss.

Want to explore further?
Will Hutchison Memorial:
http://monumentaustralia.org.au/themes/people/settlement/display/104766-will-hutchison
Will Hutchison Memorial Free Camp: https://planner.hemax.com/Place/Details?id=58941bf2-2559-40af-a4e9-92f508332fc3

MEMORIALS

We are confronted with more death than Will's the next morning
when we turn back onto the Stuart Highway and, despite roadkill
being common on this trip, I am shocked by the carnage.

Overcome

We leave as a freezing night
gives way to a dawn
crystalline bright

I am not thinking of Will Hutchison
as we hit the road
but death confronts us

Kangaroos not swallowed by water
as young Will was
but tossed like leaves along the
bitumen

They died as we slept and I count them
in a macabre game I soon abandon
defeated by the numbers

We hit one too
a big grey
already dead

Two clunks:
one from the car
one from the van

Flesh and bone overcome by metal
as Will Hutchison was overcome
by water

We have another long day ahead. The land's reds and greens run together like watery paint slashed here and there by the white of salt pans. We pass rest areas we have never stopped at and rest areas and roadhouses we have; Bon Bon and then Spud's Roadhouse at Woomera blur pass until, 541 kilometres (336 miles) later, we descend from the Arcoona Plateau back into Port Augusta.

I do not have the usual sense of loss as I believe I will be back in 2020 (which thanks to a certain virus, I won't). We fuel up and take our coffee with us as we cut through to Wilmington on the Willowie Road and then on to Orroroo. Wilmington is all gentle curves, pretty green hills and lush valleys, and the lands we left beyond the Arcoona Plateau take on the exotic blur of another world which, in a sense, they are.

Orroroo's welcoming sign directs caravaners to a side street with plenty of parking, free Wi-Fi, and nearby (clean) public toilets and we pull up and make a quick meal in the van. It is a Sunday and Orroroo's impressively wide main street (possibly the widest in Australia) is all but deserted.

This is First Nation Ngadjuri land and the approximation of their name for this area is *Oorooroo*, the meaning of which has been lost. Orroroo has a sense of greenness about it despite averaging 286 *rainless* days each year, in fact, the first pastoralists to take up land here in the 1800's left after 17 months of *no* rain at all.

We push on to Peterborough (our second stop on our outward journey where we met up with our friends *and* fixed our leaking water problem) then head south-west to the pretty historic town of Terowie. On our outward journey, I was struck by its well-maintained but ghostily empty buildings and was unaware of its free camp next to the defunct railway line.

We have 683 kms (424 miles) behind us when we pull into a broad, grassy area beside the line and set off to explore the railway buildings. They are all beautifully preserved: honeyed-stone trimmed with cream timber fretwork and topped with red and silver corrugated iron roofs.

The owners of the only other van are busy with their metal-detectors and we chat. They are long-time travellers, on the hunt for coins or other small pieces of metal-history. I think of the less desirable metal remnants we have seen on this trip: rusted machinery, abandoned cars, the tangled wire of broken fences; all strewn in less forgiving landscapes. Terowie seems kinder but new paint and a building's neat pointing can still hide struggle and deep sorrow.

Shadows grow and as the temperature plummets, we retreat to the van and its diesel heater.

Want to explore further?
Orroroo: https://www.aussietowns.com.au/town/orroroo-sa

ICE

When I was a child, water pipes were lagged to stop them freezing and bursting, and milk-ice puddles needed a decent heel-slam to crack the surface. I am reminded of them the next morning as I toss buckets of water over our ice-covered windscreen and it takes a good ten minutes of scraping wiper-blades to clear enough to safely drive away. It takes even longer for my frozen fingers to tingle painfully back to life.

We follow the same route as on our outward journey because it is quickest. South to Burra; south-east to Loxton and Pinaroo; south to Bordertown; east across the border into Victoria and its shard-like grain silos; on through Kaniva, Nhill and Dimboola to Horsham: home to one of the couples we travelled with.

We ring ahead as we hope to park outside and sleep in the van but they are having none of it. We will be in the spare room *after* we share a meal and a good bottle of wine. In the meantime, I have one last poem to write; one I have dabbled with since the wife of this couple asked me for a poem about crows.

It was a reasonable request given crows have been our constant companions (along with cockatoos, red dust and roadkill). I ponder crows' historic association with magic, mystery and death; their nonchalant hops from the paths of speeding vehicles; their surveillance of city foot traffic from lofty lamp-post roosts; their haunting of Outback cemeteries and, in particular, their odd song amongst Broome's Japanese dead.

No Beggar at the Bird-feeder

Crows hold an honoured place in tales
though our reverence might be a bribe to
ward off ill-will

Crows care nothing of such things

or their link to war and woe
and even their meal of roadkill
is taken with cool disdain
for passing cars

These bead-eyed, black-breasted bearers of bad news
 are no beggars at the bird-feeder

They sit in silent judgement high on lamp-posts
and sing in cemeteries, not with joy or sorrow
but as a soul might sing that passes
between two states

going to somewhere close or distant
that only crows can know

Coincidentally (or thanks to synchronicity), crow-song is the first
thing I hear as we pull up outside our friends' home, 684 kms (425
miles) from our frosty start at Terowie. We enjoy the wonderful meal
promised us and that good bottle of red, but as we reminisce about
our time together in the Outback, and our respective *adventures*
since parting, I experience that same odd feeling as in Burra on our
outward trip. I am back in a *place* I have visited several times before
(our friends' home in Horsham) but I am not the same person.

There is also an odd jag in *time* the next morning as we continue
the last leg of our journey. The greenness outside the 4x4 window
asserts its familiarity and the Outback's vast redness is forced to give
way to paddocks then to Melbourne's outer suburbs and then to the
Ring Road's traffic.

The strange disconnect strengthens as we return the van to storage,
take the short drive home, put the key in the door and step inside. All
is as we left it, but *I* am not as I left it, although I have little time to
digest the changes or consciously articulate them.

In less than a week we are off overseas on a different type of journey and it is several months before I carve out the time and space to consider my twin journeys: one into Australia's vast wilderness known as the Outback and the other *soul-journey* into myself.

PLACE OF REST

The way into the mind is a strip of black tarmac, I write on day one of that journey and then discover, as the journey unfurls behind me and I keep my pledge to write a poem a day, that the poems serve as a way in too; stepping-stones of bright symbols to light the way on my soul-journey. But the highway of black tarmac and metaphorical stepping-stones also allows for passage out and, firmly back in the outer world, I wonder what I have learned.

This is an easy question to answer in an outer world sense. I know far more about First Nation history and culture; European history; geology; geography; fauna; flora; the dynamics of friendships; how the van works and so on, but what of the inner world? What insights did my poetic stepping stones deliver?

Insights are defined as *accurate and deep understandings* but only half the definition seems a good fit for the inner journey. The notion of accuracy belongs in the outer world where it is rightly subject to fact-checks and verification while in the context of the soul-journey, accuracy is better judged by whether our discoveries *feel* true for *us*.

The second part of the definition, that of deepening understanding, *is* a good fit. My insights do not advance my soul-journey by revealing anything grand-spanking new but by intensifying what already resonates within me.

I had thought the metaphor of *the long graveyard of the wild and un-wary* with which I begin my story (in *The Long Graveyard*) referred to roadkill but realise the metaphor includes the *death* of our former, discrete lives too.

It also includes an understanding that we are part of, not separate/ superior to, other creatures, a notion reinforced by a number of poems during the journey. In *Landward Run* I write: *Chinaman's fingernails, bivalves, whelks and a jellyfish gold against the grey; creatures that have other ways of living and thinking, and knowing unknown to me*; and in Shining Silver: *I stare down through the glass-bottomed boat ... there is another world down there going about its business.*

This understanding of connection extends into the past as well. Crows are our constant companions in the red, sandy wilderness and Western cultural tradition associates them with intelligence, death, and otherworldliness.

When I observe them and they observe me, I sense my place in time but also experience an odd timelessness knowing I am part of the great cycle of life that came before me and will continue after. This sense is expressed in *No Beggar at the Bird-feeder*: *They sit in silent judgement high on lamp posts and sing in cemeteries, not with joy or sorrow but as a soul might sing that passes between two states going to somewhere close or distant that only crows can know.*

Death in the inner world soul-journey is very much about renewal but physical death in the outer world is, depending on our belief systems, about endings or about life elsewhere. Death (whether metaphorical or literal) reminds us our lives are finite and no type of death does this more powerfully than the death of the young. *I walk amongst the graves of those unclaimed by old age. Children barely from their cradles lie beside others old enough to dream of futures that never came* (in *Uneaten by the Sea*); *I read of a woman whose child died of diphtheria, whose new-born died a week later and whose husband died when she was thirty* (in *Onslow's Women*); *He defends those on death row ... and watches them go from small-time crims to mature young men in prison ... then hanged or shot* (in *The Man on the Radio #2*).

It is no surprise that given the limited, precious time we have, many of my poems reflect my horror at being robbed of it. *Caught Between*, compares refugees incarcerated in Australia's off-shore detention centres to food abandoned at a border Quarantine Station: *Someone has left a net of onions and a bag of potatoes propped against the side. These are legal, like refugees, but here they remain neither carried over the border nor binned. Even the ants can go where they cannot.*

My deepened understanding of the limitations time imposes on us, and that consequently, we must be active in progressing our soul-journeys, is reflected in multiple metaphors for time-inflicted ruin and decay. *Shape-shifter metal ... escaped the blacksmith's hammer and the mighty machines' compression and unforged* (in *Unforged*); *mortar ... loosed its grip slyly over the years and let the stone go back to the earth* (in *Slyly*); *at night the stars take over clean and bright and it is easy to forget that they are dust and we are too* (in *Dust*).

The outward journey through Australia's blood-rust-red wilderness strengthens my awareness that I will never share the rich cultural understanding of Australia's First Nation people developed over 60,000 years of habitation and yet, in accepting the limitations of my understanding, I am freed to delight in what I *do* understand.

Following our flight over Lake Kati Thanda – Lake Eyre, I write: *We look down as the pelicans do; see swirls of empty waterways, salt-bush, the emu-tracks of wind. But there is another seeing etched into the landscape; the scarification of initiation that tells of a knowing we can never share* (in *Silver Heart*) and in *The Quietness of Truth*: *... he walks through the crowd ... his hat part cowboy, part Akubra, his gaze all Elder. He carries his silence about him like an echo of other times, his soul scarified with initiation rites if not his skin. He has no need of bluster to know his place, just the quietness of truth.*

Despite my exclusion, there *are* points of connection I recognise when I stumble upon them. Their sacred essence is timeless even if time moulds their manifestation in the outer world. These are the churches in country paddocks where *the soul-stuff lingers* (in *Country Churches*); the water-mirrored gorges where *words are too small or too clumsy for what is revealed* (in *Cathedral Gorge*); the brilliant perfection of sunrises and sets *where clouds blaze crimson across the heavens* (in *Sunset*). These are Uluru's *sacred places where king-fishers dive and dart blue as the sky* (in *Uluru*) and Kata Tjuta's *sweep of stone that settles to rest like a beggar's cupped hands or the open palms of prayer* (in *Kata Tjuta*).

The outer world journey fixes us in time and place but the inner journey of the sacred, spirit and soul frees us, so that, as I write in *Mist*: *we are not as anchored in time and place as we believe but flashes of sunlight caught between tree shadows; fleeting, ephemeral, and unconfined.*

EPILOGUE

It is mid 2020 and I am sitting in our tiny patch of garden on a sunny winter's day. I have planted the small space with dwarf citrus: lemon, kaffir lime, and an orange with fruit that defies the odds to ripen in Melbourne's cold weather. I have lavender too, their final flowers abuzz with bees, and roses lately pruned, their last buds opening in a vase inside.

I hear a familiar shriek and look up. Our neighbour has a walnut tree and two sulphur-crested cockatoos are busy cracking nuts. Their white is brilliant against the green leaves and the bright blue of the sky. I watch them, aware of the sun's warmth on my skin and the cooler drift of a breeze and one of the cockatoos ceases feeding and stares at me.

I stare back and wonder what it sees. Then I wonder what *I* see. Snow-white plumage and a lemon-yellow crest? Yes and no. They are so much more, as I am, as we all are.

End of Journey: Seeking the Sacred, Spirit and Soul in the Australian Wilderness.

I hope you enjoyed Journey: *Seeking the Sacred, Spirit and Soul in the Australian Wilderness*. **Authors need reviews!** It is how our readers find us. I would love you to leave me an honest review on Amazon, Goodreads, or another of your favourite reader sites. If the inner journey intrigued you, read on.

Works by K S Nikakis

Available on Amazon KDP and a range of digital platforms.

Fantasy Novel Series

Angel Caste 5 Book Series – available complete in one book or as five individual books: Angel Blood, Angel Breath, Angel Bone, Angel Bound, Angel Blessed.

Angel Caste – Complete 5 Book Series - *A modern female hero on a timeless quest*

A troubled half-angel, a beautiful angel guide, a binding promise . . .

Viv is on day release from jail to attend the funeral of the thug she thinks is her father, when she comes face to face with her real father, the powerful angel Archae Kald. If finding out she's a half-angel isn't shocking enough, Viv discovers her mother isn't dead after all but lost somewhere in the tangle of worlds called the Rynth.

Determined to find the only person who has ever truly loved her, Viv goes to Kald's angel world where he appoints the beautiful Thris as her guide. Thris is kind and caring, unlike the males Viv has known before, but after living on the streets, Viv finds it almost impossible to trust.

Friendship grows as Thris trains her to travel the rifts, but the Rynth is a dark and dangerous place, even for angels and, as Thris grows increasingly tempted by Viv's emerging angel traits, disaster strikes.

Viv journeys on alone and stumbles into a war zone where she finds a lost child. She pledges to take the child to safety but, as the war rages on, deciding who is friend and who is enemy becomes a deadly game of chance.

Bound by his promise to guide Viv to her mother, Thris embarks on a desperate search for her, but a greater threat confronts them both and, in the end, they must fight not just for their own lives, but for the lives of those they love.

The Kira Chronicles - 6 Book Series – available complete in one book or as six individual books: The Whisper of Leaves, The Silence of Stone, The Secrets of Stars, The Thunder of Hoofs, The Crying of Birds, The Music of Home.

The Kira Chronicles – Complete 6 Book Series – *traditional fantasy with deep forests and high stakes*

A gold-eyed Healer, a prophecy, two brothers at war.

In seasons long past, twin gold-eyed princes sundered a kingdom. Rejecting his brother Terak's warrior ways, Kasheron led his people deep into the great southern forests and established the healing settlement of Allogrenia. The Tremen flourished, upholding Kasheron's legacy of peace and healing, and protected by the vast, trackless trees.

All Tremen delight in the healing arts, but Kira is the greatest Healer of them all.

To the north of Allogrenia, drought ravages the Shargh's land, and as their suffering escalates, the chief's younger brother seizes on an ancient prophecy to snatch the chiefship for himself. The prophecy links the Shargh's doom to a gold-eyed Healer, and Kira has gold eyes.

The Shargh attack with devastating consequences and Kira must fight to save the wounded, but the Shargh wounds rot, no matter her skill, and Kira finds herself in a deadly race against time. As the slaughter continues, she makes the horrifying discovery that the Shargh hunt her. To halt the attacks and save her people, she sets off for the North to seek aid from her long sundered warrior kin.

But the dangers beyond the forests exceed even the Shargh attacks. The Tremen detest their warrior kin but Terak's descendants have inflicted a worse fate on the Tremen. Kira's new-found love is torn apart by ancient hostilities and when trust turns to betrayal, it risks everything she has fought for.

As the battles rage on, Kira becomes increasingly sickened by the bloodshed. Desperate to end the suffering once and for all, she sets out on a quest that could cost her everything and everyone she loves.

Fantasy Novels

The Emerald Serpent – *the Celtic Fae in a fight for survival*
Book trailer: https://www.youtube.com/watch?v=bGpKxnpCEMg

Betrayal, torture, death: Etaine lives on only to destroy those who robbed her of everything she loved.

Seven years before, Etaine met fellow Ranger Cormac, the he-Eadar she believed was her longed-for true-mate. Emerald-eyed, white-skinned, and black-haired, the Eadar had formed into Ranger bands to fight the Fada, invading religious zealots determined to replace the Eadar's Serpent Goddess with their own gods of stone.

The pure blood of the ancient Eadar runs strong in Etaine and Cormac's veins, and their joining had the potential to open the Emerald and Serpent Ways to them, old worlds only true Eadar can enter. But their love affair goes tragically amiss, with catastrophic consequences.

Etaine flees and as the years pass, slowly rebuilds her life, but the Fada's attacks grow more ferocious, and the Eadar are forced to fight for their very existence. When the Fada mass to commit yet more bloody slaughter, and the bands join in a final, desperate effort to defeat them, Etaine comes under Cormac's command, the very last Eadar she ever wants to see again.

Together they have a weapon that can destroy the Fada, but to use it, Etaine must learn to trust again and Cormac to Remember. And time runs short: the Serpent rises.

Heart Hunter – *a female hunter on an impossible quest*

Fleet is a young Sceadu hunter: skilled, strong, and fast. She hunts deep into the icy mountains, seeking meat for her people, for the rains have failed and plunged the Sceaudu into hunger.

Her hunts are hard, but she has much to look forward to. Soon she will be gifted her air-name by the Sceadu's shaman, and then she will be a full adult, and free to marry the man she loves.

But while Fleet is on hunt, the old shaman dies, and the new shaman visions a very different future for her: cross the frozen, ice-locked mountains and complete a perilous quest or lose the man she loves forever.

In a moment of anger and frustration, Fleet commits a terrible wrong and sets out into the frigid mountains to atone with her life. In a journey that takes her deep into the earth's darkest places, into strange new worlds, and even into Death itself, she discovers that only she can save her people. To survive, she must draw on every shred of her hunter strength, and doing the impossible, it turns out, is just the beginning.

The Third Moon – *Science fantasy with a very human quest*

Where does the past end and the future begin?

Haunted by inherited memories of his people's dispossession and theft of their children, Warrain is just twelve years old when the nightmare repeats. But Warrain isn't living on Earth in the 21st Century, he is living on the planet Imago in the far flung future.

Five years before, Station One's Mech's got high on the opioid arrash, and in the bloodshed that followed, Warrain's scientific community were expelled from the Station, his father murdered, and his mother and unborn sibling lost to him.

The scientists carve out a rudimentary Station high in Imago's ranges, and Warrain's friends get on with their lives. Not Warrain; he climbs the Tors to stare down at Station One, dream of his mother and sibling, and plot revenge.

And then one day, everything changes. A third moon appears in the sky, one of Imago's life-forms calls him by name, and disease breaks out at Station One.

When the Mechs visit to seek help for their ill, Warrain seizes the opportunity to deal them a blow they will never forget. But the third moon brings changes that threaten them all and, to aid the life-form whose kind is being dispossessed and slaughtered, he must turn his back on the hate that has long sustained him and find another way to live.

Messenger – *a dystopic future filled with hope*

In a world made deaf by hatred, who will hear the messenger?

Severine's world ends the day her family is murdered. Being raised in the loving community of gay Travelers always marked her as an outsider, but being female puts her in mortal danger. Women are scarce, precious, and hunted.

When chance brings Severine face to face with the father she has never known, he assigns the son of his murdered best friend to guard her. They soon clash. Severine believes all men are violent brutes and Jeph resents his freedoms being curtailed.

An uneasy understanding grows but Jeph is glad to deliver her to the Enclaves, a sanctuary her father has carved out in the mountains for his women and children. But there is no safety in a world broken by war and sickness and when violence follows her, Severine flees to the northern city of Andhaka in search of a home amongst her mother's people. Jeph follows, bound by loyalty to her father, but the north holds terrible dangers for him.

It's been years since Andhaka has welcomed outsiders with anything but bullets, and to survive and to protect Jeph, Severine must learn to use her enemies' weapons against them. As the stakes rise, she comes to understand the horror of her mother's loss, and what drove her father north seventeen years before. His quest becomes her quest, but she hasn't counted on the savage legacy that war and sickness have left behind, or on falling in love.

I Heard the Wolf Call My Name – *gender-fluid shifters in search of home.* **Finalist Best YA Novel – 2019 Aurealis Awards**

Jax is on the run from his past. A shifter from the island of Rua, he is trapped on the mainland amongst the despised Off-islanders. Even worse, he is in the military, with a less than exemplary military record.

So when he is ordered to pack up his kit and is flown away in the middle of the night, he is in no position to argue. And it isn't as if he has any other place to go.

Ten years before, when Jax was just twelve years old and in bird-form high above his island home, it blew to smithereens, leaving him the only survivor, or so he believes.

The mystery flight dumps him at a new base where he comes face to face with Matiu, the boyhood friend Jax thought was as dead as his previous life. The military want Jax for an important mission and Matiu wants Jax too, but for different reasons, but there is no way Jax is going to resurrect what took him ten long years to bury. As the pressure on him ramps up, Jax flees but is confronted by something more deadly than his nightmarish memories.

To stop the other Islanders suffering the same fate as his people, Jax must finally face who and what he really is and decide where he truly belongs.

Fantasy Short Stories

Available on Amazon KDP

The Gift – A Deep Fantasy Short Story #1 – free on my website at
www.ksnikakis.com

Excerpt:

Thariel sat for a long time, surveying all around her, as if she ate the
world that would soon be memory. Then she took the harness from
the mare, and with soft words, thanked her and bade her farewell.
Her own feet she turned towards the forest, tossing her face-plate
aside as she went, so that her hair fell loose to her waist, then she
discarded her chest-armour, the sword and dagger, her bow and
quiver.

The trees closed in and she came at last to the lake Men call
Menios and stood for a while on its shore. An owl cried and a mouse
shrieked, and all around her the souls of the newly dead jostled in
their journey to the void. She stepped into the water and the new life
inside her quivered.

'Fear not, little one,' she whispered, in her own tongue. 'We are
going home.'

The Tale of Prince Anura – A Deep Fantasy Short Story #2 – free on my website at www.ksnikakis.com

Excerpt:

I should have been happy, for she was beautiful. Dark rivers of curls, skin as white as moonlight on water, breasts softer than spawn, and she loved me well. But her chamber was small, no matter the comfort of her bed, and the old feelings of entrapment rose, as persistent as gas that bubbles from rot below still waters.

I sat at the casement and listened, as I had once loitered near the watery skin of the second world and waited. The moon grew large and small many times, but it came at last, as I knew it would. The soft lament on the night-time air, the song of a soul as confined as mine. It took me a journey of many days through the depths of a massive forest to find her tower.

Stone it was and sheer, and as remote as the third world's glimmer had once been. I sang to her and she answered with sweet melodies of her own and we made love as frogs do, with our voices. And when trust had built, she let down her shining ladder of golden hair.

Glass-Heart – A Deep Fantasy Short Story #3
Finalist Best YA Short Story – 2019 Aurealis Awards

Excerpt:

Geth moved amongst his band, exchanging quiet words while they waited. Some he had fought with since the Tallon's foul ships had first found their shores while others had come later, when the burn of cot and kin had sent them from their valleys.

Hate drove them but hate was no shield against arrow and knife. It was fighting skills that kept them hale, and Geth ensured they had them aplenty. He needed them living, not just for their own sakes and his, but for what would come later. When the Tallon's stain had been scoured away, the destroyed must be rebuilt.

Kyth sat alone and he went to her and gazed about. 'The glass-heart's fled, has it?'

'I sent her to a place of safety. She will come to me when it is over.'

'Safety was what I wanted for you!'

'And what I wanted for Nyar.' Her eyes caught the star-sheen as she looked up at him. 'But you can't always have what you want, can you, Ceannasai?'

Dragon Sprite – A Deep Fantasy Short Story #4

Excerpt:

Genn rocketed straight upwards, not just because she enjoyed seeing the limitless blue sky before her, but because a Waiwin's wing shape made vertical flight harder for them. Orin didn't try to catch her but swept in circles around her, gaining height in an ever-narrowing spiral. It was a clever tactic and one Genn didn't believe he had thought of in the instant she had cleared the trees. He had obviously studied her strategies and developed a plan to counter them or so he thought.

Genn waited until the spiral narrowed to axeel, the minimum distance a Waiwin must keep from a Velven unless she accepted him, then swerved towards him, narrowing the distance between them. Orin's eyes flashed to black, shocked she had accepted him, but before he could act, she folded her wings and dropped.

The strength that had driven Orin's pursuit had surged to his wing-tendrils in anticipation of locking them with hers and he would struggle even to stay airborne until it flowed back.

www.ingramcontent.com/pod-product-compliance
Lightning Source LLC
Chambersburg PA
CBHW060006100426
42740CB00010B/1412